Pancho Segura's Championship Strategy

How to Play Winning Tennis

by Pancho Segura with Gladys Heldman

Introduction by Billie Jean King

McGraw-Hill Book Company

NEW YORK/ST. LOUIS/SAN FRANCISCO/DUSSELDORF/MEXICO/TORONTO

783787

Book design by Judith Michael.
Illustrations by Pritchett Design Associates.

1 2 3 4 5 6 7 8 9 MUBP 7 9 8 7 6

Library of Congress Cataloging in Publication Data

Segura, Pancho.
    Pancho Segura's Championship strategy.

        1. Tennis.   I.   Heldman, Gladys, joint author.
II. Title.   III.   Title: Championship strategy.
GV995.S39   796.34′22   75-43500
ISBN 0-07-056040-4

Portions of this book appeared in various forms in *World Tennis* magazine.
Tennis court diagrams reprinted by permission *World Tennis* magazine.

This book is dedicated to Jimmy Connors, Howard Schoenfeld, Stan Smith, Erik Van Dillen, Barry MacKay, Ken Rosewall, Lesley Hunt, Beth Norton, Tom Leonard, Tom Kreiss, Butch Buchholz, Alex Olmedo, Antonio Palafox, Tracy Austin, Laurie and Robin Tenney, Fernando Gentil, Ricardo Icaza, Jeff Austin, Sally Greer, Shelley Hudson, Spencer Segura, and Cynthia Lasker, who were among the pupils I coached—and who brought so much pleasure to their teacher.

Contents

Introduction by Billie Jean King

Just as Pancho Segura has been called the Ph.D. of Tennis Strategy, Gladys M. Heldman has been the premiere observer of the game of tennis these past twenty-five years. Together they make an unbeatable combination for anyone, recreational or expert, interested in learning the fine points and the basics. Jimmy Connors and many other players who grew up in Southern California benefited from Pancho's incisive analysis of different games and players (and most importantly the strategy involved in beating them), and there is not a single player in the game who has not been awed by Gladys' skill at observing, understanding and reporting the game.

When a beginner enters the fascinating world of tennis, he or she is bewildered by the new terminology that is a prerequisite to being "in" the game. The novice hears the teaching pro say: "Put more top on the ball," and the novice hasn't a clue that "top" stands for topspin, what topspin is, and how to do it. This book explains it. The beginner who has been playing two or three months doesn't know the difference between an Eastern or a Continental, which one is better, whether it makes any difference, and what to do about it. This book explains it. After the beginner has been playing for five or six months and is supposed to know what to do with the ball, he or she isn't really sure what to do. Should one blast the ball or just poop it back or try underspin or learn tactics? There is a whole new guide for those who are beginning the game, and this book provides it.

As the player gets better, he is able to absorb more and is ready to try advanced shots such as the topspin lob and the sidespin forehand approach shot. This book tells how and when to do them. When one reaches the Championship Flight, learning is never over: the game changes, players appear with new shots and new ripostes must be learned. This book explains the new styles of a Bjorn Borg and a Manuel Orantes, the new techniques of a Jimmy Connors, and the new ploys of an Arthur Ashe.

I have always believed the champion must have the mentality of a chess player, working out ploys in advance but having the skills developed to the point where the ripostes are secure. I attacked against Bobby Riggs, used change of pace and change of spins against Chris Evert, and tried to outrun Nancy Gunter. They in turn worked out their ploys, and the net result was some fascinating tennis, particularly for the participants.

The tennis player who reads this book shouldn't try to absorb it all in one sitting. There is too much varied material. Read it through first, then reread it frequently as you need. If you have lost confidence in your smash, read the chapter on the overhead and then work out your problems on the court. If you are only hitting soft, bloopy shots, read how to hit them harder, then practice what you have read. If you are on the championship level, read the story of Jimmy Connors racing in after hitting a short, low crosscourt in anticipation of the opponent's down-the-line, then try it yourself and see if you are as fast as Jimmy.

Tennis isn't learned in a week or a month or a year. It is a continuous challenge. As your skills advance from constant practice, so your mind expands to absorb new thoughts, techniques, and tactics. You won't become a great tennis player overnight, but as you read, think, and practice, you are headed in the right direction. A book on learning to play the cello doesn't make the reader an overnight concert genius, but it does enable him to know the difference between Pablo and Rosie Casals, to appreciate the finer points of the skills involved, and to acquire the proper techniques.

Have fun, because tennis is a thoroughly enjoyable game. The pleasures are in the improving, in being invited to play by those who are more skilled, in understanding what is going on in a great match, and in reaching your full potential.

Good luck, and hit lots of sidespin forehands down the line!

Foreword

never before has a book been devoted to the entire strategy of the tennis game. Until now, the closest have been several books by Bill Tilden which were marvels in their day. He wrote about spin, and what he didn't know about spin wasn't worth knowing. Tilden was the intellectual genius of the Iron Age of Tennis. The game moved into the Silver Age with Jack Kramer and his "Percentage Tennis," and the emphasis turned to pattern play. In the last fifteen years, a dozen different exponents of the game have demonstrated new styles of play, new ways to win and new combinations of attack and defense. In a way, tennis has become the thinking man's game: Jimmy Connors worked out a plan of attack and defense against Arthur Ashe—then Ashe turned around and worked out a plan of defense and attack against Connors.

A player with only a few months of experience can get much more pleasure out of hitting the ball when he has a plan. There are tactics for the beginner that will help him quickly jump to a higher level. He learns the game isn't slam-bam; matches are generally won on errors, not on winners. Most tennis players of club level think that balls should skim the net in a baseline exchange: their games improve dramatically when they start to clear the net by 6 to 8 feet, as all good players do.

Strategy in this book is given at all levels, in singles, doubles and mixed. Strokes are the bread and butter of the game—but tactics are the soufflés.

Tennis is a game of timing. The beginner has to learn to measure the rate at which a moving ball is coming to him, to comprehend automatically that the racket is a 27-inch extension of his arm, to know how to coordinate his backswing with the moving target, and to judge where the ball will bounce on the basis of how his opponent hits it. In the past it was thought that good timing could only be learned by experience and could be acquired best by players with natural ability. However, this book endeavors to speed up the acquisition of good timing. The reader will become aware of the low bounce of the underspin, the high, forward-jumping topspin, the sliding sidespin, the backspin on a drop shot, the way the ball jams into the body off a left-handed serve to the forehand, etc. The beginner and the intermediate can move rapidly into a higher level of competition, because shots and spins that would have confused them are now readily recognizable and therefore much easier to handle.

The subject of timing has been totally overlooked in previous tennis books, which have concentrated almost exclusively on strokes. Timing is as important to the advanced player and the champion as it is to the beginner. The discussions in this book show why the topspin shots of Bjorn Borg and Guillermo Vilas are so effective on clay, how Manuel Orantes won the U.S. Open with a slithering, underspin backhand, why Billie Jean King is so deadly on grass with her sidespin forehand approach shot. The great young juniors of today are frequently beaten by the masters of yesterday because the latter, despite their lack of speed on shots and in court coverage, are masters of timing through their years of experience. Jimmy Connors got a crash course in timing which enabled him to jump from relative obscurity in the Juniors to the No. 1 player in the country three years later.

Tennis instruction books in the past have dealt only with the strokes for the beginner or the intermediate. This book describes the basic strokes in the most simplified form for beginners, but as the reader advances, it explains the nuances and advanced technique of the stroke for every level of play. For example, the beginner learns to lob the ball high, the intermediate to disguise his lob, and the advanced player to experiment with the topspin lob. The beginner is taught to block the volley, the intermediate to punch and angle the volley, and the advanced player to drop-volley. The novice does best if he takes the groundstrokes at waist level, the intermediate begins to move to the ball to take it almost at the top of the bounce, and the advanced player learns to hit the bill on the rise.

This is a book for pre-teens, promising Juniors and dedicated champions, for housewives, tired businessmen and -women, and what used to be called the middle-aged. Today people are starting tennis for the first time in their thirties, forties, and fifties. There is no age limit in the game: there are tournaments for players under twelve, for women over fifty and for men over seventy.

Unless you're a beginner, you need not start this book at Chapter 1 and read straight through. Begin in the middle—or even at the end, if you prefer. Each chapter is designed to explain a specific phase of the game. If your problem is the volley, start there and then work forward or backward. Pick out a chapter from the "Strategy" section, read it, and then put it into practice. If your serve is giving you problems, check your action against the chapter on the serve. If you are changing from a slow to a fast court, consult the section on adapting to new surfaces. If your friends shun you on the court, get instant help from the chapter on court etiquette.

After you have absorbed everything and are almost perfect, lend the book to your partner and ask him to read the section on doubles.

Chapter One / Getting in Shape

nyone who plays tennis has to be in good physical condition. Beginners are often exhausted at the end of the first 10 minutes of their lesson, intermediates frequently begin to drag at the end of the first set, and tournament players often suffer late in the match from an inability to move and react at 100% efficiency. Every player needs to be totally fit for his level of the game, and the more one is fit, the easier it is to rise to a higher level.

THE BEGINNER

Most novices are soft and lazy unless they have been playing an active sport such as basketball, football, soccer, hockey, etc. The first few times they go out on a court, they are able to hop and bounce less than 10 minutes before exhaustion sets in. The quickest way to develop minimum stamina is to play four times a week for an hour at a time and to force oneself slightly *beyond* the level of fatigue. Stamina then comes quickly, and in two weeks the novice is able to last the full hour.

If the beginner plays only once a week, he or she can do specific exercises to develop endurance. The two best (because they take the least amount of time) are jumping rope and potato races. A potato race takes less than one minute. Six balls are placed on an imaginary line, approximately three feet apart. Pick up each ball, starting with the one farthest away, and deposit it in a box or wastebasket, which is placed at the point where you start. You will run 18 feet each way to pick up the farthest ball, 15 feet each way to pick up the next one, etc. By the time you pick up No. 6, which is only 3 feet away, you will have had a nice workout. If you are able to do three potato races at top speed each day, you are in good shape.

Heat and humidity are the most difficult conditions for the average beginner. A bright, hot sun is enervating to anyone accustomed to air-conditioned homes, cars, restaurants and movies, and playing tennis in the hot sun can quickly wilt the potential tennis player. If you can't be on the court four times a week in the summer, then jog or bicycle to get you better acclimated.

There is one other exercise that helps a beginner to start quickly. Stand in the privacy of your own room with a racket in your hand. The feet should be 18 inches apart and the knees flexed. The weight is on the balls of the toes and the back is almost straight. Now bounce without letting your toes leave the ground (the knees simply flex deeper with each bounce). Now push off with your left foot to move toward your right; then push off with your right foot to move to your left. Get husband, wife, child, parent, or friend to "pretend" to toss a ball to your right or left, and see how quickly you can push off with the opposite foot. The foot reacts instantaneously as the eye sees movement.

INTERMEDIATES AND ADVANCED PLAYERS

Once one begins to play matches, stamina, speed of foot, and flexibility become vital. Calisthenics such as jumping-jacks get the blood pumping in arms and legs. Using pulleys on the walls is a good exercise to teach you how to shift. Zigzag running drills develop agility and make the player looser from the waist up. In tennis one seldom runs on a straight line (it is usually on the diagonal), and zigzagging increases agility and mobility.

When I was learning to come to net, I would practice running full speed from the baseline to the service line 50 to 100 times a day. Jumping rope is also excellent—particularly jumping on one leg, since it teaches equilibrium. (Balance is the greatest asset one can have in tennis.) Basketball is a good exercise because it requires constant shifting, quick movements, and good lungs. Any exercise that puts more weight on the knees is desirable since the bent-knee player is more flexible, has better balance, and can be more deceptive. Conversely, when the knees are straight, one cannot move quickly or get under the ball easily or hit short shots as well.

Tennis requires split-second starts and tremendously fast running for 5 to 10 yards at most. During the course of a long match, a player will run 5 miles, but it is almost always in spurts of 5 to 8 yards. Fast tennis players could set records for the 5-yard dash. Therefore, running long distances is good only to develop wind power, whereas running 5 yards full speed, backward and forward, is the action one will perform on the court. Short sprints and zigzags are the exercises that are most duplicated in match play.

Of all the players in the game today, Ilie Nastase is the most limber, has the best balance and can get to the ball and come back into position better than any other player. Smith, Ashe, Pasarell, and Graebner have to get set to hit the ball well, although they hit it very hard. The fastest players are those who are most limber: the Australians Mal Anderson, Ken Rosewall, and Rod Laver and the Americans Jimmy Connors and Chuck McKinley. Laver, on a running shot, is as good as anyone in the game. In women's tennis the fastest court coverer is

Evonne Goolagong because she can change directions so well, but others who are almost as quick are Rosie Casals, Billie Jean King, Margaret Court, Françoise Durr and Julie Heldman, although Czechoslovakia's Martina Navratilova may prove to be even faster and more flexible some day (if she loses some weight).

DIET

There is only one rule on diet that should be observed by every level of player: weighing too much is bad for the heart and for mobility. A fast player becomes even faster when he takes off extra pounds. Getting down to proper playing weight is not a matter of going on a diet for three or four weeks, then going back to the old habits. It is much better to give up certain foods for life—sweets, sauces, rolls, and excessive starches.

Most people know the proper foods to eat, but for those who don't, here are the basics for a balanced daily diet:

- Orange, grapefruit, or tomato juice (Vitamin C)
- Meat, cheese or nuts (protein)
- Milk or cheese (calcium)
- Salad with oil and vinegar dressing (roughage and Vitamin D)
- Green vegetables (Vitamin A and minerals)
- Whole wheat, rye bread or cracked wheat bread (Vitamins A and B, minerals)
- Fresh fruits (Vitamins A and C, minerals)
- Eggs (Vitamin A and calcium).

There are numerous nutritionists, doctors, and health food gurus who favor a particular diet and have a large following among athletes and laymen. You may go on the trip that advocates blackstrap molasses, wheat germ, and yeast; or you may be convinced that eggs and butter will give you a high cholesterol count, which you are told is dangerous; or you may be a Vitamin E faddist with a yen for chicken livers; or you may simply be a compulsive vitamin pill popper. However, if you can acquire a taste for raw vegetables instead of sweets, for fruits and cheese instead of starches, and for foods with a reasonably low calorie count that provide vitamins, minerals, and proteins, you will be giving the cells of your body the nourishment they need without acquiring excess, undesirable fat.

Players differ in what they eat before a match. Those at the top level of tournament play generally eat very lightly, if at all, in the two hours before a match. Some will avoid a heavy meal even if they are not going to play for another four hours. There are so many differences among the top players themselves that one must regard it as a matter of individual choice. For example, Pancho Gonzalez would literally starve himself while playing in a tournament, whereas other players would keep to their customary meal schedule and simply avoid eating too heavily or too soon before a match.

AVOIDING INJURIES

Anyone who only plays occasionally, who is over thirty-five, or who is just recovering from a bad elbow, shoulder, back, etc., should do one or more of several warm-up exercises to prevent muscle pulls or knee injuries. You can warm up before going out on the court by jogging or doing slow stretching and moving calisthenics. Warm up your arm and shoulder by lifting the arms and letting them move in a wide, slow circle. If you have a tendency toward a weak ankle, rotate your foot gently and slowly for a few minutes. When exercising any muscle, do it in slow motion and always avoid sudden, sharp movements. On the court, hop and bounce quickly but hit the first few balls softly and with a big, free-and-easy stroke. Take plenty of soft practice serves before trying the big one.

The most common injury in the game is "tennis elbow," and most frequently the pain is on top of the elbow. It can be caused by picking up something too heavy or by catching the ball wrong on forehand or backhand so that the elbow receives the jolt when ball meets racket. The arm can get so tender that it hurts to pick up a glass or brush one's teeth or hold a telephone. If you have had a bad tennis elbow, hit forehands only during the first five minutes; if a ball comes to your backhand, run around it or catch it—but don't hit it. After five minutes you will probably be able to hit a backhand in front of you without feeling any twinges.

If you have any back problems, make sure you toss the ball well in front of you on serve; if you toss the ball directly over your head or behind you, you will have to lean back and this puts too much weight on your back muscles. If you have a trick knee caused from an old football injury, protect it with an elastic-and-leather brace. If your wrist or shoulder is sore, lay off for a few days since there is no way to hit the ball without reinjuring the damaged area.

Those who have been playing tennis regularly for forty years or more usually show the most common sense in warming up properly. They protect the weak knee or the weak back with a bandage or support. They warm up very slowly on the court, and when they finally take their practice serves, they hit them easily to warm up the shoulder. They never serve an American twist* since this is the most common cause of back injury. In the winter they wear heavy sweaters or warm-up suits and in summer their hats protect them from the sun. When they finish playing, they never sit around in the cold where muscles might stiffen. They take care of themselves far better than they did forty years ago—and as a result they suffer far fewer injuries.

* See Glossary.

Chapter Two / Equipment and Apparel

The three basic items a tennis player needs are a racket, tennis balls, and tennis shoes.

Standards of tennis apparel have changed so much in the last few years that white shorts and a white shirt or a white tennis dress are no longer a prerequisite for getting on most courts. There are only a few hold-outs among clubs and resorts; a middle-class club aiming for upper-class status may still bar any player wearing a colored shirt (or having a colored face). A second-class club in the Palm Springs area had a third-rate pro who barred first-rate players from stepping on the courts in color-trimmed outfits. The touring pros wear red, yellow, blue, orange, pink, or purple in solid colors, stripes, or polka-dots. It's a prerequisite for television so that spectators can easily recognize the protagonists. Lamar Hunt's World Championship Tennis (WCT), which promotes many of the major Men's Pro events, fines a player for wearing all-white (it's bad for TV) and fines the two members of a doubles team if they don't wear the same color shirts (again because of the demands by TV). The all-white rule of the early days of tennis is as passé as spats and bustles.

A beginner, particularly a young person, will probably buy a cheap racket at first, since, as the child grows and his tennis develops, he will want a slightly heavier racket with a slightly bigger handle. Adults will have to decide whether they want cheap or expensive equipment: quality means both superior materials and workmanship, and the extra cost of an expensive racket is in the quality and also the quality control. A cheap racket may have the same wood or steel or aluminum as an expensive one, and it may even last as long, but the laminations are more carefully put together and cured in the higher-priced wooden models, and the welding, riveting, or grommets show better workmanship in the more expensive metal rackets. The finishing, trim, and grip cost extra, although the basic frame may be about the same in cheap and expensive models.

Many manufacturers use their top-line unfinished frame rejects for their lower-priced models. If the frame is rejected for a meaningless wood blemish, there is no problem, but if the batch of glue was bad or the wood was not cured properly, you could be buying a lemon. So you pay for quality and quality control; your chances are better, although there is never an absolute guarantee even with the most expensive merchandise. Some rackets are more expensive to make than others, and they are the highest priced. You must decide whether you want a Rolls-Royce, a Mercedes, a Pinto, or a Volkswagen.

Some players choose a wooden racket and some a steel, Fiberglas, graphite, or aluminum racket. The top players in the world have no unanimity about wood, steel, Fiberglas, graphite, or aluminum: Billie Jean King uses a Bancroft, Jimmy Connors a Wilson, Pancho Gonzalez a Spalding, Arthur Ashe a Head, John Newcombe a Rawlings, Ken Rosewall a Seamco, Virginia Wade a Dunlop, Bob Hewitt a Fisher, Harold Solomon a Garcia, Tony Roche a Yonex, Roscoe Tanner a PDP, Margaret Court a Yamaha, and Julius Heldman a Volkl. The reason usually given is "feel," meaning the reaction when the racket and ball meet. This is a function of the stiffness of the frame and the gut tension as well. The stiffer the frame, the more controllable the ball—that is, the less fast the spring-back action of the frame to sling-shot the ball. Even before metal rackets, one could get whippy or stiff wood frames. Big servers liked whippy ones but most groundstrokers went for average or stiffer ones. Now metal rackets come in all degrees of springiness, even more whippy than the most flexible wood. My advice is to beg or borrow various rackets to try before making an investment in a type which gives you fits because you cannot control your groundstrokes.

Rackets can be head-heavy, head-light, or evenly balanced. Some players say that unless the racket is evenly balanced, the racket head will swing through too fast (head-heavy) or will lag behind the wrist (head-light). Others say the racket will do more work for you and will produce more momentum with an easy swing if it is very head-heavy. One famous player of the late 1930s, Gil Hunt, used to fasten a thin strip of lead to the tip of the racket head and then use a swing only a foot or two long. The arguments against a head-heavy racket are that it is harder to maneuver and tires the arm. If your arm can take it and it suits your timing, you probably will have a harder serve with a head-heavy racket. Most fast-hand volleyers, who must move their rackets instantly, will probably go for a head-light (as well as a light) racket. My recommendation for beginners is to pick an evenly balanced racket. Those who have played for a long time will choose a racket that best satisfies the natural timing and wrist action of their most important stroke. For some it will be serve, for others groundstrokes, and for some the volley.

Racket handles will have a letter that says L, M, or H. L means light, M means medium, and H means heavy. As a rough guide, L corresponds to less than 13½ ounces strung weight, M between 13½ and 14 ounces strung weight, and H over 14 ounces. There is no recognized standard, and so an L racket of one manufacturer need not be the same as an L from another maker—and, for that matter, two made by the same company may vary quite a bit but still both be labeled the same. Strings weigh slightly less than ¾ ounce (⅝ ounce for thin or tournament gut). All good tennis shops have sensitive scales, and the L, M, or H marking should be used only as a rough screen if you want to duplicate the weight of a racket you have and like.

The general ranges of strung weight are: children, 11–13 ounces; women, 12½–14 ounces; men, 13–15 ounces. Today the top men players are using rackets about ½ ounce lighter than they did in the 1930s. If the racket is too light, you won't realize your full power potential, but you can maneuver the racket easily. If the racket is too heavy, your arm gets tired and you may swing late. As usual, there are the exceptions. The late Maureen Connolly hit the heaviest ball in women's tennis during the era in which she played, but she used an extremely light racket. Lew Hoad, the great Australian star, still uses a racket as light as a woman's. Don Budge, one of the all-time great players in tennis history and one of the hardest hitters, used and still uses a heavier racket than anyone else.

The feel of a racket handle is the single most important factor in the suitability of a racket. The human hand is astonishingly sensitive to tiny variations in the circumference and shape of a handle. Racket handles average about 4⅝ inch in circumference, and many players can distinguish as little as .02 inch variation. Not only that, but they can "feel" a slightly different shape, which will lead to a slightly different grip, resulting in a different opening of the racket face for a set wrist. Again, it is vital to play with different handles, both size and shape, before selecting a racket. In the 1920s, handles of 5 to 5¼ inches circumference were the rage. Now men use 4⅝ to 4⅞ inches; anything smaller or larger is uncommon. Women use 4⅜ to 4⅝ inches, and children are down to 4 or 4¼ inches, when such rackets can be found. The racket will turn in your hand too easily if the handle is too small or large. Very few players like round handles because they cannot "find" their grip automatically; they prefer handles with sharp bevels so that the hand easily moves into the proper grip for backhand or forehand.

Beginners should not have tightly strung rackets because the gut wears out faster and the difference is not yet important. As the player improves and the reaction of the strings against the ball takes on more meaning and subtlety, he probably will want a tighter string job. Still, there have been some great players who have always insisted on "fish nets." John Bromwich, a great Australian player of the 1940s, used a loosely strung racket. So did Italy's Beppe Merlo, a star of the same era.

Most top players like their rackets strung with thin gut up to 60 to 65 pounds tension. If the stringing is too tight, then all the resiliency of the gut is gone and it is near its snapping point. Some rackets have plastic grommets which yield a little when first strung, and the first string job on these rackets will loosen substantially during the first week of use. Good players generally believe a tight racket is most important on volley. Another vital factor is economics. The champions use thin gut and very tightly strung rackets, which means that the string jobs don't last as long. A hard-hitting player with a lot of spin can go through two or three rackets in the course of one match.

Gut has more attractive playing qualities than nylon, but it is expensive, and it frays and breaks when used in the rain. If you use a racket strung with gut on a wet court or during a light rain, put talcum powder inside your racket cover afterward to help to dry the gut. Although just about every good player uses gut, beginners can use nylon not tightly strung.

There are two types of nylon, monofilament and braided or twisted. Monofilament nylon is the cheapest and is waterproof. But it slowly stretches, losing its spring, and, most important, it can snap without warning at a place where its smooth surface has started to abrade or where there was a minute imperfection. Braided nylon is intermediate in cost, is waterproof and does not stretch as much. It simply does not have the liveliness of gut when tightly strung. Nylon can abrade on a dusty clay court just as badly as gut.

It is difficult for the average player to tell good gut from bad, and so he usually leaves it up to the stringer. Bad gut is uneven in appearance, showing translucent "fat" patches, and is soft and too stretchy. A reputable manufacturer will not sell "green" gut that is not properly cured.

If a string breaks a week after your racket is strung, look to see where it has broken. If it breaks in the hole of the racket head, then the stringer failed to burn the hole smooth and you can probably get a new string job. Some stringers may try to foist off a repair job on you. Patching a racket is never as satisfactory as a complete string job, so insist on a total restringing in the case of a break at the hole.

If your racket breaks and you neither threw nor dropped it, you can usually get a replacement. The shop where you bought it will work it out later with the manufacturer. The one thing you cannot expect to get free is another string job, and this is where you will take your loss.

The way to tell a good string job from a bad one is by strumming the strings. The "ping" is high on a highly strung racket. If you look at the strings from along the handle, you can tell if they all have the same waviness, meaning they are all pulled to equal tightness. It is bad if they are not. After a few months, the sound of the strings will get lower, and when it gets too low you may want to get a new string job.

The minimum number of rackets a player should have is, obviously, one. Most players who are past the intermediate level have two or more, and top tournament players generally have six or more. The reason: in case a string breaks, there is an immediate duplicate replacement.

A racket will last until it goes soft in the head or warps. Good frames will last a long time—possibly six or eight or even ten years. However, if it goes through three or four string jobs, its life is shortened. Worn-out leather grips can easily be replaced. As for string jobs, tournament players with heavy spin serves, using thin gut and tightly strung rackets, will go through gut in twenty sets or less. But as the string is thicker and more loosely strung and as the spin is less, the gut lasts longer. If you don't play very much and if you don't have heavy spins, a fairly tight string job may last for a year or even two or three. It does lose a little resiliency, and if you are finicky or rich, get your racket restrung.

Tennis balls are sold three to the can, and the amount of time you will use them depends on you. As your game improves, you will be overcome by an irresistible desire to play with new balls every time you go on the court. The average player may use a set of balls anywhere from four to eight sets, depending upon whether the surface cuts up the balls (concrete or asphalt) or is less abrasive (clay, composition, or grass). Tournament players are a little more fussy and will use balls anywhere from two sets to six sets—depending upon their economic status.

Heavy-duty balls, which were introduced only during the last decade, are balls with a cover which fluffs up higher than regular balls. The cover lasts longer on hard surfaces like concrete and coated asphalt. Heavy-duty balls still have a pressurized core like the regular champion-ship ball. Tretorn balls are one brand of "pressureless" ball, made with a soft core which does not hold gas pressure. The cover is the heavy-duty type. Tretorns play differently from regular balls, just as nylon plays differently from gut. Heavy-duty balls are often used by top players in preference to regular balls on concrete, asphalt, or Laykold courts. The fuzz mats down or wears off too fast with regular balls. But on a slow, soft court, heavy-duty balls fluff up and feel like lead, and so most top players prefer championship balls when they play on clay.

There comes a time when all balls die. Tretorn balls never go dead (lose their bounce) but they ultimately lose their fuzz and then they do not have good playing qualities. Other balls can be used until their internal pressure decreases, which means that enough gas escapes from their core to the point where they bounce too low, or when the fuzz is worn off, whichever comes first. If the fuzz is smoothed down but not yet all gone, put a batch of balls in a washing machine and dryer. It will fluff them up again.

Beginners will often use balls to the point where all the fuzz is gone and the bounce is lost. This is usually because they are too new to the game to know the difference.

Once in a while you will buy a can of balls that is dead. If the can does not hiss when it is opened, the balls will be dead because there was no pressure in the can. Balls are pressure-packed; if they are not, the pressure in their cores slowly escapes. If you get a can of balls that does not hiss, return the balls at once and the pro shop or department store can easily recognize unused balls. Never buy balls that are not in a can unless they are the pressureless type, no matter how cheap they are.

The amount you can expect to spend on equipment in the course of a year depends on how often you play, how smartly you want to be dressed, and how great your desire is to play with new balls. A pair of good tennis shoes will probably cost you $30, although you may spend less or more. Some tournament players go through a pair of shoes in a week, whereas many club players will wear the same pair of shoes for two or three years. Rackets and string jobs can cost you anywhere from $25 to $200, depending upon your taste in rackets. Court fees range anywhere from zero on a public court to $50 or more in dues each month at a club (not counting initiation fees). What you spend in apparel is up to you, but you will probably want several outfits suitable for the court, one or more warm-up suits for cold weather, and a slightly jazzy, tennis-oriented outfit for display purposes.

The three important costs for a young person are balls, shoes, and racket. Shoes can be the biggest cost, followed by string jobs. By adult standards, everyday tennis for two hours could cost $1,000 per year or more, but a dedicated boy or girl can hack it for $200.

The classical shoe is a low canvas shoe with rubber sole. The good ones have some kind of arch support and cushioning. The sole can either be smooth finished (for hard courts) or corrugated or pattern-molded for better gripping on clay or grass. Basketball shoes, which come up above the ankles, are not used for tennis. They are too heavy and clumsy. Leather shoes are very popular today. The good ones feature cushioned sides as well as heels and are very comfortable and attractive, although quite expensive. There is no "best" in tennis shoes and it is a matter of personal preference.

Most players use drip-dry tennis apparel since tennis clothes are usually washed after one wearing. They come in a variety of fabrics such as nylon, orlon, polyester knit, cotton mesh, Fortrel, Kodel polyester, dacron, cotton, and endless mixtures (e.g., dacron-cotton or polyester-cotton piqué). They are priced as low as $10 (made by Abe Segal, a former South African International star) and as high as $300 (specially created costumes by the supreme tennis couturier, Teddy Tinling). The well-known names in tennis apparel are Mondessa, Quantum, Sphairistike, Puritan, Court Casuals, Paul Sullivan, Loomtogs, Fred Perry, Munsingwear, Allen-A, Adidas, Jockey, Sports Accessories, Seasport, Elke and Joianna, Point Set, David Smith, Duofold, LaCoste, Anba, among many others.

If you are a man you will want shorts (formerly white, now also in pastels and brighter colors), a shirt (formerly white, now in pastels, bright solid colors, stripes, or checks), and a sweater. For women there are tennis dresses, skirts, shorts, and shirts in white with pastel or bright trim or in a variety of colors. The most popular socks are nylon, thick orlon, or wool-nylon, since they don't shrink and dry easily. Hats or caps are protection against the sun, sweatbands are popular with many players—and all additional equipment or apparel is optional, depending upon your income, your tastes, and your own prerequisites (band-aids, elbow or knee braces, racket covers, a travelling tennis case, etc.).

Balls come in a variety of colors now. Ten years ago only white balls were acceptable; yellow balls are more popular today. In the future, when tennis courts are stained navy blue, white balls might make a comeback.

Chapter Three/Court Etiquette

If you are a beginner or an intermediate player, you may have a difficult time getting opponents and partners. However, your pleasant personality on the court and your sensitivity toward other players will get you into a variety of matches. The word gets around fast: the good guys get asked and the bad guys don't.

The rules of the court are simple. Read them now—then reread them in a month to see which ones you have forgotten.

Never ask a better player to hit with you. You will either be turned down or the better player will sulk while he ungraciously hits with you. If three good players are looking for a fourth, don't offer your services, even if you do so modestly ("I know I'm not so good, but I would be happy to fill in if you want me").

Run to pick up the balls after a rally or a point is over. If you run, you will at least get some exercise while you are learning, and your opponent won't have to stand in the sun, staring at his racket, while you leisurely dawdle over to a ball.

You are not good enough to groan. When you miss, keep quiet. If Margaret Court and Arthur Ashe don't shout their displeasure or make grimaces, why should you?

If you are not sure whether a ball is good or out, you must play it as "good." You may never return a ball, lose the point, and then ask your opponent to play it over because his ball may have been out.

Don't cross through a court while a point is in progress.

If a ball from the next court rolls into your court while you are rallying, stop your rally, pick it up at once, and return it directly to one of the players. If the ball rolls into your court while you are playing a point, replay the point after returning the ball.

Don't "call 'em close." Any ball that touches the outer edge of the line is good. If you can't see it as "out," you must play it as good. Among the champions, 98% never give bad calls intentionally; the 2% who do have infamous reputations.

Don't stall between points by endlessly wiping your glasses or tying your shoelaces or picking up stray balls. Former Wimbledon Champion Ann Jones once played a Wightman Cup match against an American who repeatedly stalled. When the two-hour match was over, Ann extended her hand for the traditional handshake and said: "Thanks for the 20 minutes of tennis."

Don't boast about your wins or alibi your losses. Chris Evert doesn't go around telling everyone whom she just beat, and Rod Laver has never offered an excuse after he has lost.

If a good player offers to hit with you, you in turn should occasionally ask someone not as good as you. Don Budge plays singles with his wife, John Newcombe regularly has a game with wife Angie, Billie Jean King plays with husband Larry, and former Wimbledon Champs Chuck McKinley, Roy Emerson, Manuel Santana, Fred Stolle, and dozens of others will play doubles with friends, relatives, and Juniors.

Never call a ball on your opponent's side unless he asks you to do so.

You cannot call a shot in your partner's alley. You can call his service line only when he is receiving the serve (and when there is neither linesman nor umpire).

Don't borrow balls. When you use someone else's balls, you are wearing them out and they are no longer of use to the lender. (It's like borrowing someone's sandwich.)

Don't tell your partner what he is doing wrong or groan when he makes an error. If you ever get to play in a doubles with the likes of Stan Smith or Charlie Pasarell or Françoise Durr, you will find they only encourage and never berate you. They attempt to make you feel good, not to humiliate you.

If you make a tennis date, be on time. The only thing ruder than being late is not showing at all. (In Men's Pro tennis, a player who is late can be fined as much as $1,000.)

Try to be consistent, because your opponents will enjoy the game more. It is better to lob every ball and get it in than to hit every ball with all your might and spray the fences with your errors.

Use a backboard or a wall or a tennis play-back net or a ball machine as often as you can or when you cannot get a game. Backboards and ball machines never miss; an opponent often does.

If you are playing badly, don't get discouraged. Review the fundamentals to see if you can discover your error. If you continue to hit badly, then run as fast as you can for every ball. At least you will get one good hour of exercise.

If you are cheerful, eager, and industrious, you will improve rapidly and get tremendous enjoyment out of the game. Your happy attitude will soon get you into many games with players better than you. Keep on smiling, working and trying, and soon you will be the better player.

Be modest in victory (don't gloat) and gracious in defeat (no excuses).

If you have made a practice date with someone and you are playing badly, don't quit when you are down 0-4.

For your own sake and for the benefit of fellow players, wash your tennis clothes frequently.

Chapter four/The forehand

Jimmy Connors can hit unbelievably hard groundstrokes, flinging himself at the ball with a totally uninhibited swing. Both feet are often off the ground on his forehand. The wrist is laid back, which is the position for maximum power, and the grip is Eastern, even verging slightly toward the Western. Connors hits his hardest forehands with just enough topspin or sidespin to control the ball.

Chris Evert has exemplary preparation for every stroke, which is the result of intensive, careful training. She holds the racket with an Eastern grip, drawn back with the racket head above the wrist and somewhat above ball height. As she swings, her right leg will come down firmly and her left leg will move forward, shifting her weight into the stroke. The racket will describe a down-and-up arc as it moves forward, providing comfortable topspin with a very firm wrist.

A player with a big forehand is always a dangerous opponent. He can do things that the player with the big backhand cannot do: he can run around his backhand (a backhand player almost never runs around his forehand); the stroke is harder to read because of the shoulder motion; and the forehand return off second serve is a much tougher shot. The "big forehand" player can hit a forehand winner from his backhand alley, leaving the rest of his court wide open because he is confident he is going to win the point. He will use it equally against volleyers and baseliners, not only because he hits it so well but because he puts the pressure on his opponent to play to a very narrow spot on the backhand side or to the strong forehand. The opponent never knows where the forehand is going to go until it has been hit; even though Ken Rosewall has a superb backhand, he can angle his forehand more and it is harder to read. A big forehand player such as John Newcombe eats up second serves, stepping around the ball to take it on his powerful forehand and knock it down the line for a winner.

THE FOREHAND GRIP

There are three forehand grips—the Western, the Eastern, and the Continental (the Australian grip is a modified Continental). A player usually stays with the grip which he was taught when he first began, and there have only been a few classic cases where a player successfully changed from a Western to an Eastern or from a Continental to an Eastern. Don Budge, after winning the National Junior Boys', worked with coach Tom Stow and smoothly made the transition from a Western to an Eastern grip. Eddie Moylan, a Top Ten player of the 1940s and 1950s, made a successful switch from a Continental to an Eastern grip. Darlene Hard, winner of many U.S. national titles, changed from a Continental to an Eastern forehand but was never completely happy or secure in her new stroke. Frankly, I wish it were possible to have

different grips for different circumstances since one could improvise so beautifully, taking high balls with a Western, wide shots with a Continental and waist-high balls with an Eastern.

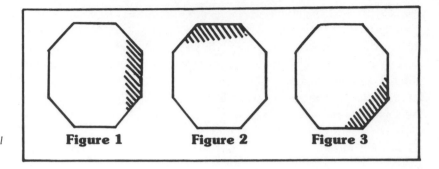

Figure 1   Figure 2   Figure 3

Eastern (Fig. 1). The butt of the palm is against the wide right side of the handle.
Continental (Fig. 2). The butt of the palm is on the top plane of the handle.
Western (Fig. 3). The palm is on the diagonal face nearest to the bottom plane of the handle.

The easiest way to "find" your grip is by placing the butt of your palm against the racket handle. If the racket is held in front of you, with the racket face perpendicular to the ground, you can find the Eastern grip by placing the butt of your palm against the wide right side of the handle (see Figure 1). For the Continental grip, the butt of the palm is on the top plane of the handle (Figure 2), and for the Western grip the palm is on the diagonal facet nearest to the bottom plane of the handle (Figure 3).

The Australian grip is not quite a pure Continental; the palm turns very slightly towards the Eastern. (A change as small as one-quarter inch may seem minute but it makes a great deal of difference in "feel" and in style.) Most players spread the fingers slightly, whether they hit with a Western, Eastern, or Continental; but there are enough famous exceptions so that there is no "absolute" in this rule. Pancho Gonzales played for years with a "hammer" grip (no separation between the fingers), and so did American star Butch Buchholz.

I recommend the Eastern or the Continental grip, although I like the Continental better because it is so versatile and makes the volley so easy (the same grip suffices for forehand and backhand). The Western was popular fifty years ago, particularly in California, and one of the most able exponents of this grip was Little Bill Johnston, U.S. National Champion in 1915 and 1919. It is very effective on a high-bouncing surface such as clay or cement (Little Bill used to wind up on a high forehand by swinging the racket around his head), but it is less effective in digging up low-bouncing shots.

Bjorn Borg of Sweden and Harold Solomon of the United States are the only famous players of this decade who use a Western. Although Borg's results have been excellent on clay (he won the 1974 Italian and French championships) and on carpet (he was the 1974 and 1975 WCT finalist), he never did well on the grass at Forest Hills, Wimbledon, or Australia. When the surface at Forest Hills was changed in 1975 to Har-Tru (a surface as slow as clay), Borg reached the semifinals. Solomon also excels on clay or carpet but has never had a major win on grass. The disadvantages of the Western grip are the difficulty in hitting low balls, the incredible problems involved in trying to volley, and the

Ken Rosewall hits his forehand with an Australian grip and a straight backswing. The wrist is laid back a little and the racket face is slightly open. As always, Rosewall's body placement and balance are excellent.

inability to pull off drop shots or to play short balls (low-bouncing shots inside the service line area) deliberately.

The Eastern grip was taught by almost every coach in the United States until ten years ago. For decades the great American champions hit solid Eastern forehand drives. If a player had a natural Continental, the coach tried to change it to an Eastern, often with disastrous results: the grip would be Eastern but the style Continental. But more Australian coaches migrated to the United States and more Australians and Europeans began to hit the top ranks with a Continental or Australian grip. Today the situation has been reversed, and some coaches now force a pupil to change a natural Eastern grip to a Continental—with the same unfortunate results.

The great masters of the Eastern forehand were generally big men such as Don Budge, Dick Savitt, and Tony Trabert. A big man can get away with an Eastern forehand because he can get so much power from a standing position. The smaller fellow has to use body weight, the momentum of moving forward and of taking the ball early. Budge, Savitt, and Trabert produced great power from a standing position with just backswing and arm, whereas Jimmy Connors and Rod Laver get their power by moving into the ball. The big Eastern players hit classical forehand drives, whereas the Continental star of today will also slice his forehand approach shot so that the ball will die after it bounces. The Continental player has more variety on his forehand because he can drive it, slice it, or, with the same wind-up, have the option of drop-shotting.

Bjorn Borg has a powerful, Western-grip forehand, often hit with an open stance. He imparts heavy topspin to the ball both by bringing the racket up sharply and turning his wrist over as he hits. Borg can hold the ball on his racket and guide it with spin and wrist action. It is not the kind of stroke one would teach, but it is the premier shot in Borg's arsenal.

THE FOREHAND DRIVE

The forehand drive, whichever grip you use, consists of a wind-up, hit, and follow-through. If there were no wind-up, it would be impossible to generate any power off a soft ball. If there were no follow-through, the weight could not transfer forward smoothly, and again no power could be generated off a soft ball. The only time one can dispense with a wind-up and follow-through is against a very hard ball such as a big serve since a "block" action allows the player to use the opponent's pace. To make your own pace, a full wind-up and follow-through are necessities.

The racket head on the Continental forehand never points down toward the ground during the wind-up or at the hit. As the racket is taken back on the wind-up, the racket head is almost always higher than the wrist. If the ball is low, you don't drop your racket head; you bend your knees. The racket can either be taken straight back or it can come back in a small arc so that the completed stroke will be almost like a figure 8. At the end of the backswing, your racket is pointing to the fence behind you. As the racket swings forward in one smooth motion, it starts from under ball level and moves forward and upward until it ends pointing to the top of your opponent's fence. The swing is from low to high to put natural topspin on the ball. In the course of the backswing, the arm is bent at the elbow, remains slightly bent during the

This Evert forehand wind-up is the perfect result of endless training and drill. The racket is drawn straight back early, the racket head is only slightly raised and the wrist is moderately laid back. The weight is on the back foot and she is just starting to shift forward with the swing.

hit, and then straightens out quite a bit as the arm follows through to the finish. At no point in the backswing and during the hit is the arm ever totally stiff, since "feel" for the ball comes through a slightly bent arm.

The wrist must be firm. If it is wobbly, the racket head will droop downward or flop weakly at the moment of impact. A solid wrist is vital when learning the forehand drive, although later the player will learn wrist motion on serves, overheads, drop shots and forehand touch shots.

The Eastern forehand should not be hit with a cocked wrist (the racket head tilted upward), although this is perfectly acceptable (and preferable) with a Continental. There are two common styles of hitting an Eastern: the wrist is laid back throughout the stroke until almost the end of the follow-through or the wrist is allowed to drop slightly (not sag) so that it will come under ball level just before the hit. As long as the wrist does not wobble, either style is safe and solid.

The shoulders and head remain on the same plane throughout the stroke. Don't tilt your head or lift one shoulder or lower it. There is a natural shoulder rotation in the wind-up, and as the left shoulder rotates back, it conceals the direction in which the ball will go. The shoulder rotation is synchronized with the motion of taking the racket back. This puts the balance and weight on the right (rear) foot. As the racket comes forward toward the ball, so does the weight, with the left foot one step ahead of the racket arm. The timing is not "step-hit" but "step, then hit." The step must be forward rather than sideways since it is impossible to get full power if the body is moving in a sideways direction. The fact that the shoulders pivot on the wind-up means that a sideways stance is unnecessary. However, avoid swinging the right hip around during or after the hit: excessive hip swiveling detracts from power, gives away the shot, and puts the player off balance.

On all low or waist-high shots, the knees are bent. The player waits for the ball with his knees bent and his shoulders slightly hunched so that he is ready to move quickly and is in a good position for a low shot.

As the player develops more facility in hitting a forehand, the follow-through will change depending upon the shot he is hitting. When he is trying a low passing shot, the follow-through will not be high but almost on one plane. On a short ball the follow-through will be short, on a lob the follow-through will be high, and on normal topspin shots the follow-through will be long and high.

TOPSPIN

Topspin is imparted to the ball by moving the racket in a low-to-high forward direction. This gives the player an ample safety factor in clearing the net and it also enables the ball to be hit with great depth. Heavy topspin is imparted to the ball either by rolling the racket over on the follow-through or by pulling the racket upward sharply. I am extremely partial to normal topspin, as created by the low-to-high motion of the racket against the ball, but there are many dangers in hitting the ball

Guillermo Vilas has a full roundhouse loop swing on his forehand, characterized by an astonishingly high backswing. His body weight is low with knees bent, but his racket is high above his head. Vilas will bring his racket down as he starts his forward swing, describing an arc that will reach below the ball, then come up and over it with pronounced topspin.

with excessive topspin by rolling over or pulling up sharply. First, an excessive topspin shot hit from behind the baseline will be shallow, and one often sees Bjorn Borg, a great topspin artist, hitting balls that land regularly in the area of the service line. Second, excessive topspin is a bad approach shot because the ball bounces high. Third, it is difficult to hit with excessive topspin against a big serve: the topspin artist tries to change the flight pattern of that ball, and in breaking the pattern he can injure his arm. Some of Tony Roche's arm problems could well be from the excessive topspin he puts on a ball. Fourth, the racket is brushing up on the ball in such a quick motion that the shot is often mis-hit or mistimed. Bjorn Borg frequently mis-hits his forehand; sometimes every fourth ball sounds as though it were hit off center.

Heavy topspin can be a good addition to the repertoire of a champion if he knows when to use it. Today's topspin artists are Borg, Solomon, Laver, Richey, Vilas, and Roche. They are all good clay court players because the high bounce that topspin takes on this surface works to their advantage. (It is a disadvantage on grass because the ball slows up.) Of this group, Laver best understands when heavy topspin is most effective; he uses it when he is standing inside the baseline, so his topspin shot won't be shallow, or when returning second serve. Heavy topspin is also extremely successful in an offensive lob, as demonstrated by such skilled champions as Ilie Nastase, Manuel Santana, and Chuck McKinley. Two women players, Billie Jean King and Julie M. Heldman, use heavy topspin deliberately on offensive lobs and for a change of pace, but their basic forehands have only moderate topspin. They are not caught in the trap of hitting every ball with excessive top.

Rosie Casals, a 5'2" player who ranks in the First Ten of the world, overdoes the excessive topspin forehand. She gets no penetration on a heavy topspin that goes short; she would get much better depth on a full, long follow-through. Tom Okker of the Netherlands used to hit tremendous topspin forehands. For a while he caught many an opponent by surprise: Okker's shot would look as if it was going out and the net man would let it sail by, only to find that the heavy spin brought the ball down inside the baseline. The geniuses of the game use heavy topspin mainly for offensive lobs, change of pace, against balls that bounce well within the baseline, or against opponents who have no adequate reply.

THE FOREHAND APPROACH SHOT

There are two kinds of strong forehands. One is the deep, forcing shot from the baseline which opens up the court and makes outright winners. It is exemplified in the classical Eastern forehands of Budge, Savitt, and Trabert. A second forehand is just as effective on the baseline in opening up the court and hitting placements but it has much more flexibility. The masters of this forehand not only hit topspin and flat balls but can slice and use sidespin as well. It is a forehand with variety because with it you can play the angles, the drop shots, the drives, and the approach

Margaret Court is attacking as she hits a running forehand down the line. The grip is Australian. The racket face is open, providing the underspin that Margaret often uses on approach forehands.

Chris Evert is hitting this Eastern forehand in a slightly cramped position, her right arm held in close to the body from shoulder to elbow. Many shots require some adjustment for bounce or position. In all other respects Chris shows the care and training that characterize her ground game.

shots. The name of the game is getting to net, and a good approach shot is basic to the forehand repertoire.

The forehand approach shot should always be hit firmly and with depth, and the bounce of the ball should be low. A player with confidence in his forehand can move into the ball on second serve, either to try for an outright winner or to put the pressure on the opponent with an aggressive approach shot. The approach shot must bounce low, since if the ball bounces up the opponent can lob successfully; if you hit the ball to the opponent's shoe tops, he must hit up. If he hits up, he has to hit with underspin. The underspin ball always rises, which gives the net man a better chance to volley it away.

When moving in on a short shot, the player with the big forehand uses no backswing at all. The momentum of his run is all he needs. If the ball is high, he stops and hits with a big swing. If he has all the forehand shots in his repertoire, he can topspin that shot or fake with a hidden drop shot or do anything else he wants because he has so much time. My last choice would be topspin, since I would be moving in and reaching out in front of me, and excessive topspin is hardest to use in such a situation.

One of the best forehand approach shots is the sidespin. The ball stays low and feels very heavy on the racket. It is hit with a firm wrist, but as the racket meets the ball the wrist is laid back far more than usual so that the racket brushes forward and to the left of the ball. The follow-through is always a clear indication of a sidespin shot: it is almost on the same plane as the hit, but the racket head points to the right while the arm and wrist have moved to the left. When experimenting with this shot, try it on a reasonably high ball and make sure you hit it well in front of you. The wind-up starts from the same plane as the level of the ball; if you start from a higher plane, the ball travels downward and will not clear the net or will go short.

The first exponent of the sidespin forehand was Jack Kramer. He hit every forehand approach shot with sidespin down the line, to the backhand of a right-handed player. The ball slithered and stung when it hit the opponent's racket. Billie Jean King used the sidespin forehand approach shot over and over in her famous match against Bobby Riggs. Her body position was magnificent: the ball was taken well in front of her and she was always moving in. Kerry Melville Reid of Australia uses the forehand sidespin shot regularly, not only to approach the net but in rallies from the baseline.

CONCLUSION

The mark of the great forehand is how often it is used aggressively. The big forehand players will step around any shot in their left court that is reasonably slow and will go for the winner with a hard forehand that is perfectly disguised. Big forehand players invariably run around second serves to go for the put-away. This has a second benefit: the opponent tries to hit for too narrow a spot on the backhand or too narrow a spot on the forehand side. If your opponent starts to press on second serve because of his fear of your big forehand, he will begin to double-fault. No one takes better advantage of second serves than John Newcombe; he puts the pressure on his opponent to serve better or to take the consequences, and that's a tough position to be in when the score is 30-40, second serve.

Today's big forehand is more than a grooved baseline shot hit with great power. It is a forehand of variety that can be hit short and low or hard and deep, that can have topspin, slice, or sidespin—and, above all, that can be hit on the dead run as an approach shot.

When most players are stretched this wide, they can only play a defensive shot or pop up a lob. But Jimmy Connors has the stroke equipment (and the killer instinct) to go for a winner on a wide, high forehand. He flings himself at the ball, and his strength and agility give him surprising winners from a defensive position.

Chapter Five / The Backhand

Rod Laver is hitting a sliced crosscourt backhand with a full follow-through, a shot used in a baseline rally. In the first drawing, Rod has completed his backswing and body preparation for the shot. His weight is settling on his right (back) leg, the racket is behind his head with the racket face open, and the left shoulder and hip are turned to face the net.

In the early stages of development, the backhand is a much more difficult shot to master than the forehand, but as the player advances to a higher class, his backhand often turns out to be the better shot. There are several reasons. First, the backhand is played far more often than the forehand. Second, the backhand is the more natural shot because the right shoulder automatically turns in on the backswing. The mechanics of the stroke seem easier, provided the elbow does not jut out and the wrist remains firm. If the right shoulder pivots, if the arm swings freely, if the ball is taken well in front of the body, and if the wrist remains firm from wind-up through follow-through, this stroke can become a consistent and aggressive weapon. However, I find moving to the left not as easy as moving to the right, and my judgment in moving to the left is not as good, probably because I am a "forehand player."

THE GRIP

Unlike the forehand, there is no multiple choice of grips on the backhand. The old Western backhand with its awkward and often painful distortion of the arm has disappeared. Everyone has the conventional Eastern or Continental backhand grip (they are practically identical), with the exception of French star Françoise Durr. She hits her backhand with an Eastern forehand grip and has her forefinger pointing up the racket handle. Most players would find it painful, since the wrist takes the brunt of the impact.

Players who use the Continental grip do not have to change grips: the forehand and backhand are identical. The Eastern forehand player switches to the Eastern backhand by moving the butt of his palm around the handle approximately a quarter of a turn so that the butt of the palm is on top (see Figure 1). In "the good old days" the thumb pointed

As the forward swing starts (second drawing), the right foot is planted to launch the weight transfer forward, the left arm starts to uncoil with the racket face still open, and the hip and shoulder start to turn.

In the third sketch, the weight continues to transfer forward and the body turns through the hips. The arm has straightened, the wrist is cocked and firm, and the racket face angle is carefully tailored to provide the underspin required.

Rod's left arm is fully extended on the follow-through in the fourth sketch. The racket face is almost level with the plane of the court. The weight has transferred to the front foot.

The finish of the follow-through in the fifth sketch indicates Rod's confidence in this shot. He has hit through the ball rather than jabbing or slapping at it. The back foot moves up as he gets ready to hop into position for the next shot.

straight up the handle (this usually means the hand must turn to the left an extra ⅛ inch turn), but most players today find this too stiff a grip; instead they slant the thumb across the racket just as one would in a handshake, and the other fingers are slightly spread. Some players bunch the fingers together in what is called the "hammer grip," but the majority of good players space the fingers to get more "feel."

THE DRIVE

The biggest defect among beginners is leading with the elbow: the elbow juts out and becomes the pivot so that only half the arm is used. Actually, the right shoulder should be the pivot: the stroke is based not on elbow or wrist motion but on the entire arm swinging from the shoulder.

As the right shoulder turns in, the weight moves onto the left (back) foot. At the finish of the wind-up, the racket head is pointing directly to your back fence. When you take the swing, think of throwing your racket to the top of the fence, with the shoulder as the pivot point. Normally, if the shot is thought of as a swing from the shoulder, one need not worry about a sagging or limp wrist; the wrist takes care of itself if the shoulder does the work. When problems occur and the elbow starts to lead or the wrist sags so that the racket head points to the ground, an easy cure is to put the left hand on the racket and hit the ball with two hands, just as thought it were another forehand.

Any tennis swing should feel natural—neither cramped nor stiff. In a natural motion, the wind-up must have a bent elbow, since it would be unnatural and awkward to stretch the arm out stiffly. As the arm swings forward, it straightens but never becomes rigid. At the moment of impact, when racket meets ball well in front of the body, there is a slight bend in the elbow. At the end of the follow-through, the arm is almost but not quite straight.

The knees are bent so that you are ready for any low ball and the shoulders are hunched so that you are well balanced. Now you are ready for any low ball but you can straighten if you must take a high one. On a high ball, the wind-up starts on a higher plane, but the same action is used. Players with good backhands can hit the ball at ankle level, knee level, waist level, shoulder level, and even higher, while still having that confident feeling of swinging from the shoulder.

THE THREE BACKHANDS

The basic methods of hitting a backhand are flat, topspin, and underspin. The flat shot has no spin at all, and only gravity brings the ball down into court. The topspin ball rotates in a forward motion and the underspin in a backward direction, and it is the spin that pulls the ball down into the court. The flat shot has the most pace; the topspin shot, because of the forward spinning motion, also has good pace; underspin has less pace and is easier for the net man to volley away because the ball moves upward as it travels across the net. The well-

John Newcombe has a carefully produced backhand, hit with a minimum of spin, which he guides with good accuracy on approaches to the net. He does not hit hard, relying on preparation, timing, and wrist control for placement. Here he runs forward, using his body momentum to impart some speed to a backhand approach guided down the line. The shot is hit well in front of the body and is a chip (a shot with very little backswing and an open racket face).

rounded player should have all three shots and should know when to use them—topspin for passing shots, because the ball dips when it crosses the net and the pace is hard; underspin against low-bouncing balls to make them rise and clear the net; flat against short, fairly high balls to hit the put-away; underspin (also called slice) to pull off delicate angle shots; topspin for backhand lobs because when they finally bounce there is a forward motion; flat for power, as when one hits directly at the net man; lots of underspin to create a perfect drop shot; topspin for safety on a deep crosscourt; underspin for safety on a deep down-the-line, etc. To put it another way, flat is for power (at the expense of control), topspin is for passing shots, lobs, and deep baseline exchanges, and underspin is for low, short balls under net level, for touch shots, and for change of pace.

The backhand topspin is the safest shot, although every good player will also add an underspin backhand for low balls and approach shots. Among the great players with outstanding backhands are Don Budge, Dick Savitt, Ken Rosewall, Tony Trabert, Frank Kovacs, Rod Laver, Pauline Betz, and Billie Jean King. All but Rosewall used top-spin, although most of them could also underspin at will.

HOW TO HIT WITH SPIN

In flat shots and topspin shots, the racket face is perpendicular to the ground and the strings meet the ball head on. The racket face tilts slightly for underspin so that the strings come under the ball. Because there is no upward trajectory on a flat ball, one can only hit flat when the ball is *above* net level. The racket action is a downward movement (from high to low) on an underspin or slice backhand, with the racket face tilted slightly so that it can brush under the ball. The racket action is an upward movement (from low to high) on a topspin backhand, and the racket face is perpendicular to the ground throughout. The racket action is on one plane for the flat shot. In other words, the wind-up is high on an underspin but the follow-through is low; the wind-up on the topspin is low and the follow-through is high (the racket ends up pointing to the top of the opponent's fence); and the wind-up and follow-through on the flat ball are at ball level, which should be at least 4 feet from the ground.

The fault of most backhands is too much underspin. The racket face is slanted too much, causing the ball to rise. Until the last decade, most teaching pros (Tom Stow being one of the few exceptions) claimed it was too difficult to teach the topspin shot to the average player. As a result, there were numerous terrible backhands on the circuit, including my own. Among the great players with backhand weaknesses (because they could not topspin) were Fred Perry, Jack Kramer, Budge Patty, Jaroslav Drobny, Neale Fraser, and Lennart Bergelin. Patty probably had the weakest backhand but eventually he did acquire a topspin lob. One weakness of having only an underspin backhand is the inability to lob effectively: the ball does not travel forward after the bounce.

Virginia Wade uses heavy underspin on almost all her backhands. Her control with underspin is better than on the topspin she uses for some passing shots. She has excellent depth and is particularly effective on underspin approach backhands. Her wind-up is high, with an open racket face. From here she will slice under and through the ball.

Arthur Ashe can stretch and get down to the ball when he has to, particularly on his backhand (one of the few weaknesses in his great game is a tendency to stand too straight for low forehands). On this low backhand he is well balanced, with a low center of gravity, and his racket is below the ball as he swings forward and up with a short but firm stroke.

The best shot in Arthur Ashe's repertoire, outside of his famous serve, is his topspin backhand, which he hits freely and with confidence. The topspin is provided by the upward motion of the racket, the face being very slightly closed at the hit. Arthur can also chip accurately on his backhand, shortening the backswing so that the shot is little more than a block.

The outstanding shot in Guillermo Vilas' repertoire is his topspin backhand, a full and free swing from and to anywhere in the court. His backswing starts low (in contrast to his forehand) and he swings sharply up and over the ball with outstanding accuracy in direction and with good pace. While he can hit underspin backhands, he prefers full topspin even on high balls, ending his swing high above his head.

Manuel Orantes used an underspin backhand to great effect in the finals of the U.S. Open against Jimmy Connors. In the semifinals Connors had eaten up the high-bouncing topspins of Bjorn Borg: he hit down on them and often followed to net. He could not use the same attack effectively against Orantes' low-bouncing backhands. The balls were bouncing *under* net level, which meant Connors had to lift the ball on his return. When Connors tried to come to net, he could hit neither as hard nor as accurately because the low-bouncing shots of Orantes did not set up the way the high-bouncing balls of Borg did. Orantes' underspin backhands had uncovered a Connors weakness.

Variety on the backhand is ideal. Only the big men of the game (Budge, Savitt, and Trabert) could afford to topspin the drive practically all the time. Rod Laver, a much smaller man, could hit for winners or slice intentionally. He had power and control; he could use topspin or underspin. When an opponent got grooved to his speed, Laver changed to spins. Tom Okker also has a good variety on the backhand, using topspin and underspin.

The best backhand approach shot is the one with variety. The player should be able to hit flat, with topspin or underspin. This gives him the option of driving or drop-shotting, going for the bullet or the sharp angle, making the ball bounce high or low. However, one should never forget that the topspin backhand is the basic shot, and, until one has perfected it, there is no point in learning variations. The latter come easily once the primary shot has been learned.

Manuel Orantes depends on control and deception rather than power, and his backhand has plenty of both. Most of his backhands are hit with a rather short swing, usually with slight underspin, and Orantes obtains what power he has by his excellent weight and body balance. Here he moves forward into a low backhand, hit as a short chip, with almost the same motion he would use in taking a low backhand volley.

Chapter Six / The Two-handed Shots

Players with two-handed backhands can drop the racket head on low balls without losing control. Then, if the racket is pulled up sharply, pronounced topspin is produced. Harold Solomon can drop his racket head and make amazing sharp crosscourts in this way. In contrast, most one-handed backhand players use underspin to handle low shots, and so it is quite difficult to hit sharp crosscourts.

The two-handed backhand is so popular today that one wouldn't think twice if a beginner or an intermediate was taught (or picked up) a two-handed grip. The 1974 U.S. and Wimbledon Champion, Jimmy Connors, and the 1975 Wimbledon Champion, Chris Evert, hit with two hands on the backhand side. So do Bjorn Borg (1974 Italian and French champion), Harold Solomon (he made the 1975 World Championship of Tennis Finals), Frew McMillan (former World's Doubles Champion with Bob Hewitt), Cliff Drysdale and Eddie Dibbs (WCT stars), Billy Martin (a National Junior Champion), Laurie Fleming Rowley (a Virginia Slimsite), Jeanne Evert (a U.S. Wightman Cupper), Carrie Fleming (a U.S. Junior Girls' Champion), and several dozen young Floridians. Zan Guerry, a former Junior Champion, was so impressed with Solomon's two-handed backhand that he relearned his own with two hands. In the past, fewer pre- and post-World War II players tried this grip because it was not considered "classical," but in Australia Vivian McGrath in the 1930s and John Bromwich in the pre- and post-World War II years were highly successful in international competition. For a long period of time one only rarely spotted a backhand two-hander, although Peaches Bartkowicz won the National Junior Girls title three years in a row in the 1960s and Mike Belkin of Florida won the National Boys and the National Juniors in the same decade.

There have been far fewer two-handed forehands. I have always used it and Frew McMillan hits two-handed on the forehand as well as on the backhand. Jimmy Connors, a lefty, has in my opinion two forehands—a one-handed forehand on his left side and a two-handed forehand on his right (backhand) side. I cannot think of any others. Recently Nana Sato of Japan was having problems with her forehand. She closed the racket face just before the hit and could not prevent herself from doing it. In desperation she took to hitting with two hands, which enabled her to hit a crisp, firm forehand. However, her coach in

Japan felt the two-handed shot would not give her a big enough reach (this is true) and so she is hitting one-handed again. This leaves her with the same old problem.

I am right-handed, so I hit my two-handed forehand with the left hand by the end of the handle and the right hand above the left. If my left hand were on top, I would shorten my reach. The two-handed shot is hit like the one-hander, but I put more body and shoulder motion into the stroke, I get closer to the ball, and the shots are extremely firm because of the support of the second hand. I can slice (get under the ball) by turning my wrist; the wrist is not floppy, however, because of the two-handed support. I can also hit flat or with a little or a lot of topspin.

Many players with a two-handed backhand will let the racket head drop. It is almost impossible to drop the racket head very low on a one-handed shot since the angle of the wrist makes it wobbly. Two-handers Harold Solomon, Billy Martin, and Eddie Dibbs (and Chris Evert on occasion) will drop the racket head and still hit firmly because of the support of the second hand. Without that second hand, the shot would be a loser. I never dropped the racket head on my two-handed forehand because I bent down to the ball. The reason Solomon has so much trouble on grass when the bounce is low is that he drops his racket head instead of bending: thus he is shoveling rather than stroking.

There are many reasons to hit a backhand with two hands. The support of the second hand overcomes the problems of a weak wrist, and it gives precision and disguise to a shot. The two wrists reinforce each other to hold firm even when hitting a hard or deep shot. This wrist solidity brings precision. Backhand errors spring from a wrist that cannot hold firm against a hard impact or from a wrist which moves slightly as the ball is hit even if it is not a hard shot. The two-handed backhand also has disguise. Changing the direction of a two-handed drive is accomplished by hitting the ball a little earlier, or later, or by swiveling both wrists together to make the racket head come through faster or slower. This last-minute action makes it very tough to anticipate the direction of the hit.

Beginners can develop terrible habits on the forehand or backhand side, and almost always they are corrected by temporarily hitting with two hands. The two-handed shot naturally pulls the front shoulder inward on the wind-up. It almost always makes the weight come through on the shot and almost invariably prevents the elbow from leading on the backhand. Jean Hoxie, the late great Hamtramck coach, started all her young players with two-handed backhands because many of them were too small to hold the racket head up. Most of her players eventually ended up with one-handed drives, although Peaches Bartkowicz stuck with her two-handed backhand and achieved the remarkable feat of winning the national title in her age division every year from age eleven through eighteen.

The big disadvantage of the two-handed shot is lack of reach. Cliff Drysdale and Jimmy Connors will hit very wide shots with one hand only. The two-handed player has to be a little faster or must hit with one hand when he is fully extended.

I am hitting a two-handed forehand on the run, having held the forward motion of my racket for an instant to direct the ball down the line. As I hit, my weight will come forward. The two-handed stroke provides the wrist brace required for control whether the shot is hit early or late, down the line or crosscourt.

The left arm, held close to the body, acts as a brace to insure the precise racket position and reinforce the right arm and wrist in Harold Solomon's two-handed backhand. Harold comes up and sharply over the ball, using a lot of topspin, and his two-handed action permits him lots of sharp angles and disguise without losing accuracy.

There is really very little difference between Jimmy Connors' two-handed backhand and my two-handed forehand. Both are aggressive, almost flat power strokes from the right side of the body. Jimmy launches himself at the ball, rushing net behind the resultant bullet whenever he can. The two-handed technique allows a hard, flat shot to be hit with maximum directional control. As Jimmy hits the ball, his left leg will swing forward as he starts his run for the net.

Chris Evert follows through on her two-handed backhand hit down the line, ending with the racket head pointing to the sky. With the same wind-up, Chris can hit the ball an instant sooner and close the racket face, producing a sharp crosscourt topspin drive.

On the two-handed backhand, the player invariably hits with a backhand grip on the right hand and an Eastern forehand or Continental grip with the left (supporting) hand. However, a player could use an Eastern forehand with his right hand since he has so much help from the second hand. The problems are reaching for a wide one on the backhand with one hand (and having the wrong grip) or eventually deciding in favor of a one-handed shot and having to learn a new grip.

The follow-through of the two-hander is very much like that of the one-hander. Most of the follow-throughs end up pointing to the opponent's fence. However, I sometimes wrap my racket all the way around my neck, and Cliff Drysdale will do pretty much the same thing on his two-handed backhand. *Chacun à son goût.*

There are some peculiarities in the two-handed style. Practically all of them are hit closer to the body than the one-hander, particularly when the player has plenty of time. If a one-hander did this, the shot would be cramped. One sometimes sees wrist-snap on a two-handed shot; if the same style were used by a one-hander, he would be "hooking" the ball instead of coming through smoothly. Two-handed backhand players like Drysdale can face the net in an open stance and hit the ball solidly; it is almost impossible to pivot and hit the ball well from this position with one hand. Screwy wind-ups are possible on two-handed shots, and one only has to see the curlicues that Eddie Dibbs makes to realize the solidity the second hand gives to the shot. Two-handed players can approach the ball with a closed racket face, then simply turn both wrists to straighten the racket face just before the ball is hit. Solomon and Dibbs both approach the ball with a closed racket, which is deadly for a one-hander.

If you want to play with two hands, you will get firmness, disguise, precision, a natural weight transfer, and the ability to hit with several kinds of spin. Some players already have all these attributes in a one-handed shot and, in addition, they have a bigger reach. If you are lacking firmness (your wrist is floppy), precision (hard balls jolt you because the wrist is not strong), and/or a proper weight transference (your hips swivel backwards as you hit), I recommend trying the two-hander either as a temporary or permanent alleviation of your current problems. Remember, a two-handed shot is not an irrevocable commitment.

When I hit my two-handed forehand without having to move, I approach the ball with a closed stance, drawing the racket straight back with both arms outstretched, then swinging straight through the ball with only a hint of topspin. My stroke is basically an Eastern forehand with an assist from the left hand and arm.

Chapter Seven / The Serve

The hardest shot for a beginner to learn is the serve because it requires perfect coordination. Both arms are moving at the same time: the left arm and hand rise slowly to toss the ball to an exact spot while the right arm and racket swing in an accelerated motion to meet the ball and hit it with power and accuracy. Not only do the arms have separate rhythms, motions, and functions but the weight must shift, the shoulder come through and the wrist snap forward with exact precision. The beginner need not freeze at the thought of combining all these movements. He can start out with a simplified grip and an abbreviated hit which will enable him to serve the ball into court almost immediately.

THE NOVICE SERVE

Many beginners (and almost all young people) do not have the wrist strength to serve with the Continental grip. They start with an Eastern forehand grip while recognizing that it is a temporary expedient. The swing and the weight transference can be minimized so that the emphasis is on the toss and hit only.

All players, beginners or advanced, use the same stance on serve. The body is almost sideways to the net. In the forehand court, the right (back) foot is usually a little more to the right than the left (front) foot. In the backhand court, the right (back) foot is more to the left of the left (front) foot. In both cases, the shoulders are lined up diagonally with the opposing service court. The feet are slightly spread (about 12 to 18 inches apart). The right hand grips the handle (the beginner uses the Eastern forehand) and the racket throat is gently cradled in the finger tips of the left hand. The racket head points to the opposing service court. Both arms are bent (the right arm at a 90° angle), and the racket is held at slightly above waist level. The racket is almost

1. This is the start of the forward-back-forward, roundhouse, rock-and-roll service action that I advocate, particularly for smaller players. Both arms are extended toward the net and the weight is on my front (left) leg as I lean forward.

2. My body straightens and the weight shifts to the back (right) leg. As the racket arm comes down, the toss arm comes up. Both arms move in unison, although the motion of the right arm will shortly accelerate.

3. Now my knees bend and the racket arm swings almost straight back as the ball is tossed by thrusting my left arm upward. At this stage my racket is well behind my body, in a more accentuated style than most players use, evidencing the full, free swing I prefer.

4. Here I am into the coiled crouch. The knees are flexed even further and the back is arched like a spring. My right elbow has bent to start the racket head down behind my back.

5. From here on all the action is upward and forward. The knees start to straighten, providing an extra power thrust, and the back does likewise, as the racket head reaches down to its lowest spot by cocking the wrist. I use the toes of my left foot as a base to push off and up.

6. The knees are straighter, the back is straighter, the weight is on the toes and the racket arm is coming up, leading the racket head at this stage. I am going to get my full height on the hit.

7. The foot-knee-body spring is almost completely uncoiled as I hurtle myself at the ball. The only pronounced angle left is between arm and racket, with the forthcoming wrist snap to provide the last ounce of acceleration to the racket head.

8. Everything is as straight as possible, and as high as possible, as I jump into the air to hit the ball. This full extension is only possible as part of a full wind-up and follow-through sequence.

9. Both feet are still off the ground as I continue my swing with the racket moving forward and down. The eyes follow the ball and the shoulder comes through; otherwise the rest of the body has not moved.

10. The pronounced forward extension of my arm and racket head here is the exemplification of the forward-back forward principle on service. The arm and racket are still swinging—forward, down, and around—quite freely.

11. The downward follow-through is completed and at the same time I have landed on my left leg, preserving my body balance. Players who do not jump on serve (plus some who do) swing their right leg through and land on the right foot, a full step into court.

12. At the end of the full, free swing, with the racket around to the left side of my body, I use my left foot as a pivot. I can shove off to move forward, left or right or to stop in place.

parallel to the ground (the head points very slightly upward), and the racket face is perpendicular to the ground.

The beginner will now do two things only—toss the ball and hit it with a simplified motion. He will keep his body almost motionless for the first dozen sessions to avoid all the extraneous contortions that generally encumber a novice's serve. His knees won't bend and his weight won't shift backward. The only movement he will learn at this stage is a follow-through. The serve will look a little stiff but it will be free from wild wiggles and bows.

The simplified hit means an abbreviated swing. The beginner lifts his right arm *without a backswing* to the point where the racket head is "scratching" his lower back and his elbow is jutting forward. He is now in a perfect position to hit. As soon as the tossed ball is in the air, his right arm comes forward and straightens at the same time. The arm and racket form a straight line at the moment of impact, and the hit is slightly in front of the body. Because the ball is hit in front of the body, the right shoulder comes forward naturally. The follow-through is a full one, with the arm and racket finishing in a big sweep that ends behind the left leg.

THE TOSS

All players (beginners, advanced players, and champions) use the same toss motion. I am going into it in great detail because it is the *sine qua non* of a good serve. Additionally, it can be learned by a beginner in very quick order if he will practice it every day for a week. Once he has it, the rest of the serve is easy, since the tossed ball will always go to the identical spot.

The ball is almost always held by the finger tips: it rests evenly just inside the tips of the thumb and the first two or three fingers, with the pinkie acting as anchorman. (When two balls are in the toss hand, the top ball rests on the thumb, forefinger, and middle finger.) The ball is never held inside the fingers or in the palm. It is gripped in the same way one would grasp a glass of water if one were holding the bottom of the glass. The position of the fingers never changes during the toss: they point to the right and slightly upward (approximately at a 45° angle) and simply release the ball (which is impelled by the arm) when the toss arm is totally extended in the air.

The upward motion of the arm is what causes the ball to go up, and the fingers do not release the ball until the toss arm is up almost as high as it will go. No one can achieve accuracy on the toss if the ball is released too soon (when the arm is extended only halfway).

There are large variations in the action of the toss arm before it reaches the fully extended position. Almost every good player starts with the tossing hand at slightly higher than waist level and reasonably adjacent to the racket throat or racket face. In other words, the tossing hand is held 12 to 18 inches in front of the body and slightly to the right of the left shoulder as the action begins. Many players then allow the toss hand to drop down to the leg and then bring it up again in one long, smooth action to time it with the long wind-up of the racket arm.

A large group of players allows the toss hand to drop only slightly; a much smaller group does not allow it to drop at all. The latter procedure is more difficult to learn, since the left arm tends to move downward at the moment that the right arm begins its backward swing. But the downward motion of the toss hand serves no purpose, and the less there is of it, the better the chance for an accurate toss.

The tossing hand starts 12 to 18 inches in front of the body and slightly to the right of the left shoulder. When the ball is hit, it should still be 12 to 18 inches in front and slightly to the right, approximately 35 to 40 inches above head height. Therefore, the less you do with your toss arm, hand, and fingers in the form of swinging the arm sideways, moving the wrist, or flicking the fingers sideways or backward, the better. The aim is to raise the arm slowly until the elbow is almost straight, at which point the ball is released from the upturned fingers. If the fingers are always pointing to the right and upward, no sudden correction is needed at the last minute.

The toss is badly neglected by the lower echelon of players, even though it is basic to a proper serve and can be practiced anywhere, at any time. It can be practiced by itself until it is perfectly grooved, then practiced together with the racket arm. It should be so grooved that a thousand tosses will always end in the same spot at the same height. It should be the one factor you can always depend on, and it is up to you to make it that reliable.

The most common toss errors among inexperienced players are caused by gripping the ball inside the fingers so that it is not easily released; letting the ball go at shoulder level instead of when the toss arm has straightened (the longer the ball has to travel, the less the control of its direction); moving the toss arm far too quickly so that the ball shoots up too high and the server has to wait for it to drop; rotating the toss arm so that it swings over to the right, which makes it impossible for the toss to be in front; moving the fingers at the moment the ball is released, which means the ball will not follow a straight trajectory; braking the arm motion before it is completed so that the toss is too low and cannot be hit by an extended racket arm; and moving the wrist when the ball is released, which usually causes the ball to go backward and makes it extremely awkward for the server to hit.

The easiest way to see for yourself is to watch the champions on a television screen, in play at your local courts or in stop-action pictures. The greatest variation you will see is in the start, when quite a few of the champions will let the toss arm drop way down (a rhythm motion for them) before bringing it up again. Vijay Amritraj has an extremely long toss motion and a beautiful, powerful, natural serve. Do not try it unless you have Vijay's talent. Watch the simplest, most precise tosses and copy them. In all cases of good serves you will see that the toss is in front and slightly to the right of the body. This is necessary for anyone following his serve to net. For example, how can you toss directly over your head if your whole motion is netward bound? Even if you are not following your serve to net, *pretend you are* so that you get a forward impact on the hit.

Many a good server has a toss that seems too low—until you realize that the racket arm is fully extended. Roscoe Tanner seems to have a low toss because the action is so fast. He never has to wait for the ball to descend, and, because he is so gifted, he can even hit the tossed ball while it is still on the rise.

Look at the great players who have never grooved the toss and who occasionally toss so badly that they catch it, say "Sorry," and try another toss. One in fifty will have every shot except the toss, and usually the explanation is that the player was originally a baseliner who tossed to his or her right (for slice) and not enough in front; the old toss to the right was grooved and the "regrooving" shows brittleness when the pressure is on. They have to think "I'm coming to net behind serve" to get the toss well in front.

Torben Ulrich, a mad Dane with many sane ideas, has a toss so foolproof that he can practice with his serve at night on unlit courts without a moon. Can you?

ADVANCED PLAYERS

As a player gets older and stronger, he should use the Continental grip on serve. It allows him to snap his wrist, to slice, to hit flat or with American twist. It is very difficult to spin a ball with a forehand grip, and the only champions in the last few decades who have served with a forehand grip are Alex Olmedo, Ted Schroeder, and Shirley Fry.

The advanced player also can take a much fuller swing. The right arm and racket usually make a full circle before the back-scratching action. The arm sweeps all the way behind the body, then drops behind the back and comes forward with increased momentum. There is also much more body movement: the weight rocks to the back feet, then comes thrusting forward. The smaller the player, the better it is to have a full swing, a big rocking motion, and a hurling forward of the weight and body at the hit. I have always used a hurtling action to achieve power, and I believe a small player like Harold Solomon would have a bigger serve if he used this type of action.

The better player can use a more closed stance on a serve to disguise the direction. In the backhand court my right foot is not behind my left foot but almost on the same line. Now my opponent cannot tell whether I am going to serve to the left, right, or center.

THE THREE SERVES

It is ideal to have three serves—the flat, the slice, and the American twist. I do not recommend the American twist as a basic serve because so often it sets up with its high bounce and slower speed for the opponent. The taller the player, the more easily he can hit the flat serve and get it in court; I seldom use it because I do not have the height and will miss too many first serves. The slice serve gives excellent control and can still be hit with good pace.

Arthur Ashe's famous serve demonstrates the full reach and use of height as Arthur's arm and racket are fully extended. This serve is a flat cannonball (no spin of any kind), with only placement and gravity to bring it into the right spot.

The toss on the flat serve is in front of the body and slightly to the right. The racket face is flat (not slanted in any direction) at the moment of impact. In order to clear the net with safety and land deep in the boundary of the opponent's service court, the server should be 6'4" with a big reach. Small players cannot hit totally flat; even fairly tall players use a small amount of spin on what is called their "flat" serves. The flat or cannonball serve should be used only when you are leading: it provides more power but it causes more errors. It is particularly effective when the server goes for the center line or directly at the receiver's body to jam the follow-through.

The slice serve is also tossed to the right and in front of the body. For more pronounced slice, the ball is tossed even more to the right. The racket face comes around the right side of the ball but obviously with a forward motion as well. It is the best basic serve since the ball moves sideways as well as forward after the bounce.

The toss for the American twist is directly over the head or over the left part of the head, and the follow-through is across the right leg rather than across the left. The racket moves from left to right behind the ball, although there is still a lot of forward motion. One major liability of this serve is the strain it puts on the back: the knees bend and the back arches just before the hit. A second liability is the ineffectiveness of this serve if it is not hit with great depth. Third, it is sometimes a good serve to the opponent's high backhand, but then it is usually a set-up if it goes to the opponent's high forehand: if it must always be served to the backhand, its limitation is the lack of variety. The American twist is a good second serve (it can also be used when you want to throw in a second serve for a first serve). It is also effective against a small opponent because he has to hit it at head height. Still, it is an easy serve to read, and the opponent can step around the ball and take the net away from you.

The American twist has become the forgotten serve of the 1970s. The players who used it best were stars of the past—Henry Prusoff and Les Stoefen in the 1930s, Frank Kovacs in the 1940s, Neale Fraser in the late 1950s, and Chuck McKinley in the 1960s. It is still a useful shot for variety or against a particular opponent. It can also be effective in doubles since the ball slows up and it gives the server much more time to get to net.

THE BIG SERVES IN TENNIS

The best serve I have ever seen in tennis from the viewpoint of perfect rhythm, effortless motion, and effectiveness was that of Pancho Gonzalez. The toss was smooth as silk, the knee motion classical, the cock of the arm impeccable, the arc made by arm and racket totally fluid—and the ball came off the racket like a bullet. In his best playing years, one could predict that, if Gonzalez was down 0-40 on serve, the first serve would always go in. It always did.

Other players with great serves were Jack Kramer and Lew Hoad. Among the smaller players, Bobby Riggs had a superb serve, as did

Chuck McKinley.   Rosie Casals also does very well for 5'2".   The two biggest serves in the game today—John Newcombe's and Roscoe Tanner's—are unique.   Newcombe rocks forward and then backward (the type of action I advocate for small players), while Tanner has such a fast action that it seems he is taking the ball while it is still rising.   Colin Dibley of Australia serves bullets.   Virginia Wade and Billie Jean King have very tough serves.   Wade's arms are not synchronized (the motion of one starts before the other), but the power is excellent.   King does not have quite as much power, but she moves the opponent around well and can change her spins.

What counts most in evaluating a serve is how strong, deep, and consistent the second serve is.   When Rod Laver turned pro, he discovered his second serve was too short.   Hoad and Rosewall ate him alive, winning 24 out of 25 consecutive singles matches.   It took Laver three months to develop a better second serve.   Colin Dibley has too big a second serve because he double-faults too much.   Newcombe has the best second serve for length, consistency, and accuracy, although it let him down in his big head-to-head match with Jimmy Connors (he served eight double-faults).   Vladimir Zednik has the biggest serve for sheer power, but it is not consistent enough; he wound up in the cellar at the end of the 1975 WCT Tour.   Clark Graebner had a great serve, but he could not get to net well behind it.   Stan Smith has always been known for his big serve, but he has lost some pace in recent years.   Arthur Ashe has a perfect serve in the forehand court because it pulls the opponent very wide to the forehand.

In 1930 John Doeg won the U.S. Nationals on service alone.   In 1961 Mike Sangster of Great Britain got to the semifinals of Wimbledon and of Forest Hills on a cannonball serve.   Sangster used to practice his serve three hours a day, three times a week.   His groundstrokes were wild and his volley highly erratic, but in the days before tie-breakers it was difficult to beat him.   So there is good reason for calling the serve the single most important stroke in the game.

Jimmy Connors has an excellent serve, utilizing his full height.   Perhaps the best feature of this serve is Jimmy's ability to keep his opponent guessing on direction, spin, and attack.   Jimmy mixes all his options, keeping the receiver off balance so that he cannot get set for the return.

THE CHAMPIONS' SERVES

Once the toss, action, and hit are grooved and sound, the serve still has to be practiced.   I like to use markers, placing them deep in the service court in the middle, right, and left.   Depth is one of the keys to good serving: if the ball is shallow, the opponent can step in and take the net.   Rosewall had a short second serve.   Gonzalez, Jimmy Connors, and I would come in behind it and rush him, threatening to volley his volley.

The ball must be moved on serve.   Do not always serve to one spot and let the receiver get grooved.   Let him worry about where you are going.   I go to the backhand a lot in the forehand court, but I do not set a pattern; if I served 90% to the backhand, the opponent would be grooved.   Still it is dangerous to serve to the forehand in the forehand court at 30-all: the receiver may get more angle than you, and it is hard to read his forehand.   I make it a practice not to serve to the forehand in the forehand court on a vital point: if I try to pull the receiver wide on the forehand, I might miss on first serve. Now I am in the position of throwing in a second serve on a vital point, and, if it is not hard or deep enough, he can run around it, putting me on the defensive.

On 40-30 (the closing point), I often serve right at the body to jam the player. There is much less risk in serving to the body, since the serve cannot go wide. Most players tighten up on second serve, and this is the reason that a second serve must have good length.

In serving in the ad court, there is not as much danger if one serves to the forehand. At 40-30 I will sometimes deliberately serve to the forehand because almost always the return will come to my forehand volley, enabling me to go for the crosscourt volley winner. Newcombe in the ad court will often serve to the center line because he also has confidence in his forehand volley.

STRATEGY SUMMARY

Get the first serve in on vital points. The tendency of most players is to try too hard on first serve when the point is critical. Play your safest first serve when the chips are down—if you miss, you put more pressure on yourself to hit a good second serve. Be more consistent on first serve when you are behind in the game score. Save the "big serve" for when you have points to burn—30-0, 40-15—or when the score is 0-0. Do not serve wide to the forehand in the forehand court except at 0-0, 30-0, or 40-15 (never at 30-all). Mix up your serves not only by changing directions and spins but by serving directly at the body as well. Practice with markers so your second serve is not a sitter. Throw in a second serve first for change of pace. Keep your opponent off balance by preventing him from guessing or reading you.

Chapter Eight / The Overhead

T he overhead resembles the serve in that the ball is hit with the arm extended upward, the "hit" motion is the same (a forward motion of the shoulder and a wrist snap), and the grip is identical (almost a "backhand" grip). The overhead differs from the serve in that the wind-up is usually shorter, the follow-through is not always as full, the player frequently must move, run, and/or jump to get into position, and, on short overheads, the ball can be hit flat and with a decided downward swing. The overhead, unlike the serve, can be hit from any area of the court—by the net, in midcourt, at the baseline, or even well behind the baseline on some bounce-overheads.

BEGINNERS AND INTERMEDIATES

A player who has no confidence in his overhead can develop "feel" for the moving target by first grooving himself on set-ups—short, easily reachable balls that are lobbed to him while he is at net. The lobs should be short enough so that, instead of having to leap or move back, he can hit the ball *in front of him* with a partially downward motion. He learns to judge how long the extended arm-racket line is, and this teaches him the feeling of the height of the ball at the time he should hit it. By the time he has hit 15 or 20 set-ups, he is finding his range. *Judgment is best developed against set-ups,* and only then can the player start moving back for deeper and therefore more difficult lobs.

The beginner should aim for a sideways stance and point toward the ball with his left arm and hand. This automatically lowers the right shoulder and puts the weight on the back (right) foot. Since the shoulder comes through on the hit, the weight automatically moves forward, which gives power to the shot. The action is a shortened version of the serve: instead of the long, sweeping arc of arm and racket swinging

The stop-action catches Rod Laver in the middle of a leaping smash, just as his racket meets the ball. Rod is fully stretched out as he hits but his wrist is in the process of snapping forward to direct the shot and add to the power of his arm motion. When he began his leap, Rod's left foot was planted behind his right, but he has scissored in the air and his left leg is now moving in front.

back, the racket is simply picked up and dropped behind the back. The player can then hold this position (for one or two seconds, if necessary) until the lob gets within range. The follow-through is also shorter than that of the serve, and the racket often stops when the right arm has come down after the hit (it does not necessarily have to sweep past the left leg).

The grip is going to be a challenge to the novice. It is almost a back-hand grip, which means the player will have to *twist his wrist around* in order to hit the ball flat. If he forgets to turn his wrist, his overhead will sail way over to the left. The grip will not feel natural until the novice has used it in three or four practice sessions. But this grip will allow him to snap his wrist forward, and this is what will eventually add power to his overhead.

After the player has acquired a good eye for set-up overheads, the lobs can be *slightly* deeper so that he is either forced to move back a few steps or to leap for the ball. His timing may suffer a set-back since he has to run to get under the ball or jump to reach it. Whenever he loses the feel, he should go back to the set-ups to regain his confidence, then start on lobs where he has only to move back one or two steps. Since any novice must crawl before he can walk and walk before he can run, a novice tennis player must learn the stationary overhead, then the two-steps-back-and-hit overhead before he tries to smash high lobs or crack bounce-overheads.

The most common errors of beginners are: facing the net; not letting the racket head drop behind the back on the backswing; taking too big a swing when fine timing is required; holding the racket with the wrong grip; stopping the follow-through a foot after the ball has been hit; and hitting down so much that the overhead goes short or even into the net.

ADVANCED PLAYERS

The better player whose overhead has gone sour can sharpen up by hitting set-ups. He goes back to the fundamentals, making sure that his side is to the net, his swing is not too big, and his weight is coming forward. When his eye and his confidence are back, he practices more difficult overheads and can increase the freedom and length of his swing.

As the lobs get deeper, the alternatives are: shuffling backward with the side to the net for slightly deep balls; running back with the side slightly turned to net for much deeper balls; and/or leaping in the air with a scissors-kick jump-overhead. The backwards-skip is actually a three-step shuffle *without* a hop. The right leg goes back one step, the left leg goes back to a position just in front of the right one, then the right leg goes back once more while the left leg actually comes up in the air and points forward. As the left leg is up, the racket is scratching the back and is about to start its forward motion. At the hit, the weight comes down on the left leg and the right leg swings over. When the lob is much deeper, the player runs back with his side to net (so that he can follow the ball while still being in position) until he gets under the shot,

Jan Kodes is attempting one of the most spectacular shots in the game—a leaping backhand overhead. This is a desperation stab, to prevent a well-placed offensive lob from becoming a winner, but some of the top players have such powerful and agile wrists that they can leap up, with their back to the net, and place the shot remarkably well with a wrist snap.

VI-4

at which time his weight should be on his right leg and his left leg should go up. At the hit, the right arm and shoulder come forward and, if a leap is required, the right leg scissor-kicks; if no leap is required, the left leg comes down and the right leg swings over on the follow-through.

Overheads hit by advanced players should never be babied. They should be hit for the opening with moderate to hard pace or they should be hit with as much sting as the player can control. Advanced players are too good to "push" overheads; at worst, they should take a medium swing for a deep or an angled area. Only when they are in the back court will they frequently opt to give up speed for spin.

Most right-handers hit their overheads to their right but those who have mastered slice will hit more often to their left. For lefties, reverse these directions. Particularly in doubles the sharp angle of right-handers to the right and left-handers to the left is used all the time. Champions are able to hit overheads in either direction, but when the lob is tough they will usually favor one side.

All short lobs should be hit flat unless the right-hander wants to go to his left; in this case he will put a little slice on the ball to guide it. Lobs taken at mid-court are usually hit flat, since there is much power to be gained that way without much risk. Deep lobs that are taken in the area of the baseline should be sliced since the distance to the net is now so great that players are not tall enough to hit flat and still clear the net with safety.

Each player will find whether he hits his overhead better when his feet are planted or when he jumps. Some players would much rather jump than move back; others have a better feeling of security when their feet are planted. To each his own, depending upon the rhythm he has acquired.

Deep bounce overheads should be hit like spin serves. Judgment is learned through practice, and only through hitting hundreds of bounce overheads does the player develop confidence in his ability to judge the ball. Players hit thousands and thousands of forehands and back-hands in order to groove their groundstrokes; they should hit thousands of overheads in order to groove this particular shot. Such practice is exhausting but it gives the player the put-away when the occasion arises.

The top players have almost all developed bigger, fuller, freer swings on the overhead. Usually the swing is as big as that on the serve. They have the timing so they don't have to wait with racket cocked back as beginners must do. They still turn sideways on the wind-up, but as the shoulder comes through, the body is facing the net (this is also true on the serve). Beginners often think top players face the net on overheads because they look only at the moment of impact rather than at the wind-up as well.

The advanced player who has a weak overhead suffers a tremendous handicap, since the opposition quickly learns the soft spot in his game. There is only one remedy: practice. If a beginner can learn a decent overhead on a set-up, an advanced player can learn a good overhead off a deep lob. The most common error for those who don't practice overheads enough is hitting too soon, which makes the ball go straight

Top players swing freely on smashes, blasting the ball with a full swing. They often leap by choice, using a coordinated backswing, leap, and scissors-kick rhythm. At the end of this action the left foot is on the ground while the right leg is out behind. Mike Estep is one of those who take a full, roundhouse clout, and he ends up with his racket almost to the ground on the right side of his body.

Jimmy Connors has made a heroic leap, but the lob is already over his head and it will be difficult to reach it and snap it forward with any power because the ball will be behind him. He can probably hit it with no more than medium pace, but his powerful wrist can direct the ball where he wants it.

down. Practice will show you how long to wait and will give you the confidence to smash the ball accurately.

TOURNAMENT PLAYERS

The tournament player has more options than the advanced player in his choice of overheads. When he fails to work out an overhead strategy, or when he does not play to the score, he can lose a critical point which may mean the match. For example, I use the crosscourt overhead to the opponent's forehand whenever I am behind the service line. At 30-all I will also go for the crosscourt to the forehand to open up the court. At 30-0 or 40-0 I go for the opponent's weakness. If I am inside the service line, I go mainly to the backhand. Many players, when hitting an overhead from the left side, will go down-the-line; I go to the backhand deliberately because I have more room. It puts me in a better position—my opponent has to run and therefore will not be able to return as well. If I go down-the-line, my opponent has too much open court to aim for on my forehand side. I slice when I want to angle the ball. I hit a flat overhead when I am hitting down the center, and I hit down the center when I want to prevent my opponent from coming in. The flat smash has more power and the center shot enlarges my safety factor.

Only a few players are better on the overhead when they have to reach for the ball. It is a gift that most players do not have. The best was Ted Schroeder, a player who never let the ball bounce and who leaped and smashed incredibly well. He could hit the overhead on the run going backward! Lew Hoad had one of the biggest overheads in the game from behind the baseline. He generally chose to go down the center with tremendous speed. Three smaller players also have notable overheads—Ken Rosewall, Chuck McKinley, and Jimmy Connors. Rosewall, whose serve is rather weak, has perfect timing on his big overhead. The depth is excellent. Chuck McKinley had a great overhead for a small guy: he could leap three feet off the ground and hit bullets. Jimmy Connors is also a great smasher.

Those players at the championship level who had relatively weak overheads would go for placement rather than speed. The smash was Don Budge's weakest shot. Bobby Riggs, Frankie Parker, and I were never considered great smashers. Parker, to make up for his lack of sheer power, used the short overhead that bounced inside the service line area. It is a dangerous play that I almost never try, but Parker was good at it. It is a difficult shot because it requires so much touch and perfect control, but it is effective because the opponent expects a deep ball and the smasher then fakes him. After the great players turn fifty, the first thing they lose is power on the overhead; they try to compensate with better placement.

When hitting an overhead every tournament player should consider the graphic position and the strength of the opponent's groundstrokes. It will determine whether the player will hit flat or with slice (I have never seen an American twist overhead). In any case, the smasher will conceal the direction. Many players will let the ball bounce on a big point such as 40-30 or 30-40. At 4-all, 40-30 in the fifth set, I would let the ball bounce because it is vital not to miss the shot and important to close out the game. If you hit it on the fly you can misjudge the ball, and if you misjudge it at this point you may tighten up and lose the match.

I saw Onny Parun playing Raul Ramirez in South Africa. Parun had 5-2, 40-0, and Ramirez was off somewhere in his alley. The New Zealander went for a down-the-line winner, missed the overhead, and lost the match. If he had let the ball bounce, he would have won the point. The moral: do not make a show-off shot or aim for the lines on a vital point; give yourself plenty of room to get the ball in.

The players with the best backhand overheads that I have seen are Stan Smith, Lew Hoad, and Ham Richardson. All three had tremendous strength and could belt the ball. I tried to avoid hitting backhand overheads, although it was not always possible. When the opponent hits a perfect backhand crosscourt lob, it is difficult to move back without leaving your right court open. To me it is one of the toughest shots in the game, but it is a shot that everyone must have. Since power off the backhand overhead is so hard to develop, the player must go for depth or angles. Hit for the alleys to make the opponent move laterally and to make him reach for the ball.

Arthur Ashe has just hit this smash a little bit to the left of his head, and he has turned his wrist so that the racket head will sweep toward his right. This jackknife action, with the right leg forward, the body slanted slightly backward to balance the forward tilt of arm and racket at impact, is typical of overheads in top tennis.

Chapter Nine / The Volley

This is the end of my low backhand volley. There is practically no follow-through; the arm and racket are held firmly as the ball is blocked, with a forward motion of less than a foot. The ball is controlled and directed upward to clear the net by means of the open racket face, which imparts the required underspin to the shot when coupled with a downward motion of the racket.

In addition to crouching with his knees, Rod Laver is bending at the waist to get down to this ankle-high forehand volley. The grip is Continental, the arm is almost straight, and the racket is brought parallel to the ground by the sharp wrist angle.

The volley is a punch, not a stroke. It starts without a wind-up and with the racket in front of the body. It is the shortest stroke in the game since it consists only of a short forward motion like a boxing jab. Drive volleys and long volleys should not even be attempted until the punch volley is acquired. The shorter the punch, the better the volley will eventually be.

The average player with only minimum tennis experience tends to take a backswing as soon as the ball nears his racket. This wrecks the stroke. The only way to get rid of the unwanted backswing is to start in a ready position with the racket well in front of the body, then place the left hand directly behind the right (racket) hand to prevent the right hand from moving backward. By the tenth or fifteenth try, much of a player's tendency to take a backswing will have disappeared.

The beginner's volley motion should be 6 to 10 inches long. It starts with the arm and racket well in front of the body. The arm is slightly bent, and at the conclusion of the stroke it will be straight. The racket is slightly in front of the hand (closer to the net), and the racket head points upward and to the right on the forehand side, and upward and to the left on the backhand side. The racket does not point straight to the sky (a 90° angle) but slightly upward (20° to 45°). On a high volley, the tilt of the racket will be 45°; on stretch volleys, the racket will often have no upward (or downward) angle; on low volleys (below net level) there will be no upward or downward angle—but the racket *face* will tilt slightly skyward to enable the player to lift the ball up and over the net. In no case does the racket ever point downward: on low balls, the legs spread and the knees bend, almost touching the ground, so that the racket can be at ball level. If the legs do not spread, the body is off balance, and tennis is totally a game of balance.

Most players use a Continental (backhand) grip on the volley because on fast exchanges there is no time to change grips. The beginner will find, in a quick exchange, that he is hitting a backhand volley with a forehand grip, and there is nothing more awkward or ineffective: the elbow points in the air and there is no power or accuracy. If you are not fast enough to change from forehand to backhand grip at net, use the backhand grip only. The first time you try it you will feel helpless, because the position of your wrist must change with the new grip. Flatten out your wrist (lay your hand back) and try to hit volleys down-the-line, since the tendency when the grip is first tried is for all volleys to go crosscourt. After the first practice session your wrist will feel stiff, but if you try the new grip for five minutes every day, by the end of the week you should be hitting forehand volleys with pretty good control.

Control is the key to the volley, not power. If you have control you can volley deep or angle-volley; if you have no control, you can only pray the volley will go in. The harder the ball is hit at you, the harder it will come off your racket if you use the 6-inch punch and take the ball well in front of your body.

Most beginners and intermediates are afraid they will be hit when they are at net and the ball is coming hard at them. This is because they are looking everywhere except at the ball: they are watching the opponent's eyes or movements instead of "seeing" the ball come off his racket. If your racket is in front of you, and if you try only to block the ball, you can protect yourself easily against almost any shot hit from the baseline. Your reactions must speed up when the opponent is at net, particularly in doubles when exchanges are fast, but you can work up to this level gradually. First, feel confident at net when the opponent is on the baseline, no matter how hard he hits. Your Continental grip makes you ready to handle a ball on either side, your eyes keep you alert, and your racket is so far in front of you that you can block back any ball.

The idea of the volley is to close in before the ball begins to drop. If you are standing halfway between the service line and the net (the proper position for the net man) and a high ball comes to you, do not wait for it—move in to the point where you are practically on top of the net. In your anxiety to kill the ball, do not forget that backswings are verboten: you are going to punch the volley well in front of you. The longer your volley punch, the less chance you have to make an angle volley and the easier it is for your opponent to read you.

If a high ball is coming toward your right, you do not move to your right to volley it; you move *forward* and to the right so that the ball does not drop. High balls are what you are waiting for, since they give you the chance to put the ball away. If you let the ball drop, your chances for a clean winner become much worse.

When you are standing at net, you are not there for decorative reasons. In singles you have to cover the entire net, which means you must anticipate the direction of the ball. In doubles you want to lure the opponent to hit to you so you feint to fake him: you make a movement to your right, hoping he will hit to your left, since you are ready to spring back. Because you have so much territory to cover in singles and so much cutting off to do in doubles, the ready position becomes extremely important.

Careful preparation pays off. In fast play at net it may not be possible to move the legs into the recommended classical stance (the left foot in front for a left-handed backhand), but it is possible to bend the knees, get down to the ball, open the racket face slightly and hold the wrist very firm. All this Rod Laver has done on this beautifully executed low backhand volley.

Arthur Ashe has stretched wide for a backhand volley. He has maintained good body balance and, of necessity, has bent his knees to get down to the ball. Arthur blocks the ball at his side, with minimum underspin for control imparted by the slightly open racket face.

Stan Smith leaps to his right for a high forehand volley, with the racket head high. The stroke is a short swing, with practically no spin. Stan likes to play close to net, where his reach allows him to kill a lot of balls.

You cannot wait for the ball with stiff legs or feet close together. You should look like a racer, ready to take off in any direction. That means your feet are spread, your knees are bent and your center of gravity is low (close to the ground). Now you are ready to spring forward and/or sideways. The racket is held in front of you, with the racket head tilting slightly upward and the fingers of the left hand supporting the racket throat. Most important, your eyes are on the ball. In a fraction of a second you are ready to hit a forehand or a backhand. If the ball comes straight at you, hit it with a backhand volley; you would have to be a contortionist to hit it with a forehand volley.

Whether the ball comes to your ankles or above head height, there will be no backswing and your feet will be far apart for balance. Low balls should always be taken without a backswing and with a short forward motion; high volleys can always be punched well in front of the body, although when your volley is very secure you may add a drive volley to your repertoire.

The drive volley is almost as large as a full forehand groundstroke. There is a backswing, starting at or above shoulder level (most forehand groundstrokes start at waist-level). If you are on top of the net, the follow-through will be slightly downward; if you are in midcourt, the follow-through is usually on the same level as the hit so that the ball will go deep. The strength of the drive volley is in its depth and pace. The weakness is it is not as precise as the punch because the stroke is so long, and you cannot get sharp angles or turn your wrist at the last minute to drop volley.

Most of the top players in the game today have too long a forehand volley. It is a good foot to two feet long rather than 6 to 10 inches. This means the player can only volley for depth and has eliminated his chances to angle volley or drop volley. I infinitely prefer the short underspin volley, which can be punched flat by turning your wrist (laying it back slightly) or can be angled sharply. When you want to angle a forehand volley, the wrist is not laid back at all: the ball is taken well in front of the body, there is no backswing and the entire punch is only 6 to 8 inches. The racket face is slightly open for spin control, and as a result you can get incredible angles. The action is like the old-fashioned chop but with a smaller stroke.

Arthur Ashe, Stan Smith, Charlie Pasarell, and Clark Graebner have such long forehand volleys that they can never play short deliberately. They hit their volleys just like groundstrokes, but with no backswing at all. They start their swing at approximately body level rather than a foot in front of the body. Their only alternatives when they volley are down-the-line or crosscourt; they have cut themselves off from short balls, sharp angles, and drop volleys.

The player who uses the short action punch volley becomes a master of angles and of low volleys. Since he uses underspin on all his short crosscourt volleys, the low volley (under net level) is the easiest shot in the world for him. He is used to opening the face of his racket and he can guide the ball down the line or crosscourt with the same ease. Best of all, this action makes it incredibly easy to drop volley and get an extremely sharp angle at the same time. If Arthur Ashe could master

John Newcombe can put away almost any volley he can reach because he likes to play so close to the net. Here his stretch forehand volley is blocked without any spin because the shot is above and close to the net.

Not all of Jimmy Connors' backhand strokes are his lethal two-handers. Sometimes he lets go of the racket with his right hand just before he hits the ball, particularly on low shots, and of course he uses only one hand when stretched wide. Jimmy is blocking this low backhand volley with an open racket face and slight underspin.

Ken Rosewall takes this beautiful low backhand volley in front of his body, on a line with his right foot. His right arm is almost straight, pointing down in front of his body, and the sharp angle at the wrist brings the racket almost parallel to the ground. The racket face is very slightly open to provide a minimum of under-spin for control.

Both precision and grace are apparent in every Rosewall backhand. This low volley is guided down the line by opening the racket face and holding the racket head back slightly. The wrist is totally firm, and the body placement and balance are perfect. The shot is taken in front of the body.

Billie Jean King demonstrates the low forehand volley to perfection. Her legs are far apart and she has knelt to get her racket below the ball without dropping the racket head. She will block-punch the ball well in front of her body with a firm wrist. Billie Jean has the best fundamental preparation for volleys, particularly on low balls, of any player in the game today.

Bob Lutz has a distinctive but very effective backhand volley. It is hit with the racket head high and the wrist cocked, at his side or even slightly behind his body. This shot is perfectly disguised, with a slight wrist adjustment at the last minute giving the ball its final direction.

Stan Smith stretches for a low backhand volley. His balance, arm, wrist, and racket are excellent, with the tilt of the racket face indicating just the right amount of underspin for low volley control.

Adriano Panatta moves to his left, crossing his right foot over, for a backhand volley. His backswing is high and longer than necessary, and the racket face is open. Panatta's swing will be downward, imparting underspin to the shot.

this volley, he would be an infinitely more dangerous player. John Newcombe knows this volley but tends to drive his forehand volleys too much. The best forehand volleyers in the history of the game—Budge Patty and Jack Kramer—excelled in the short underspin volley. It was what made Louise Brough, Margaret Osborne duPont, and Sarah Palfrey Danzig such great champions in singles and doubles.

Although great forehand volleys are rare, top tournament players generally have excellent backhand volleys. John Newcombe is an exception, perhaps because he has such a great forehand volley. Newcombe's backhand volley is not really weak; it's simply not up to his forehand standard.

The good backhand volleyers underspin all low balls and generally hit either flat or with underspin on the high balls. I choose underspin because of the degree of angle I get, but it takes more wrist control. The minute you choose to hit flat, you have to hit deep; with underspin you can hit deep or short angles. The flat backhand volley is like a backhand drive with no wind-up. It is extremely effective on high balls or hard balls.

The best backhand volleys in the game today belong to Ken Rosewall, Tony Roche, Billie Jean King, and Evonne Goolagong. Roche has the hardest, firmest backhand volley, but Rosewall's first volley on the backhand side is so good that he puts his opponent in either alley or behind the baseline.

Newcombe and Connors have the best forehand volleys in the game because they do so much with the first volley. They hit it harder, firmer, and deeper than anyone else. When Connors played Rosewall in the 1974 U.S. Open final, his first volleys were so forceful that he swept through most of his service games without giving the Little Master a chance to hit a good passing shot. It was the worst major defeat that Rosewall had ever suffered. Ashe for years had a forehand volley weakness, but in 1975 he took a big jump forward: he got down lower for the shots and he played more for depth and placement than sheer power. As he cut down on his volley errors, he jumped to the top of the world rankings. His greatest display was in the 1975 Wimbledon final against Connors: his forehand volley was unshakable and precise. Ashe's weakness had been converted into a strength.

Chapter Ten / The Lob

*Cliff Drysdale's two-handed backhand is a
powerful and well-disguised shot, but
he must have his right arm close to his body to
produce an offensive stroke. Here, when
stretched wide with both arms extended,
he has to resort to a defensive lob.*

There are two kinds of lobs—defensive and offensive. The defensive is a high, deep ball, either hit directly down the middle of the court or over the opponent's backhand. It is usually a sky-ball, hit with no particular spin, and it is designed to get the player out of trouble. The offensive lob is marked by pronounced topspin and excellent disguise. It is a passing shot designed to win the point from the net man. If a player had his choice, he would always hit an offensive lob, but sometimes he is pulled so wide out of court and has so little time that all he can do is throw up a sky-ball and get back into position.

The defensive lob is used (1) when the player is pressed by the net man and cannot possibly attempt a good passing shot, (2) when the player has had to run very wide for a shot, leaving the rest of his court totally open, and (3) when the ball is hit so deep and/or so high that the player cannot comfortably stroke the ball back. It is then the safest shot. This lob should be hit very high and as deep as possible to allow the player to get back into the center of the court and anticipate the return.

The defensive lob can be learned in a few minutes. The stroke is exactly the same as a groundstroke, except the racket face opens up, tilting skyward instead of being perpendicular to the ground, and the follow-through starts sooner: instead of letting the arm and racket sweep forward and up, the forward movement is cut short and the arm and racket move upward almost immediately after the hit. Of course there must be some forward motion or the ball would not even reach the net. If your lobs are going short, you have pulled up too quickly and have not allowed your arm to come forward enough. A few minutes of experimenting will give you the feel of how much you must open the racket face and how soon after the hit you can start pulling up. Take a good, healthy swing—the ball has a long way to travel from one baseline to the other.

A defensive lob is a loser if the net man can hit it away or if the base-liner can come in and take the ball as a high volley. Lobs must be high and, if the net man has a good overhead, they must be deep.

The defensive lob becomes an offensive weapon when it has disguise. It catches the net man off balance: he is moving forward or playing too close to net, and by the time he sees the ball is a lob it is too late to move back. Disguised lobs serve a double purpose: they are not only excellent passing shots but they keep the net man from moving in too close. The farther back the net man plays, the easier it is to pass him and the harder it is for him to put away the volley.

Learning to disguise the lob is almost as easy as learning the lob. The trick is not to open the racket face until just before the lob is hit. Most beginners and intermediates open the face as the backswing ends and the forward motion begins, and this is a dead give-away. The skill of the game is in preventing the opponent from reading you. Ten minutes of practice will give you a good start in acquiring a disguised lob.

The topspin lob requires much more skill and excellent timing, but it is the best lob of all: after the ball bounces, it travels so fast that even the quickest players cannot run it down. If it goes over the net man's head, it is a winner. The topspin lob has two other factors working for it. It offers complete disguise, and it can be badly misjudged by the net man: he lets it go, thinking it will sail out, but the heavy topspin brings it in.

The topspin lob is not hit with an open racket face. The lob action is derived from brushing the racket upward at the moment of impact while still coming forward. Some players impart so much topspin that the follow-through ends with racket and arm almost directly over the shoulder. The long, full sweep of the groundstroke follow-through is gone: racket and arm move sharply upward and only slightly forward. The unskilled player will mis-hit far too many topspin lobs and lose too many points, so he should forget this stroke until his abilities are better developed. The skilled player should try to acquire this shot at once, since it is one of the most useful and aggressive shots in the game. If he cannot acquire it on the backhand, he should at least develop some topspin and a controlled trajectory, which can be offensive in every way except for the fast-forward bounce.

The great topspin lobbers of the game—Manuel Santana and Chuck McKinley in the 1960s and John Newcombe, Ilie Nastase, and Jimmy Connors today—have tremendous strength in their forearms. They get under the ball and pull up sharply at the last minute, and they hit their best lobs on the run. The average player cannot topspin when he is late or pressed because he hasn't the time; Newcombe, Nastase, and Connors are so quick that they can topspin-lob while moving laterally or forward. These men are great lobbers because they know *when to lob.*

The best place to lob from is the area between the service line and baseline. The net man figures you will lob when you are well behind the baseline, but if you are inside the line and lob him he gets confused. The next time he comes in, he doesn't know whether to crowd the net

Betty Stove is hitting a high, wide backhand lob with her back to the net. Almost all top players develop the wrist strength and agility to permit them to execute this maneuver, which is called for surprisingly often.

or not. Sheer speed doesn't bother the net man as much as lobs which keep him back and give you more room to pass him.

The lob is never tried from inside the service line. The choice here is a passing shot, a short angle, or a hard one directly at the net man.

The best time to try a lob is at 30-all or 30-40. The server tends to crowd the net too much, and he won't try too tough a volley because of the score. If the volley is short, Newcombe and Nastase will come in as though they were going for the winner; at the last second they fake you and hit a lob. I saw Connors playing Jeff Borowiak, and at 30-40, match point, Jeff came in and volleyed short. I knew and Jimmy knew that Jimmy was going to lob. The position was perfect, Connors had anticipated the short volley and he made a winning lob.

Topspin lobs can be hit off the backhand as well as the forehand. Defensive lobs should also be hit off either swing. They are vital shots to every player's repertoire and yet one sees far too little of them in the average match. Some players are "too proud to lob"; they think it demeaning not to hit every ball with all their might. Bobby Riggs won a Pro Tour against Don Budge with a defensive lob, Tom Okker got to the finals of the U.S. Open with a topspin lob, and Rod Laver uses the lob intelligently and frequently. I lobbed so extensively that Pancho Gonzalez nicknamed me "Sneaky."

The champions who stay at the top (not the fly-by-nights) are the great lobbers. They know when, where, and how to use it. Fortunately it is a stroke that even a beginner can learn.

Ilie Nastase is on the defensive, stretching as he runs wide to his right to throw up an underspin lob. His grip, close to the Continental, is way down on the handle, the end of the palm extending past the butt.

Chapter Eleven
The Touch Shots: Drop Volleys, Half-Volleys, Drop Shots, and Lob Volleys

After a player has mastered the groundstrokes, punch volley, and lob, he must acquire a half-volley and a drop shot. It is impossible to attempt a net attack without a half-volley, and the drop shot becomes vital for wrong-footing an opponent, drawing him to net, or breaking up his rhythm. The drop volley and the lob volley are not prerequisites in the making of a champion, but they give finesse and polish to a game and they are worth valuable points. Ilie Nastase and Billie Jean King are superb at all the touch shots, but many a player has used touch shots to compensate for a particular deficiency in his game. Julie Heldman, a baseliner, makes up in great part for her lack of confidence at net by her ability to drop-volley, half-volley, drop-shot, lob-volley, and change her spins and her pace.

HALF-VOLLEY

The half-volley is not a volley at all; it is a groundstroke with almost no backswing. When a player comes to net on serve, he almost never gets to the net position (halfway between the service line and the net) in time for the first volley. Usually he takes the first volley two or three steps behind the service line. Frequently it is not a volley at all; the ball has already bounced just in front of him, and the net rusher is forced to hit the ball as it is rising and before it gets to knee level. The net rusher must get good depth or he will be dead on the next shot. He half-volleys, which means he hits a groundstroke without a backswing and with his knees bent so the racket head will not drop. If he stood straight and simply dropped the racket head, he could only shovel the ball back in a high arc, which would give the opponent every opportunity to pass him.

The half-volley, like every other stroke, is hit in front of the body. The swing starts at the side of the body rather than behind, and the racket and arm travel up after the hit to give natural topspin to the ball. It is the topspin that enables the low ball to clear the net. Although arm and racket travel upward on the follow-through, the finish is not quite as full as the finish on a groundstroke nor is it as high. On a groundstroke one starts at waist level and finishes at shoulder level; on a half-volley the start is below knee level and the finish is usually at or slightly above waist level.

The intermediate who is learning this shot should concentrate on three things: getting down to the ball, starting the swing by the side of the body, and watching the ball to see the bounce. The biggest problem may come in an involuntary backswing. The remedy is to tuck your elbow into your body and even put your left hand behind your right (hitting) arm to prevent the right arm from going back.

As with any stroke, practice develops control, accuracy, and depth. The more you come to net, the more you must half-volley. Your return must clear the net low in doubles, and it must go deep in singles. You open the racket face slightly when you half-volley from midcourt and you follow through slightly higher when you half-volley from the back court. Both have the purpose of enabling the ball to clear the net.

There are other times when the half-volley is useful. You may be trapped on the baseline by a very deep volley or approach shot from the opponent. You have no chance to move back and so you must half-volley. If you can hit the ball in front of you and keep your wrist firm, your half-volley will utilize your opponent's pace.

The half-volley should be avoided when both players are on the baseline trading groundstrokes. Some players half-volley from this position because of laziness: they will not take the two steps back to get ready for a very deep ball. The groundstroke is the safer shot—so hop back when the depth is good, then step in for the groundstroke.

DROP SHOT

The drop shot should be executed from inside the service line, although there are exceptions to the rule. When a baseliner has a weakness on low, short balls because he cannot put the ball away, a drop shot followed by a lob or passing shot is a perfect strategy ploy. In women's tennis the drop shot has been used against particular players even when the drop shotter is in the back court. Doris Hart used it on return of second serve against all baseliners. Billie Jean King used it often against baseliner Nancy Gunter to tire her out early in the match; Nancy would win the point but pay for it in exhaustion later in the match. Virginia Wade drop-shots Chris Evert's forehand from the baseline; Chris always gets to the ball but seldom puts it away. Chris herself uses drop shots from just inside the baseline at unexpected times, and because her disguise is so good she often pulls off a winner. But the general rule is to drop-shot only when close in and to drop-shot more in the beginning of the match than at the end. When a match is in the last set, the opponent will run for "impossible" shots; he will also be expecting drop shots if his opponent has been doing so earlier. Many a player has gotten a big lead on drop shots early in the match, only to lose it later when the opponent got grooved and anticipated the drop shots that had been winners earlier.

A player who underspins on his backhand or chips on his forehand has a much easier time disguising his drop shot. The exact same action is used. The player who only drives must work much harder to mask his shot since it would otherwise be so easy to read. The drop shot is a 6- to 10-inch underspin shot hit with a downward motion. If the ball is at waist-height, the racket travels from slightly under shoulder-height to under the level of the ball. The racket face is tilted skyward to put underspin on the ball. The follow-through is short because the object is to hit the ball with as little forward motion as possible—just enough to make the ball go over the net and die. If the ball bounces forward, the drop shot is ineffective. You have not used enough underspin. If the ball clears the net by several feet, the racket face is open too much.

Before learning a drop shot, the player should be able to hit underspin backhands and either punch volleys or chip shots on the forehand. Every player who advances to high intermediate level eventually learns an underspin backhand because it is the easiest and most natural way to hit a low backhand down-the-line when coming to net. Every player can also learn a punch volley in pretty quick time. However, a player who knows neither of these shots will have a frustrating learning period in trying to acquire a good drop shot. Assuming that the backhand underspin and punch volley have been acquired, the drop shot now is relatively simple. Practice it first without disguise until you know exactly how much the downward motion of the racket should be, how much the racket face should open, and how short the follow-through should be. When you can regularly hit undisguised, obvious drop shots, you then can work on "hiding" your shot until just as the ball is hit. The secret of the successful drop shot is disguise, although the more you drop shot, the more the opponent will be on his toes, ready to run in. Do not start the action with a slanted racket face but come under the ball at the last second. If your wrist control is good enough, your racket can come under the ball and then pull *toward your body* so that the hit is with backspin: when the ball bounces, it shoots backward rather than forward. Some players can actually make the ball bounce back to their side of the net. A large percent of top players hit all their drop shots with backspin.

The reply to a drop shot is either another drop shot to the side farthest from the opponent or, if the opponent is in the service line area, a deep ball to the side where he isn't.

THE DROP VOLLEY

The drop volley requires much more skill than the drop shot because the "drop" is made against a ball in the air. There is much more forward motion on the ball coming to you, and in hitting it you must put a tremendous amount of backspin on the ball to make it travel 6 to 8 feet in the other direction, then stop dead. The forward motion of arm and racket is countered by coming way under the ball (literally—under the bottom of the ball) while the *weight moves backward*. The weight transfer is occasionally visible on a drop volleyer by a backward flick of his shoulder or what looks to be a jerk of his arm or hand. Any forward motion ruins the drop volley because there should be no forward motion after the ball has bounced.

If you try drop volleys repeatedly and have small success, you have a reasonably good alternative in the sharp angle volley that has a fair amount of forward motion which you direct sideways. The farther you are drawn wide on the court and the closer you are to net, the easier it is to hit an excellent sharp angle volley. You turn your wrist in the direction in which you want the ball to go, and you can make it travel sideways, almost parallel to the net, if you know the short punch volley with underspin. It is as effective in doubles as it is in singles, even if all four are at net, because the underspin mixed with the short punch action makes the ball travel under net level. The drop volley is more spectacular, but the low angle volley, in the hands of a player less skilled than Nastase, is much safer.

THE LOB VOLLEY

The lob volley is one of the least used shots in the game because it must be performed when both opponents (or all four opponents) are at net, it is incredibly difficult to do off hard volleys right at you, and the consequences of not lob-volleying high enough are deadly. However, there is an important place for it—and it is much, much easier to execute than it sounds. Any player who knows the underspin lob and can volley reasonably is able to lob-volley in no time at all.

The lob volley is a lob hit off a ball that has not bounced. It is a shorter stroke than the groundstroke lob (no wind-up and a 6- to 10-inch action), and it is hit with the racket moving in a very slight upward pattern, with the racket face almost wide open (pointing to the sky). Try it a few times against a partner who is practicing with you while you both are at net. Try it against a reasonably easy ball, and after six or eight tries you will discover the amount of open racket face and forward motion that you need. In doubles it becomes an outright winner if you pick the right volley on which to try the shot. If you misjudge the ball, duck fast and start making lame excuses to your partner.

USING YOUR TOUCH SHOTS

The players who know the touch shots seldom use them enough. I learned to play tennis on clay and used the drop shot frequently off return of second serve on clay from either side. I always drop-shot crosscourt to pull the server wide, and at the same time I moved *inside the service line* to put more pressure on the opponent and to close the court on him. He would be hitting from a position below net level, and because I was inside the service line he could not play me short. There are plenty of weak second serves in the game—Chris Evert's, Harold Solomon's, Lesley Hunt's, Eddie Dibbs'—and since Chris, Harold, and Eddie hang back on the baseline, the drop shot brings them in where they least want to be.

Some of the methods I use can be helpful to those who do not "think" drop shots. I always drop-shot off a drop shot because I figure that, if the other guy ran my tail off, I'll run his off, too. I never drop-shot from behind the baseline unless I am 40-0 and can spare the point. The ball has to travel a much greater distance, and the opponent will have a graphic communication of what is happening. I drop-shot when I am going forward because I can then fake my opponent best: he thinks I am going to hit deep (which I can if I see him moving forward), but I am inside the service line and in the best position to make a drop shot. I never drop-shot at 15-30 or 30-40 unless my opponent is way behind his baseline or out in the alley, and even then I know I have to make a perfect shot. I never try a drop shot off a hard ball that bounces at the service line—it's traveling too fast and I can't take the speed off it. If I see that my opponent has anticipated my drop shot and is moving forward, I lengthen my long chop or even try to hit through the ball.

The players who could use the drop shot best but who never try it are Manuel Orantes and Guillermo Vilas. Both are excellent clay court players who have fine, deep groundstrokes that elicit short returns. Between them they have taken almost every clay court title in Europe. As good as they are, the drop shot would make them even better.

Generally, small players drop-shot more often than tall players (Nastase is the tallest player on the circuit to drop-shot regularly), and this is usually because tall players are not that flexible. The smaller player seems to have more elasticity in his arms.

Some players drop-shot far too often. Dave Freeman, a former Junior Champion of the 1930s, and Gil Hunt, a First Tenner of the 1940s, drop-shot so frequently that we would move up to anticipate their plays. Ilie Nastase, when he gets nervous, hits far too many drop shots and drop volleys because he has lost the confidence to go for the put-away on groundstrokes and volleys. He becomes overenamored of the shot at the expense of the score, trying a drop volley at 30-40 or a drop shot at 15-30. A bad drop volley by Nastase against Roscoe Tanner in the 1974 U.S. Open gave Tanner the match. The whole court was open and the score was working against Nastase; it was the perfect time *not* to drop volley.

My guides for drop volleys are aimed at percentage play. I never drop volley a fast, low ball because I cannot take the speed off it; I would not serve, come in, and try a drop volley off Arthur Ashe's hard return. I never drop volley from No Man's Land (the area between the baseline and the service line), but only when I am inside the service line. When I hit a short, low shot to an opponent who drop volleys, I anticipate the shot by moving in. I never drop volley on 30-40. I never try a drop volley when I am moving laterally because it requires perfect balance. Even though I will not try the shot when moving wide, Manuel Santana could pull it off because he had such perfect balance. (A player who practices enough can eventually do it, too.) I drop volley crosscourt when my opponent is in the center. I like to drop volley against balls that are between waist and shoulder height. I reach forward when I hit a drop volley so the opponent will think I am playing long (about to hit deep). I use a little reverse spin so that the ball will bounce very short.

Although many tournament players have an adequate drop shot, very few can hit with enough backspin to stop all forward motion or even make the ball bounce backward. They do not practice drop shots, although they practice every other shot. I learned my drop shot by playing mini-singles (the service line becomes the baseline) three times a week, a half-hour at a time. If you try the mini-game, you will develop tremendous control in keeping the ball short through underspin, backspin, and a shortened follow-through. The hardest of all in this game is to run at full speed, stop (to be in balance), and then hit a backspin drop shot.

The drop volley requires much more art, control, balance, and nerves than the drop shot. It has to be perfect. It is the supreme test of ability. The best exemplars of the shot were Welby Van Horn, now a famous teaching pro in Puerto Rico, and Whitney Reed, who was ranked No. 1 in the United States in 1961. Today's top drop volleyers are Ilie Nastase and Billie Jean King.

Chapter Twelve / Footwork

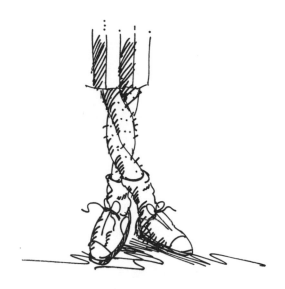

Good footwork on a tennis court accounts for speed in reacting to a moving ball, proper balance when one gets to the target, and the vital weight transfer just before the hit that gives power to the shot. Footwork is important in all sports: a batter could never hit a home run if his feet faced the pitcher square on, a boxer could not deliver the knock-out punch while stepping sideways or backwards, the golfer could not drive 250 yards while balanced on one foot, the running back could not avoid a tackle if he were not able to change directions instantaneously, and the basketball player would never be a scoring threat if he were not light on his feet. Still, many beginner and intermediate tennis players neglect footwork because they assume this is the least of their problems. They are wrong: without proper footwork the player has slow reactions, bad balance, no controlled power, and ungraceful strokes.

The factors that make for good footwork are:

- Being bouncy on the balls of the feet, with knees flexed slightly and the back straight
- Being able to push off quickly with the right foot to move to the left, and with the left foot to move to the right
- Hopping or bouncing to get into position
- Skipping to move sideways
- Stepping forward (toward the net) with the left foot in a slightly open stance on forehands
- Stepping forward with the right foot in a slightly closed stance on backhands.

The *bounciness* (being on the balls of the feet) keeps the player from being flat-footed and sluggish. When you are bouncy, your knees bend, but your back is reasonably straight. If you do bend from the waist, as many players do when receiving serve, your knees must bend deeply to keep your center of gravity low and to retain good balance. If you bend from the waist and are almost stiff-legged, a slight push could topple you forward, and your balance is precarious. To become bouncy, practice in front of a full-length mirror with a racket. Hold the racket in front of you: your feet should be a good 12 to 18 inches apart and your knees slightly flexed. Now bounce on your toes (not your heels). Don't jump; your feet should never come off the ground more than a few inches.

While still standing in front of the mirror, practice *pushing off quickly*. To move to your left, let all your weight come down on your right foot (the ball and the heel) and push with your right foot to move to your left. The right knee is bent (don't push off straight-legged). Now try moving to your right, pushing off with the left foot. Come back to the ready position, facing the mirror with knees bent, feet 12 to 18 inches apart, and your weight on the balls of your feet. Move to the left; move to the right. If you are pushing with the opposite foot, you can "feel" the impetus you get in starting fast. This is an exercise that is easily practiced indoors, and it will quicken your reactions as you learn to "push off" as soon as the ball leaves your opponent's racket.

A good player is never flat-footed when he approaches the ball. He *hops or bounces*; his weight is never on his heels. If the ball takes a crazy hop or skids into his body or away from him, he is bouncy enough to move his body quickly. Good players are nimble: even when they are exhausted and the match is in the final stages, you will see them bounce or hop—the *sine qua non* of approaching the ball properly. A bounce or hop (not a jump) pulls you toward or away from a too wide or too close shot.

When you are on the baseline and you want to move six or eight feet to your left or your right, *skip sideways* if the ball is not coming too fast. Whether you are going to the left or the right, your body faces the net as you move so your eyes can follow the ball. If the ball is coming to your right, start with a push-off from the left foot and a step sideways with the right; the left foot is then brought sideways so it almost touches the right foot, and again you push off with the left foot; the right foot steps right again, the left foot is brought next to it, and once more you push off. The "skip sideways" is therefore a series of push-offs to get you to the ball in a gliding fashion. Good players never walk to the ball: they always either hop to it, skip sideways or run full-out.

When the ball comes to your forehand, the object whenever possible is to transfer your weight forward to give natural power to the shot. This means your *left foot moves toward the net* just before the moment of impact. If your left foot moved toward your right alley (a closed stance), your weight would be moving sideways; if both feet faced the net square on (open stance), the chances are there would be no weight transfer at all. (Top players will frequently hit with an open stance because they make the left shoulder do the work, but this is most inadvisable for those who are learning.) Your left foot should step toward the net in a *slightly open stance:* you are neither totally sideways (facing your alley), nor are you facing the net with both feet on the same imaginary line. Your left foot is a step closer to the net than your right foot, and your shoulders are almost sideways.

When hitting a backhand, the *right foot steps toward the net* and both shoulders are sideways to the net. If your right foot crosses toward the alley, you have blocked yourself from hitting with power because your weight transfer is sideways rather than forward. If you were to draw a straight line from the baseline to the net, then if your left foot were on that line, your right foot would be even with or 6 inches off the line. (Almost a closed stance.)

If your footwork is good, you will do much better against *deep balls and hard balls*. Intermediates are often unaware that deep balls are their nemeses: they are off balance or pressed when they return a ball that bounds within a foot of their baseline. The proper riposte to a deep ball is to jump, hop or skip two to six feet behind the baseline, then step forward for the hit. The intermediate does not move back because he has planted his feet, and so he must either half-volley the ball or let his weight fall backward as he hits. The correct ploy is to hop backward so that one can then step forward.

Hard balls come too fast for the player who has neglected his footwork. He cannot start fast enough because he does not "push off." Even if he runs at top speed for the ball, he may end up on the wrong foot or with his weight moving sideways. There will be occasions when the ball is hit so hard and wide that the player can barely touch it with the wrong foot stretched out (the perfect time to hit a high defensive lob), but far more often the player will be able to get to the ball by timing his steps so that the correct foot moves forward just before the hit.

If you are always in proper footwork position for medium-paced balls, the chances are you will more often be in proper footwork position for hard shots.

Chapter Thirteen
The Return of Serve in Singles

Arthur Ashe demonstrates the Ready Position to receive serve. The knees are flexed, the legs are 18 inches apart, the body is in a slight crouch, the racket is held with a forehand grip with the racket throat cradled in the fingers of the left hand, and the racket head points across the net.

The easiest way to judge whether your return of serve needs improvement is to count the number of return-of-serve errors you make in the course of a set. Unless the serve is tremendously good or the server an excellent volleyer, you should not make more than one or two return-of-serve errors per set. You are probably making six or eight or even 12, except against players who are much weaker than you. When you play against someone much worse, your return-of-serve errors may dwindle to two or three; when you are up against someone much better, they rise to the phenomenal number of eight or ten (not counting pop-ups to the net man). The reasons you return badly against a good player are: (1) he or she has a better serve than you are used to and (2) he or she pressures you so much if you don't make a forcing return that you try to hit too good a shot.

The return of serve should be reasonably forcing as well as consistent. If the serve is weak, the return of serve should dominate the point either through an outright winner or a shot that has the server stretching or puts him out of position. If the serve is strong, your ability to make a good return is really tested: if you can only pop up (hit a high, short floater) or whack the ball mindlessly, hoping it will go in, your problem may be caused by one or more factors, each of which adversely affects return of serve. You may be waiting stiff-legged or off balance or with your racket dangling or pointed too far to the left. You may be standing too close to the baseline or too far to your left to protect your backhand. Perhaps you only see the ball when it is too late or you wind up after the ball has bounced or you cut short your follow-through.

Here is a quick way to find out your return-of-serve weaknesses. Take the test to learn the theory, then go out on the court and put your knowledge into practice.

RETURN OF SERVE TEST (SINGLES ONLY)

Score one point for every correct answer. You are a sharp analyst and should have a good return of serve if you score 26-30. You may have a fine return of serve but you are either lazy at analysis or careless if you score 20-25. Anything below 20 indicates inexperience *or* lack of understanding in tennis techniques.

The Ready Position

1. When waiting to return serve, should you bend from the waist or from the knees?
2. Should your racket point straight in front of you or should it point slightly to the right or left?
3. Should your feet be touching or a few inches apart or 12 to 18 inches apart?
4. Does the left hand play any part in the Ready Position and, if it does, should it be on the handle or the throat?
5. Does it matter if you wait with a forehand grip or a backhand grip?

Where to Stand to Receive

1. When receiving in the forehand court, should you stand halfway between the alley and the center service line, almost by the alley or three feet to the left of the alley?
2. Is it better to stand three feet behind the baseline or just inside the baseline against a spin serve?
3. Should you stand in on a hard serve to take it on the rise or should you move three feet back and take it at the top of the bounce or just as it is beginning to drop?
4. When receiving second serves, should you *always* move in one or two steps?
5. If a serve is short, should you generally try to hit it with your forehand, *even* if it means running around your backhand, or is this a function of whether your forehand or backhand is stronger?

Concentration on Returns

1. Should you watch the whole motion of the server or should you concentrate only on toss and follow the ball?
2. If you follow the ball in flight, should you be able to see it bounce or should you just guess as to where it will bounce?
3. Should you be able to hear spin as well as see it?
4. Should your body be relaxed or tensed for the return?
5. Is it possible to make a really good return of serve if your opponent serves before you are ready?

The Drive Return of Serve

1. Should you pivot your shoulders and hips on a forehand return of serve?
2. If you are driving a return of serve, should the follow-through be as big as in a regular groundstroke?

3. If your opponent serves a wide ball to your forehand in the forehand court, and you decide to drive the return, should you hit a deep crosscourt, a deep down-the-line, a deep one down the center or any one of the three?
4. Is it better to drive a return of serve down the line or crosscourt or should you mix them up?
5. Should the drive return of serve be taken by your side or in front of you?

Blocks and Chips

1. Should a block return of serve be used against an American twist serve, a spin serve, a hard serve or any of the three?
2. Which would you use, a block or a chip, when you plan to follow your return of serve to net?
3. On a block return of serve, do you take a small or a big wind-up and a small or a big follow-through?
4. Would you ever block a short, low serve?
5. Against a cannonball serve, where you are standing 3 feet behind the baseline, would it be better to block or chip or can you do either?

Return of Spin Serves

1. Will a right-handed slice serve to your forehand in the forehand court move to your alley or into your body?
2. Will a right-handed American twist serve to your backhand move you wide on your backhand or will it break into your body?
3. Will a left-handed slice serve to your forehand move you wide on your forehand or will it break into your body?
4. Does a good American twist serve bounce higher or much lower than a regular spin serve?
5. Will an underhand serve hit with a lot of spin bounce to your right or your left?

THE ANSWERS

Ready Position

1. Most good players crouch down, bending from the knees and from the waist.
2. Generally the racket points slightly to the left since it is unnatural to break the wrist and point the racket straight ahead. However, if you put down "straight ahead," score your answer as correct since a number of tournament players hold the racket that way.
3. The feet are 12 to 18 inches apart.
4. The fingers of the left hand cradle the throat of the racket, thus aiding in a quick shift of grip. Many players keep the left hand on the racket as they start the backhand wind-up; the left hand moves up

toward the handle and releases its grip either early or midway in the wind-up.

5. This is an individual choice. Some wait with the forehand grip and some with the backhand.

Where to Stand to Receive

1. Almost by the alley.   If you don't stand way over, you will be aced on the forehand side in the forehand court and on the backhand side in the backhand court.
2. Inside the baseline against spin.   The farther back you stand, the more the spin can pull you wide.
3. If it is a hard serve, it is better to move back at least three feet. C. M. Jones of England, who has coached many players, states that even the champions return big serves just as they are beginning to drop rather than at the top of the bounce.   Only a player with a great eye and amazing reflexes would try to take a hard serve on the rise; the percentages are against successful returns when the receiver stands close in.
4. Not *always*.   Some players hit their second serves as hard as their first.   However, the receiver has a psychological edge when he moves in a step or two to return second serve.
5. The player with the big forehand should run around a short serve to go for a winner or a forcing shot off return of serve.   It puts tremendous pressure on the server to hit the backhand line on serve.   John Newcombe received this way in the ATP tournament final at Tucson against Arthur Ashe's second serve, which isn't exactly weak.   Other players are so confident of hitting winners or forcing shot returns of serve off the backhand that they never run around the ball.   Unless a player's forehand is shaky, it is a good idea to take the optional ball as a forcing forehand because it presses the server to try for more pace, depth and accuracy and results in more service errors.

Concentration on Returns

1. Most players find it impossible to watch the whole service action and still concentrate on the toss and the flight of the ball.   Unless you are one of the rare ones, try only to watch the toss and then to follow the ball in the air.
2. Your chances of a good return go way up if you can see the ball bounce.   All your efforts should be concentrated into seeing the bounce; otherwise you are a dead duck.
3. Near-sighted players hear spin.   Experienced players who see very well depend on their eyes, but many believe they hear spin also. All good, near-sighted players can hear when a ball is hit off-center and can recognize with their ears the sound of a spin serve as against the sound of an almost flat serve.
4. Relaxed.   When the body is tense, it fights the ball: the legs are too

rigid for easy, quick moves and the arm too stiff to swing forward freely.

5. If you are lucky. This serves to point out how important concentration is in receiving. You must be in the Ready Position, all extraneous noises (and thoughts) must be blocked out and your eyes must be focused on the ball as the toss begins. A "quick serve" catches you before your mind, body and eyes are ready.

The Drive Return of Serve

1. The shoulders pivot *on the wind-up,* and as a result the hips pivot very slightly. Beginners sometimes swivel their hips and shoulders as they hit. A good cure is to concentrate on keeping the side to the net while still allowing the weight to come forward and to avoid any pronounced hip swivel.
2. Yes. If you stop the follow-through in the middle, you are not letting the racket do the work.
3. All three have their place. The down-the-line or the crosscourt can be outright winners if hit hard; a return deep to the center allows the receiver to get back into position.
4. Mix them up; never let the server get grooved.
5. All shots, including the drive return of serve, should be hit in front of the body.

Blocks and Chips

1. Blocks are best against hard serves. They utilize the power of the hard serve in making a hard return.
2. A chip shot. It slows the ball down and the receiver can move behind it to a position at net. Blocks are *not* approach shots.
3. A very small wind-up and follow-through. A block is like a flat volley.
4. No. Short, low serves should be stroked (with topspin to make the ball rise over the net) or chipped (if the player is following the return to net).
5. Block the cannonball serve and it will go back hard. If you chip the return from a position three feet behind the baseline, it slows up the ball and gives the advantage to the server. However, Pancho Gonzalez did use the chip return to great advantage, angling it so the server had to both stretch and volley a low, dipping ball.

Return of Spin Serves

1. It will move to your alley.
2. It will move you wide on your backhand.
3. It will break into your body.
4. Much higher.

5. A slice forehand underspin (sidespin) serve will bounce to the receiver's left. It is conceivable that someone like Bobby Riggs might hit a slice *backhand* underspin serve, and then it would bounce to the receiver's right.

Chapter Fourteen/Hitting with Power

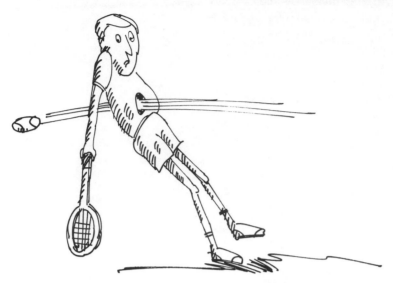

Every budding tennis player would like to have natural power, that seemingly effortless swing used by champions that makes the ball go like a bullet. Once an intermediate player has learned to keep the ball in court fairly regularly, he starts experimenting with the power game. The stroke gets bigger (and wilder), the body is hurled at the ball, footwork is often forgotten, occasionally a grunt or ferocious grimace is added to give the ball sting, balance is lost as arms and legs hurtle around the court, and the net result is certainly not an effortless swing. The ball goes harder than usual, but it often careens crazily since direction and control have been sacrificed to achieve more pace.

Intermediates striving for power are consistent only in their types of errors: the big first serve regularly goes two to eight feet out (it is not even a close fault), the high volley and set-up overhead frequently smash into one of the doubles opponents ("I'm sorry," explains the slugger, "*but I never know where my shots are going*"), and the groundstrokes are either big winners or big losers. The intermediate "power" player has given up form, footwork and fluent stroking whereas *controlled* power demands all three.

Power with precision is achieved by: hitting the ball in the center of the racket, taking the ball well in front of the body (or, not recommended, hitting it by the side of the body with a wrist flick), using a full wind-up and follow-through, keeping the wrist firm and having the entire body weight shift forward *just before the moment of impact*. Since the ball is going to be taken one to two feet in front of the body, the rhythm is "step forward, then hit," not "step forward as backhand with the right foot. The same stroke is used when hitting a soft shot or a hard one, but the momentum increases and the forward motion is much more pronounced.

The shoulder plays a big role in adding power to groundstrokes. On the forehand, the left shoulder moves in toward the net as the left foot steps forward. On the backhand, the hit is actually from the right shoulder as well as the right arm: the shoulder moves toward net and acts as the pivotal point for the entire arm. Note that *the body and hips never pivot*: such action would remove rather than add power. In the case of both forehand and backhand, the forward-moving shoulder has a slightly downward slant (if it pointed upward, the weight would automatically shift to the back foot, thus preventing forward momentum).

It is impossible to get real power if one only "arms" the ball (i.e., if the body is not moving forward) or if the stroke is not completed. If the arm does not swing through fully but instead stops right after the hit, the stroke is a jab rather than a full punch. Put a cushion a foot in front of you and jab it with your closed fist, stopping your swing as soon as you have hit the cushion. Now hit the same cushion with a full swing that continues through, and you will feel the additional power you get. To get power on the court you must not only finish the stroke but you must have the *confidence* to swing freely rather than tentatively. "Swinging freely" does not mean letting the wrist flop; it means letting the arm swing through until it winds up high in front of you, with the racket pointing to the top of the opponent's fence. Don't let the racket swing further around your body or your neck since it causes you to lose balance and you are unable to get ready for the next shot.

Too much underspin on the backhand removes rather than adds power. The ball rises and hangs in the air because underspin causes the ball to rotate *backward*. Flat shots (those with no spin) plus topspin and sidespin potentially have much more power. Most players avoid hitting the ball without any spin (a flat shot) since, although the power is potentially great, there is less control because only gravity pulls the ball down. A low ball, if hit flat, will either go into the net or, if you aim above net height, it will sail out. Only high balls can be hit flat; high, short balls can be hit flat and downwards. Topspin can be achieved by starting with the racket below ball-level and finishing with the racket well above ball-level. A ball well below net level can be hit very hard and still clear the net and land in court provided there is sufficient topspin on the shot. Sidespin forehands not only have potential power but they carry sting as well (the ball feels "heavy" on the opponent's racket.) It is frequently used as a coming-in shot, with the player moving forward as he hits. The racket action is sideways: instead of the racket head pointing high at the finish, the wrist stays laid-back (flat), the arm motion is *into the body* and the finish is just slightly higher than ball level, with the racket head pointing slightly to the right alley. The rules for spin, when power is the object, are:

- Avoid heavy underspin on the backhand.
- Use flat (no spin) shots only on high balls or, even better, on high, short balls.
- Topspin shots are safe, controllable power shots.
- Sidespin adds extra sting on forehand coming-in shots.

The player who is looking to add power to his game will find it easier to use the opponent's power than to manufacture his own. If the opponent hits hard to you and you meet the ball in front of you with a clean hit (no underspin or very little), the ball will go back with a good pace. However, if your opponent sends over a soft, mushy ball that simply plops and waits to be hit, you may have trouble manufacturing your own pace unless you remember how to create power:

- Hit the ball when it is one to two feet in front of you.
- Take a full backswing and a full follow-through.
- Hit with topspin (start low, finish high) or sidespin on the forehand.
- Step forward (left foot forward on a forehand, right foot forward on a backhand) and *then* hit the ball.
- Lean in with your shoulder (left shoulder on a forehand, right shoulder on a backhand) and make sure this shoulder is pointing slightly downward.
- Don't pivot your hips or your body.
- Don't let your wrist wobble or flop.
- Since it is a soft, mushy ball, you have plenty of time to hit it in the center of your racket.

If you have failed to get power while still following these directions, there is a defect in your stroke which is preventing you from achieving pace through weight transfer. These are the possibilities:

1. You are not using the full arm and shoulder. Instead of your shoulder being the pivot point, your elbow is. This is very common in untrained backhands where the elbow leads on the shot or, just at the hit, the elbow becomes the pivot point. The entire arm must swing freely from the shoulder.
2. You may be stepping forward and your shoulder may be pointing toward the net but your hips are moving backwards. The best correction is to keep the back ramrod-straight, bending only at the knees. Otherwise the "hips backward" motion prevents your weight from moving into the ball.
3. Your footwork may be bad and you may be facing the net on your forehand. Good players can hit forehands with a totally open stance, but intermediates should use a half-open stance: the left foot must step toward the net and the left shoulder should lead. The danger of an open stance for a less experienced player is the hip-swivel or hip-rotation. Lock your hip on the hit so your shoulder and body can move but your hips do not swerve.
4. You are stepping sideways on your forehand or backhand—your left foot is crossing toward your right alley on the forehand or your right foot is crossing toward your left alley on the backhand. As a result, your weight is going sideways rather than forward.
5. Your racket face is not perpendicular to the ground at the moment of impact. It is tilted slightly open and so the racket face is sliding under the ball. In spite of your forward momentum, therefore, the ball rotates backwards after you have hit it. Stop your motion during the hit and check to see if your racket head is actually perpendicular to the ground.
6. You have a double wind-up. You take your racket back in plenty

of time but then, just as the ball bounces, you make an extra little backward movement instead of a totally forward motion. The cure: as the ball bounces or is about to bounce, make sure your arm does not go back again but only moves forward. Once you are aware of your double wind-up, concentration will help you get rid of it.

7. You have followed through with a laid-back wrist which prevents a full, free swing. This is the easiest of all to correct: check to see at the end of your swing if your racket is pointing directly in front of you to the top of your opponent's fence. If it is pointing to your right on the forehand or to your left on the backhand, your wrist has not come through. Concentrate on the finish and the hit will then take care of itself.

It is easiest to get flowing power against balls whose spin you understand. You may misjudge a player's chip or underspin or left-handed spin, and until you can instinctively know how your opponent's spin will move after the bounce, you will mistime the ball and end up stretching sideways or hitting behind you or cramping your stroke, any of which will result in loss of power. Practice your power shots against balls you understand, which means against balls whose bounce you can predict. Don't give up playing against opponents who have tricky spins (how else will you learn what spin does to a ball?), but if you can't judge the spin well, don't expect smooth power.

Chapter Fifteen / The Proper Way to Practice

The number of hours one practices does not necessarily determine the rate of improvement. Hitting the ball as hard as one can straight down the center and taking the ball on the second bounce is not an effective practice pattern. The courts are crowded with young athletes who think the essence of the game is banging the ball with all one's might and that if they bang it long enough and hard enough, one day all their shots will go in. There are also masses of older beginners who practice four to six hours a week and who improve at an extremely slow rate because they neglect to practice footwork, stroke control, depth, and placement.

Most top players have developed excellent practice patterns. These are designed to speed up footwork and reflexes, work the kinks out of strokes, develop more accuracy and control against heavy pace and spins, build up stamina, acquire more power, touch, and/or spins and to achieve instinctive reactions to the opposition's patterns. Top players do not stand flat-footed when they are practicing. They never stroll casually around the court picking up balls after a rally. (They run.) They don't lose concentration because they are "only warming up." Above all, they don't practice with anyone who isn't serious about practicing. The worst kind of warm-up opponent is an indifferent one—a wild slugger, a bored competitor, an unenthusiastic foot-dragger, someone who wants to play instead of practice—and who then gives it less than 100% of his effort when the set begins.

Practice sessions, depending upon the stage of one's development or whether there is a particular stroke or footwork problem, vary enormously, but all have these factors in common:

- Concentration must be complete; an hour of hard practice is worth five hours of foot-dragging.
- The player is never flat on his heels. He bounces, jumps, hops and runs full-out.

- After a ball is netted, another ball is put into play immediately. There is no pause between rallies (and certainly no conversation).
- All shots are taken on the first bounce.
- From the moment the player steps on the court, each shot has a purpose—the first few hits to warm up the arms and legs and to get one's timing and thereafter to work on a particular phase of the game—crosscourts, return of serve, lobs, volleys, overheads, serves, backhand approach shots, drop shots, forehands, down-the-lines, etc.

The better players practice patterns that are impossible for beginners: drop shots and lobs or "one at net and two on the baseline." Novices will waste a lot of time practicing serves and returns of serve: many serves will be netted and the receiver will sometimes have to wait six or eight shots for a serve to come over the net. Each level requires a different kind of pattern—one that will result in hitting the maximum number of balls to achieve the greatest amount of improvement. Beginners, for example, will get much more out of a practice session if they work with a basket of used balls rather than the three new balls that top players use.

PATTERNS FOR BEGINNERS

Most novices tire quickly. At the end of five minutes they are often down to a slow crawl. At this point it is better to stop for a moment and get one's breath than to drag around limply. Novices are notoriously as slow as snails and they cannot advance into the intermediate category until they have learned to run to pick up every ball. The most important pattern for the beginner, therefore, is to pick up his feet, move fast, run, hop, bounce and skip. Walking to pick up a ball is verboten.

Some practice patterns for beginners are:

- Both players stand on the service line, each holding several balls and with several others in pockets. One starts the rally. The target here is control, not power—to keep the rally alive, not to put the ball away. The ball must be hit inside the service line so the opponent can return it. The emphasis is on seeing the ball at all times, taking a backswing early, hitting the ball in front of the body and following through.
- After the players can maintain a rally of ten shots without missing, they move back so they are now half-way between the service line and the baseline. Again the object is control, not power, and to keep the ball in play. The player does not stand still while he waits for the return; he bounces and hops.
- One player stands at net while the other stands a little behind the service line. The net man volleys his return while the opponent hits forehands and backhands. Neither player should forget the objective, which is steadiness and returning the ball directly to the opponent. After five minutes the positions are reversed, with the

net man moving back and his opponent coming in to volley.

- When both players are consistent enough, rallying starts from the baseline. However, if there is too much loss of control and if the players are wildly spraying balls all over the fence, they move back 4 feet each so that the rallies will be longer.
- The players move to the *same side* of the court and each *separately* practices serves, with one serving into the forehand and the other into the backhand court. This is another reason to have a full basket of balls since far too much time is wasted if one has to pick them up constantly.
- When the players are able to rally from the baseline and to get a sufficient number of serves in to make it worthwhile, they play a practice set. The aim is not to put the ball away for a winner but to get it back over the net. Since this is a practice set and not a match, all efforts are concentrated into keeping the ball in play. Each player tries to see the ball early, move quickly, take an early backswing and hit a full stroke. As soon as one player hits the ball, the other player starts moving. After each point is over, the balls are picked up *quickly*. If the players tire badly, they rest for one minute, then continue at full speed.

PATTERNS FOR INTERMEDIATES

An intermediate is defined as a player who seldom double-faults, has a reasonable forehand which he can hit at will crosscourt and usually at will down-the-line, an unreasonable backhand (but he gets a good percentage in unless pressed) and some experience at net, although the volley is not precise and the overhead slightly shaky. Intermediates have experience: they do not desire to play with beginners and prefer not to play with other intermediates. Among the shots they have not yet acquired are: a half-volley, a drop shot, a drop volley, a topspin lob, a deep slice serve to the backhand, a sidespin forehand that they can alternate with a topspin forehand, a backhand slice that they can alternate with a topspin (they have one or the other—not both) and a penetrating approach shot. Intermediates can whack balls away for placements; their problem is they make far too many errors and, on too many occasions, the opponent gets the ball back. Intermediates know an enormous amount about the game, since 90% of the players today are beginners, but they quickly find out what they don't know when they come up against an advanced player or when they talk tennis to the tournament players. The best thing an intermediate player can do since he has come this far, is to work like hell on his game for a year in order to get to the advanced stage.

The intermediate who is keen to take the big jump to a higher class must, first, recognize his own weaknesses and, second, sublimate his desire to stick with what he has (the big bash forehand volley taken on the dead run or the "cannonball" first serve that lands four feet out or the poorly constructed backhand that has no chance of becoming first class) in order to develop a stronger game. Each intermediate has a style of his own—attacker, defender, basher, unorthodox retriever—but he must learn to round out his game, play percentages, acquire accuracy and move twice as fast as he ever thought possible. His practice sessions are going to be extremely rewarding because he will no longer try to show the practice opponent how hard he can hit but how well he moves, sees, concentrates and controls. His patterns are designed to improve strokes and footwork, and if one or both are bad, a series of lessons are in order so that he knows what to work on. Assuming he takes these lessons, his practice patterns would be somewhat like this:

- For the first few minutes he hits forehands and backhands down the center to get his timing and warm up his arm. He bounces, hops, stretches and takes a full swing.

- For 15 minutes he hits forehands. He concentrates on seeing the ball well so that he can take it in front of him. He remembers what his pro has told him about the swing. For the first five minutes he hits forehand crosscourts and for the next 10 minutes forehands down-the-line. He is interested only in depth (hitting the ball as close to the baseline as possible). He tries to groove the down-the-line, and gradually he feels the difference in the positioning of his shoulders and feet and the point at which he takes the ball: the down-the-line requires slightly quicker timing and so is more difficult to execute against a hard, deep shot.

- During the next 15 minutes he endeavors to do the same on his backhand—crosscourts (the more natural shot) and down-the-lines. Pretty soon he will realize the timing on forehand and backhand is a fraction of a second different. Therefore, when he has a great day on his backhand, his usually reliable forehand may go off. This sense of timing is only acquired by practice. It is like rubbing your stomach with one hand and patting your head with the other at the same time (two different kinds of timing are required). Once you get it, you understand the two different rhythms.

- Now one player takes the net for 10 minutes and the other the baseline. The net man tries to volley deep down the center from both forehand and backhand side. Every fifth or eighth or tenth ball, a lob is thrown up and the net man works on his overhead. If he starts with simple, short set-ups, he develops a rhythm and confidence. Gradually the lobs are made more difficult—higher and deeper—but basically his aim is to acquire an extremely consistent overhead on short set-ups. After 10 minutes the positions are reversed and the net man now tries to hit low, hard shots down the center, alternating occasionally with a lob. Now he is trying to keep the ball low (not to go for depth) since this is the kind of shot he will hit in match play when his opponent comes to net.

- Intermediate players have good returns of serve so serves and returns can be practiced. One player serves 40 balls while the other returns, but this is more than just serving into a rectangle or returning the ball haphazardly. The server hits 20 serves in the forehand court—10 to the opponent's forehand and 10 to the backhand. Meanwhile, the receiver returns five down-the-line and five crosscourt, then five down-the-line and five crosscourt. No longer is the server (or the receiver) just hitting; each serve and each return has a purpose. The intermediate has now grown two inches in stature; he is learning placement on serve and return of serve. Serves and returns are also practiced in the backhand court. Depth as well as placement counts: a serve deep down the center is about to be acquired by the intermediate.

- The last phase of the session is a practice set or two. Everything the intermediate has practiced he now tries in this set—deep crosscourts off deep shots and sharp down-the-lines off short balls, service placements to the backhand and return of serve deep to the backhand or wide to the forehand. On short balls the intermediate clears the net well (to get depth) and follows in behind the shot to make his volley. The intermediate begins to realize that to get depth, he must clear the net by 5 to 10 feet. However, when his opponent comes in, he lowers his trajectory (to make the net man volley low) or raises it by lobbing.

PATTERNS FOR ADVANCED PLAYERS

It is not a bad idea for the advanced player to read about the practice sessions for intermediate. He is not so advanced that he no longer has any intermediate weaknesses. A realization of his own weaknesses is the panacea to his problems. How good is his down-the-line or with what depth does he hit his second serve?

The advanced player has many more shots than an intermediate and he reads his opponent far better. He moves in the second he knows his opponent has drop-shot. He runs around his backhand to clout a forehand return of second serve. His backhand is both consistent and accurate (often it is his best stroke). If he doesn't volley well, he compensates with an extremely strong baseline game; if his groundstrokes are unsteady, his volleying is impressive. He does not bang a shot to impress the gallery. He thinks on the court and very often he reacts instinctively, which is one step better than thinking.

The advanced player's practice sessions are far more strenuous than those of the intermediate because he misses fewer balls and he both starts and runs faster. Depending upon how advanced he is, here is what he can practice:

- First there are the usual crosscourt and down-the-line drills. Now these are alternated with occasional drop shots: the player runs in to get the drop shot and his opponent lobs deep. After ten or fifteen drop shot-lob patterns, a player begins to round into mid-season form. It is strenuous since the player must hit the fifteenth as well as he did the first. Another excellent pattern is down-the-line alternated with an occasional *sharp* crosscourt (one that goes short and wide). The receiver runs wide for the ball and goes down the line deep, following the shot to net. No ball is ever taken on the second bounce.

- One of the best patterns for advanced players is the approach shot off the short ball and the sharp crosscourt volley. Both players hit from the baseline until one player accidentally hits a short ball. The other player (A) then approaches net with a down-the-line deep to the baseline—sidespin is used on the forehand and underspin on the backhand. Player B tries a low passing shot and Player A responds with a sharp crosscourt volley. This pattern is practiced off all short balls for at least 15 minutes. It grooves approach shots and makes the crosscourt volley automatic.

- Both players now stand two steps inside the service line and volley at each other, gradually increasing the pace. After a few minutes one player takes two steps in while the second player (B) remains in the same position. Player A has to speed up his reflexes on the volley while Player B has to do more half-volleying. The positions are then reversed.

- Serves and returns of serve are practiced for 10 minutes or more. The first player hits forty serves but a maximum of two in a row to each court (the second ball is his second serve). In other words, each player is practicing not just his first but his second serve, and if he "double-faults" or serves too short, he is instantly aware of it. In turn, the receiver is "up" for the second serve and is ready to pounce on it if it lacks spin or is short.

- If either player has a weakness, this shot is practiced for the next 10 minutes.

- For the finale, they play one or two practice sets, working on approach shots after short balls, crosscourt volleys, lobs, overheads and passing shots. The whole pattern is one of intense concentration: how does one improve if one is lackadaisical?

PATTERNS FOR TOURNAMENT PLAYERS

The tournament player will use the practice format for advanced players with additions of his own. He may jog 2 to 5 miles a day, finishing in the stretch with a sprint, or he may jump rope, do pushups or any other gymnastic exercise designed to strengthen his leg, arm, stomach and wrist muscles. Additionally, he will practice longer and harder than the advanced player. Conditioning, accuracy, timing, touch, power, and speed of foot are the factors that distinguish him from his lesser tennis brothers, and any easing of the program will affect his game adversely.

The category "tournament player" encompasses a vast group of champions—the junior star, the Satellite Circuit player, the College No. 1, the Davis or Wightman Cupper, and the top Wimbledon and Forest Hills competitors. The club or parks champion is on the lowest level, followed by the city winner. Thereafter, in the national and international level, the heights a player reaches depends on how good he is on his worst day and whom he can beat through fight alone when his strokes have failed him or his timing is off. A great player may lose on occasion to a lesser one but never to a terrible player. The more he keeps himself in top condition through regular practice, the less chance of losing to a player ranked many notches below.

Some tournament players have few ambitions. They are happy to distinguish themselves in their own city or state and do not want to make a professional career out of tennis. Others like to reach the top or near top, but they are bored with practice and semiresigned to their fate as "permanent qualifiers." The ambitious and eager who cannot seem to get enough tennis are the most likely to improve—with two provisos. First, their practice patterns must be designed to take the wrinkles out of weaknesses such as a serve with no bite or a shaky overhead or an inability to leap for the volley; and, second, they must have the nerves to go with the heart, and this they can only work out through coming back just as fiercely and eagerly after each loss.

The tournament player will use the same practice patterns as the advanced player, but added to these are conditioning exercises and long hours of work (often with a coach) to iron out the weaknesses. The patterns are simply practiced for longer periods of time (3 hours a day instead of one or two) and are mixed in daily with several practice sets in singles and doubles. Additionally, he plays between 15 and 30 tournaments a year. If done with total concentration, the prognostication is: steady improvement and a much wider experience of match play, which means a better chance to win.

Chapter Sixteen
Can Rallying Ruin Your Game?

There was once a promising young player who was known on the circuit as "The Rallying King." No one looked better in the warm-up—clean, crisp groundstrokes deep to the baseline, sharp, hard volleys when he stood at net, and a loose, easy overhead action when he asked his opponent for "A couple of lobs, please." He was so good when I first warmed up with him that I knew I was going to be in for a helluva match.

I was wrong. He was only a rallier. As soon as the match started I discovered he didn't have an inkling about how to play. I was no longer hitting the balls to him with the same even pace; he was match-soft, could not return serve with any consistency, misjudged wide shots, had no control of his angles, and was only a duffer.

There are too many young players who rally several hours every day to "groove" their strokes—but who omit playing practice matches. They are forgetting the forest for the trees. They don't miss a ball in the rally but they miss every ball as soon as they begin to play. Even if they are working on changing a stroke, they cannot indefinitely "warm up." The test of changing a stroke is to try it out in practice sets (not in tournaments!) rather than groove it indefinitely in rallying.

Rallying Kings have a peculiar mentality. They rally so nicely that they become afraid to play. They do not know how to play—and they won't admit to themselves that the game consists of much more than just returning a ball that the opponent is feeding you.

There are two varieties of "rallying coaches." One is the coach who is afraid to play himself. He rallies indefinitely with his good pupils because he never misses in a warm-up (he couldn't beat Joe Schlunck in a match). The other is the coach who wants his pupil to have perfect strokes before he ever attempts to play. The pupil will therefore become a Master Rallier and a poor player.

The importance of rallying can never be understated. It is like the necessity for knowing how to play a hand of bridge. Match practice is the bidding and rallying is playing the hand. If you wind up in three clubs when you should be in four hearts or if you bid four spades and make six, or six diamonds and go down three, you are not on the road to becoming a Life Master, no matter how well you pull trumps.

How much you should rally and how much you should play practice sets is determined by your own game. Here are specific examples:

- You have a forehand weakness. Your tendency is to stretch your arm to full extension, thereby losing control. Recommendation: Rally at least a half-hour every day, concentrating on tucking your arm in so that you don't flail wildly at the ball. Then play at least one practice set, concentrating the same way. If you don't play the practice set, you may *rally* with a tucked-in elbow but as soon as you *play* you may flail away at all forehand returns of serve and at wide forehands.

- You are learning a nice punch volley but you are still in the learning stages. Recommendation: Stand at net and practice your punch volley for at least three 5-minute intervals during a half-hour rallying session. Then play a practice set to find out if you know how to come in to net (on what ball, how fast to run, where to stop, how to leap) to see if you can put the whole thing together.

- You have a weakness on second serve and you are working on depth, spin and placement. Recommendation: After you have rallied for 10 or 15 minutes and feel limber, serve a box of balls, starting slowly and building up so that you don't strain a shoulder muscle. Rally 10 minutes more and serve some more balls. Then play a practice set and see if your second serve is useful when the chips are down.

- You are learning a good drop shot. You have been telegraphing your move and you are now trying to disguise your motion. Recommendation: Rally for 10 or 20 or even 30 minutes, trying at least fifteen or twenty drop shots (off short balls) at various intervals. Then, when you play a practice set, see if you still retain not only the execution of the drop shot but the riposte to your opponent's return.

- You are a tournament player. You are taking a week's rest and only want to keep in shape. You are not sure whether to take a three-day or seven-day layoff or whether to rally each day or play some practice sets. Recommendation: You are now in such a high echelon of competition that you must judge by trial and error what is best for you. Mentally you may need a total rest from the tennis scene. Physically you might require some stamina exercises or warm-ups for your limbs such as jogging, setting-up exercises, or even rallying. Only you can determine what you need—because only you know that practice without concentration is not only useless but can actually make you "stale."

- You are a coach. One of your pupils has a major weakness—a late wind-up on the backhand. You are not sure whether he should take a week off to work only on the backhand since he has so many "playing" weaknesses as well. Recommendation:

> Every player is a different personality. It is worth the 10 or 15 minutes to discuss the backhand problem with your pupil to find out if (1) he cares enough to work hard on developing a better backhand and (2) if he understands that working on it by rallying alone is not sufficient. The everyday rallying session on hitting backhands early *must* be followed up with at least one practice set when his entire objective is not only to hit the backhand early but to control it as well.

Rallying is more than just warming up the arm, moving the legs and getting a "feel" for the court, balls and the conditions. To any one who has a weakness, it is a work period and it is invaluable. However, it only offers the limited practice of hitting a ball that comes to you without any of the pressures that appear when you play a set. It is like throwing a football to another fellow when only the two of you are on the field. Do you throw it well? But how are you going to throw it when three guys are rushing you and one of them is just about to knock you over?

Rallying Kings are a dime a dozen and champions are rare. No champion ever made the grade without hours of rallying to develop his strokes—but he also never made it without those vital practice sets.

Chapter Seventeen
Adapting to New Surfaces

A player who has learned his tennis on one set of courts—clay, for example—has enormous difficulty switching to another surface—such as concrete. He loses his rhythm, times the ball late, and feels jerky, uncoordinated, and frustrated. Even the top players, who "find" their timing after hitting three or four balls on a new surface, have problems in adjusting their whole game from a slow court where sliding is possible and the bounces are uneven (clay), to a fast surface where the ball often skids, the bounce is much lower and unreliable (grass), to a medium surface where there are no bad bounces, it is impossible to slide, and spins are only moderately effective (Laykold or Plexipave).

Adapting to a new surface requires a change in rhythm and style of play. And you can adjust your game only if you know what is going to happen when the ball comes to you with topspin, sidespin, and underspin; how high it will bounce on a deep, high ball, how low on an underspin, and how fast on a hard ball (will it "jump" at you or slow down more than you anticipate?); whether the footing is secure when you change directions; how wide a crosscourt undercut backhand will veer; how deep and high a heavy topspin groundstroke will come at you; whether it is possible to run down almost any shot if your reflexes are quick enough and your feet fast enough; and if even a medium volley can be a winner or if hard volleys are "gettable." If this analysis sounds too technical don't let it frighten you off; there is a method of adjusting to new surfaces for every level of the game.

Top players make the fastest adjustment. Hitting a few balls gives them the general "feel" of the court. The significant adjustment for them is in style of play: attacking more on a fast surface; waiting for openings and playing more consistently on a slow surface; utilizing more spins on courts where spin is most effective; compensating for bad bounces when the court is rough; drop-shotting more frequently when the ball "dies" on the court, etc. Beginners and intermediates make the slowest adjustment since their timing is thrown off by switching from a fast to a slow court or vice versa. Often it will take a full week for a novice to adjust to an entirely new surface. His biggest problem is to control his frustration and to analyze why he has mis-hit so many balls and how he can make the correction.

BEGINNERS AND INTERMEDIATES

John Smith has been playing for a few months on a Sportface or Sport-eze carpet which is medium-speed. He is going to play on clay (slow) for the first time.

John finds he has lost his "feel." Sometimes the ball bounces into his body and he cramps his arm so that he can't take a full, free swing. Often his timing is so bad that he has to stretch forward to hit the ball; even then he barely gets it before it bounces a second time. He often misjudges what looks like an easy shot and hits it while bending double from the waist. He feels awkward, helpless, and angry at himself for being so unathletic and inept.

Since John's experience has been limited to one surface only, he is going to have a hard time grooving his timing to a surface that is only a little bit slower but where the bounce is uneven. These thoughts will help him adjust much faster:

- He must take a slower backswing. The entire backswing, not just one segment of it, is slowed down slightly. If he takes his regular backswing, he may have to come to a complete halt just before the moment of impact. This makes the swing jerky instead of flowing.
- He must move *forward* for every ball. If he does not move forward, the ball will start to drop faster than he has anticipated, and then he will be forced to bend or lean forward in order to hit it before it bounces a second time. Sometimes he will have to move a good two steps forward so that he can hit the ball at waist level; if he only moves one step forward, he may make contact at ankle level.
- He can never plant his feet because the ball may take a bad bounce. Clay is never perfectly smooth, and if the ball hits a bad or rough spot it may bounce into or away from John. If he has planted his feet, then he has to twist his torso and cramp his arm into his body or extend the arm so straight and stiff that he loses all control. John has to be bouncy, on his toes, ready to hop sideways in either direction depending on the crazy bounce of the ball.
- John has to have a happy outlook. As soon as he gets discouraged, frustration goes into his feet (they refuse to move) and his right arm (it moves sluggishly, almost reluctantly). He must regard changing to a new surface as a challenge which will take work and enthusiasm and which will help him become a far better player.

If John moves from clay (slow) to cement* (fast), his frustration will

* The word "cement" stands for "Portland cement concrete." It is the most common surface in California, where the courts are usually very fast. However, "cement" can be very slow if it is heavily troweled to make the surface rough.

be even worse unless he has prepared himself for the necessary changes in stroke and timing. Now the ball will be coming at him so fast that half the time he will be late; instead of hitting the ball in front of him, he will often "hook" it slightly behind his body. He has no timing; his backhands go into the left alley and his forehands into the right alley, a sure indication that he is taking the ball late.

Instead of taking a full, free backswing, he must *shorten the entire swing and start it earlier.* Instead of a semicircular wind-up, he cuts off the preliminaries and takes the racket straight back. He starts his forward swing *at once.* He should try to hit crosscourt exclusively. Even then, he will find that his shots will never go in the crosscourt alley (in the left alley for a forehand, in the right alley for a backhand). When the shot goes into the wide crosscourt alley, the player is taking the ball too soon.

To make a quicker adjustment, John should prepare his mind, which in turn will prepare his eyes, arms, and legs. These ideas will be helpful if John is a positive thinker:

- Adjustment to fast courts is never easy. John must face the challenge happily since a pessimistic attitude will adversely affect his eyes, arms, and legs. The mind is the transmitter of thoughts; an arm or a leg never operates independently.
- The ball is going to come twice as fast as expected. John has to face the fact that he will often be late, but occasionally he will hit the ball well in front of him. And, if he continues to try to speed up his reactions, he will hit more and more balls in front of him.
- John has to shorten his backswing and should start the forward swing *before* he thinks he should. Surprisingly, John will seldom if ever take the ball too early.
- The eyes must work with more concentration and faster than ever before. John has to train himself to see the ball come off his opponent's racket (he can no longer wait with his feet planted until the ball has crossed the net). He then has to move in the direction the ball is going and should try to get there well ahead of the ball. His efforts should be geared to getting there *too early*, and it will frequently turn out that he has reached the spot just in time.

ADVANCED PLAYERS

Many advanced players have similar, but not as pronounced, adjustment problems with a new surface as do intermediates. Even though the advanced player has more experience, a change of surface can be quite traumatic to his timing. Players who cannot make an immediate adjustment should give careful reading to the suggestions for less advanced players.

FAST COURT ATTACK AND DEFENSE

Once the advanced player has acquired the timing for a slower or faster surface, he must adjust his style of play. On fast surfaces: he cannot afford a weak second serve; he must take advantage of every short, high ball by either putting the ball away or hitting it deep and coming to net; his passing shots must be harder, lower, more disguised, more angled since his opponent can more easily put away the volley; his defense must be clever and designed to keep the opponent guessing since the aggressor always has the advantage when the court is fast; and he must step up his pace slightly (never to the point of pressing) because the court favors the harder hitter.

There are two kinds of fast courts—one with perfect bounce (cement) and one with an unpredictable bounce because the surface is not perfectly even (grass). A third type of fast court, wood, is so rare today that it is scarcely worth more than a mention; spin is incredibly effective on boards—a left-handed slice serve to the forehand jumps into the body, an underspin backhand moves wide and low after the bounce, and a heavy topspin forehand "takes off" with a high forward bounce.

Grass and cement—particularly cement that has been finished with a glass-like patina (no rough troweling to slow it down)—are much faster than most carpets, compositions, asphalts, and acrylic-painted surfaces such as Laykold or Plexipave. However, even though grass and cement are noted for their speed, a slow, high ball will not have more appreciable speed on grass and cement than it does on clay, asphalt, or acrylic surfaces. Therefore two push-ball artists or retrievers paired against each other will not find the pace of cement or grass any different from that of clay or Har-Tru.

A ball hit on grass ordinarily has a low bounce, a ball hit on bad grass often takes a bad bounce, and a ball hit on wet grass frequently does not bounce at all. One can never position oneself firmly on grass since the bounce is never totally predictable. The knees must bend far more than on any other surface; the worse the grass, the more the knees must bend.

Underspins on grass "take off" with a sideward motion and must be handled with an extremely stiff wrist since the ball is skidding sideways from the racket. For the player who is not yet secure, an underspin backhand crosscourt should be returned crosscourt, because the ball is moving to the left of the receiver and, at worst, the leftward spin will bring it slightly more to center. He will have worse luck if he tries to hit it down-the-line, because the leftward spin will carry it into the opponent's alley.

Sidespins are also extremely effective because there is forward as well as sideways motion after the bounce and, moreover, the ball feels "heavy" on the receiver's racket. A forehand down-the-line sidespin will come to the receiver's backhand and move forward as well as to the left. This is best handled with a very stiff wrist and with a crosscourt return to counteract the sideward bounce: the ball is moving to the left and so a down-the-line return may go into the alley, whereas a crosscourt will, at worst, go toward center.

Spins are effective on fast cement but underspin will slow up the ball appreciably, so topspin and sidespin are the preferred shots. Obviously underspin must often be used on low, short balls and on many backhand approach shots, but the hard topspin backhand on a fast court is more aggressive and is hard for the opponent to reach. Heavy topspin on the forehand is extremely useful because of its forward motion: even if the shot goes short (a few feet beyond the service line), the forward motion is so great and the bounce so high on cement that the average opponent cannot come in but must play the ball from the baseline. A deep, heavy topspin forehand often forces the opponent to a position 6 feet behind the baseline.

There are three spots from which to return serve on a fast court: 3 to 6 feet behind the baseline against a very hard serve; on or in the area of the baseline for a heavy spin serve (in order to hit it before the spin has pulled the ball wide); and 2 feet or more inside the baseline against short second serves. The short second serve presents the receiver with his opportunity to step around the ball and smack a forehand down-the-line (usually) or sharp crosscourt (occasionally).

SLOW COURT ATTACK AND DEFENSE

The slower the court, the easier it is to return any ball. A great player can on occasion run down a ball that has gone past him or chase an angled overhead into the next court and retrieve it before the second bounce. Patience and speed of foot is the name of the game on very slow courts, although there is still opportunity for attack.

On slow courts the slugger is at his worst, the retriever at his best, and the clever, heady "chess player" can more easily use his bag of tricks.

The net rusher has to have a superb serve if he is to follow it to net regularly. (Today more and more top players with big serves are coming in behind serve on clay or Har-Tru and doing better than they would if they stayed back.) If the serve is not superb, the net rusher will find himself ruefully staring at a steady stream of passing shots. More often he will have to work his way to net by forcing a short shot from his opponent, then hitting it with both depth and pace to a corner. If the opponent retrieves it, the net-rusher may have to leap high to smash a sky-ball lob. Overheads are harder to put away on slow courts, and very few bounce-overheads smashed from behind the baseline are outright winners. The net rusher must therefore be patient because he can be driven back from the net by high lobs and his short volleys become set-ups to the passing shot artist. He must wait for the short balls or, when he can, volley the high ball and come in behind it.

The consistent player has a field day. If he is fast, he can throw back hundreds of balls. If he hits deep as well, he is going to be extremely tough for all but the very best players. If he is accurate on passing shots when pulled wide and can also put away a short ball, then he is going to win almost every clay court tournament. His name is Guillermo Vilas. Her name is Chris Evert. The only players capable of beating consistent passing shot artists such as Vilas and Evert on slow courts are aggressive players who are almost as consistent (Connors and Borg, for example, among the men, Court and Goolagong among the women) or an equally consistent and determined player (Manuel Orantes).

The "chess player" also does extremely well on a slow court. This player relies on change of pace and change of spin to create openings. A backhand is sliced down-the-line, then mixed with a harder backhand crosscourt, a high looping forehand, a drop shot, a forceful down-the-line forehand, a delicate lob, a deep-down-the-line, and even an underhand serve with tremendous spin. The aims are to keep the opponent off balance, to disguise what is coming next, to prevent rhythm by mixing up loops with drives, with spins, with angles.

The advanced player who comes from a fast court to clay must "think clay," i.e., getting back many more balls, primarily, and going for fewer outright winners if the percentages are proving fatal. He need not stop aggressive tactics but he cannot afford unnecessary errors. He may be able to create openings (short returns) with a big topspin forehand, which is always an effective shot on clay. If he drop-shots well, he may rely on a drop shot—lob—drop shot pattern to exhaust and wear down the opposition.

If he is lobbed, he may not go for the overhead winner, particularly if he is much closer to the baseline than the service line. When he gets a short lob, he will always go for the winner (which is often an angled overhead), since he will never have a better opportunity. If he knows how to slide, he slides into wide balls. He "thinks" clay—which means the emphasis is on consistency, depth, retrieving, creating openings, and taking advantage of openings when they present themselves.

MEDIUM-PACED COURTS AND MAVERICK SURFACES

Clay, Har-Tru, and a number of other composition surfaces are slow. Grass, cement, and wood are fast. Asphalt, acrylic paints, carpets—surfaces neither fast nor slow—lie somewhere in between. Here the adjustment is mostly for spin. As an example, Laykold and Sportface play almost identically except for the way the surface takes spin: underspins are more accentuated on Sportface and will pull the player wider.

Carpets also vary, with Sporteze (or Sportface) faster than Supreme Court, and Supreme Court accentuating spins much more than Sporteze. A player who does not understand spins will experience extreme frustration his first time on Supreme Court. Bolltex (another carpet) is easy to turn and run on; Uni-Turf is more difficult when you want to change directions; one can slide on Har-Tru or other sandy-topped surfaces, but a player can break his ankle if he tries to slide on a carpet or a hard surface.

When coming off a fast court to a medium court, the player has more time to hit the ball but he must remember that he has to move *toward the ball*. Read the paragraphs in this chapter with regard to changing from a fast court to a slow one. The same applies in the change from fast to medium, with the additional factor of learning to recognize what happens to the bounce after spin shots are hit.

Maverick courts are the most confusing to intermediates. Tennis Quick, a popular European surface, is extremely slow and has its own peculiar bounce on drop shots and underspins. Le Club in Fort Lauderdale has two courts which behave like no other courts. A combination of forehand topspins and backhand underspins is guaranteed to drive an intermediate player up the fence—until he gets used to them.

Carpets that were installed a few years ago when some carpets were then in the experimental stage will play a prominent role in bringing the visitor's game down 30 points. A maverick court gives a bounce off a spin that is comparable to no other on a "name-brand" court. When you play on a maverick surface, give yourself *at least a week* to learn to react to the challenging bounces. You will adjust faster if your mood is happy, if you never plant your feet and instead keep hopping, and if you watch the ball like a hawk so that you can improvise at the last minute. Watch that bounce so that you can be the perfect all-surface player.

Chapter Eighteen
Learning through "Spectating"

If you have ever sat next to a top tournament player during a big match, you will find out how much he knows about tennis compared to your own limited experience. His remarks might be: "Why did Pasarell serve wide to Solomon's forehand at 30-all?" or "Virginia Wade's serve pulls a player so wide that she is the only woman who can safely serve wide to the forehand—at 15-40." He might comment on the technical aspects of the play: "If only Ashe would bend his knees on the volley, he would not miss so many low ones," or "Emerson is hurrying his serve so much that he is rushing himself out of the match." The astute tournament spectator is also aware of tactics: "Tanner shouldn't try to hit with Connors; he would be better off to try to break up his rhythm"; "Borg always goes for the crosscourt when he is rushed on his passing shots"; or "Rosie Casals is crowding the net—a few good lobs would make her play back farther." He also notices spins ("Navratilova slices so much on her backhand that it sits up for Evert when Martina comes in"); fastness of reaction ("Ramirez has quick hands"); stroke production ("Heldman gets a lot of power from stroke-volleying, but if she used a punch volley a little more she'd have a much better safety factor").

What do you see when you watch a match? Are you merely keeping the score—or are you aware of style and tactics? The pleasure you will get from understanding what is happening and why will be increased by the fact that your own knowledge of the game is expanding.

The average spectator can recognize only a few ploys: Arthur Ashe is going to net on every serve, Stan Smith is making a lot of errors (off what shot? on which side?), John Newcombe is serving a lot of aces and/or doubles, and Eddie Dibbs is making some great gets. The spectator can easily train himself to look and analyze, and at the end of the match he will find that he can make a reasonably good analysis of what he has seen. First, he should understand what is happening on serve and return of serve, the two most important single shots in the game:

1. Is Ashe getting most of his first serves in?
2. In the forehand court, does he always or almost always serve to the backhand? What happens when he serves to his opponent's forehand? Does he ever "jam" the serve at the receiver?
3. If Ashe is following his serve to net, what return is Newcombe attempting?
   a. Down-the-line crunchers off the forehand?
   b. Angles or dinks off the backhand?
   c. Chips or blocks or drives?
4. What is the difference between Ashe's first serve and second serve? Does the second serve fall short and is Newcombe able to step around it and return with a forehand, or does Ashe have enough spin and depth to prevent Newcombe from taking advantage of it?
5. Where is Newcombe standing to return serve? Is he on the baseline or 2 feet back, and does he take two steps in if Ashe's first serve is a fault?
6. What is Newcombe's stance on return of serve and does he hop at the moment of the service hit and then move quickly in either direction?
7. On return of serve, how many times does Newcombe hit into the net, hit over the baseline, pop up a set-up, or lob?
8. If Newcombe lobs, is it a defensive shot or does his ball carry tremendous topspin? Are his lobs falling too short or too long and how does Ashe handle them?
9. Where does Ashe stand when he serves into the forehand court and where does he stand when he serves into the backhand court?
10. Is Newcombe mixing up his returns of serve—drives, dinks, and lobs? Is he returning better off the forehand or backhand?
11. If Ashe is following his serve to net, is his first volley usually down the line or crosscourt and does he get good depth off it? On which side is he volleying better?

The first volley of the incoming server is often hit for depth in order to elicit a short return which the volleyer can then put away. Sometimes the receiver will pop up, and the server will then put away his first volley. Sometimes the receiver will return so well that the server must either stretch the full length of the court on his first volley or dig up the ball from his shoe tops. Many servers choose to half-volley the first return, then close in at net. Which tactic is Ashe using? Is he getting in fast enough to volley the return, or is he half-volleying the first ball and then moving in?

What is Billie Jean King's style? Is her toss in front or to her side, does she take a full, circular wind-up, is the hit at the top of the toss, and are one or both feet on or off the ground at the moment of impact?

Does King stay back on second serve? If so, is she winning more than 50% of these exchanges? And does her opponent, Chris Evert, always or almost always return the second serve?

If both your eyes and your attention are good, you will be able to spot and describe the style of both players—whether the grip is Continental or Eastern, whether either player uses a little or a lot of spin on forehand or backhand, and whether the players vary their spins or hit almost every ball the same way. If there are any baseline exchanges, are both players trying for depth, are they succeeding and does the ball clear the net by 5 to 10 feet? When a ball skims the net, does it fall short (less than 6 feet from the baseline)?

Here is one easy way to judge the power of a player such as Connors. If he hits to the corner, is it an outright winner or can his opponent lope over to get it? How fast does his opponent have to move in order to get to the ball?

Overheads, among top players, are usually winners, but is it because of the speed or the placement or a combination of both? After watching Guillermo Vilas for an entire match, can you describe where he generally hits his overheads—and can you generalize by saying where most good lefties hit their overheads?

When a player comes to net behind serve and continually makes good volleys off the low returns, do you know what he or she is doing? Have you noticed that Billie Jean King and Rosie Casals get down within an inch of the ground to volley a low, dipping drive? Do you notice, on the volley, how much or little of a wind-up is taken and where the ball is hit (how many feet in front of the body)?

Many good players have only a limited repertoire. The strokes that take touch are the drop shot, the drop volley, the lob volley, and the offensive topspin lob. Does Bjorn Borg use any or all of them? If Rod Laver uses them, can Borg guess them—or are Laver's drop shots bounding too high or his drop volleys hitting the net or his lob volleys going a little short?

If you find, from the above, that you have not been following a match as well as you could, try girl-watching. The top players hit with less power than the men but they are often more consistent and have greater variety. Roscoe Tanner's serve is too fast for the average spectator to analyze; often the play is too quick to recognize what is happening. The slightly slower women's game will give you a better opportunity to analyze and to learn, although a top men's match on clay will give you the chance to examine and study strokes, tactics, the various ploys, and style.

If you have watched great matches as a "thinking spectator," you should be able to answer most of these questions correctly:

When Arthur Ashe played Jimmy Connors in the 1975 Wimbledon final, did Ashe go for a lot of service aces? (*No, he served at three-quarter speed to make sure his first serve went in.*) Did Ashe try to force Connors by hitting hard to the corners? (*No. His tactic was to hit short, low, and often to the center to force Jimmy to hit up and make his own pace; Connors is at his best when he is run wide on a hard shot.*) Did Ashe ever chip his forehand in a baseline exchange in this match? (*Not in this match—but he did in the final of the Fireman's Fund of 1975 against Guillermo Vilas, to the surprise of many spectators. He beat Vilas in a baseline duel.*)

Is Chris Evert ever caught off balance or leaning backwards when her opponent throws in a deep, hard shot? (*Almost never. If she can get to the ball, she is always prepared. She is one of the few players who never seem to be off balance.*) Is Chris considered a relatively weak volleyer because she misses a lot at net? (*No. She seldom makes a volley error. However, she does not hit her volleys as hard as Margaret Court, with as much angle as Evonne Goolagong, or with the touch of Billie Jean King—nor does she have the anticipation or leaping ability of Martina Navratilova. Still, she never misses an easy volley and puts away all set-ups.*) Is Chris fast on getting to a drop shot? (*Yes, but she doesn't always have the correct riposte which means she frequently gets passed on the next shot. It is one of her few failings.*)

Does Bjorn Borg ever start his forehand wind-up above head level? (*Yes, quite frequently. He has one of the biggest loops in the game: he can start above head-level, swoop down and finish the stroke well above head-level.*) Does Borg often slide on clay? (*He can slide 10 or 15 feet into the ball on a clay or Har-Tru surface.*)

When an opponent serves to John Newcombe's backhand, does he ordinarily drive it crosscourt or down the line? (*Ordinarily, neither. He prefers to hit low, angled dinks and chips to force the incoming server to volley up. He seldom goes for the drive return of serve, which would end the point either way.*) Does Newcombe serve a lot of doubles? (*He serves more doubles than most top players other than Rosewall, but he also serves more aces and wins more points off his deep second serve.*) Does Newcombe ever play cautiously on the forehand volley? (*He goes for winners on this shot but is incredibly consistent with it.*) What is Newcombe's favorite serve? (*He has no pattern on serve. He not only varies the spot to which he hits, often jamming it at the player, but he also varies the spin to pull the receiver wide.*)

As much as I watch tennis, I never finish learning. Neither will you. Formed opinions will change, the unorthodox becomes the accepted and you recognize that the New Champion can pull off shots or use a style that the Old Champion said would never work.

Chapter Nineteen
"Do's" and "Don'ts" of Strategy

If you are going to be a strategist, and there is no challenge in simply clobbering the ball or trying "touch" shots that don't work, you must know the cures for the sins you have committed. If you are making errors by hitting your backhand into your opponent's forehand alley, you are taking the ball late. The cure: take the ball earlier and try for the crosscourt. If you are missing your crosscourts by hitting too early (they are going wide), then aim for the center. If you are netting too much, lift the ball more by starting low and finishing high. If your problem lies in hitting long (over the baseline), perhaps the face of your racket is opening too much; try to keep the racket face perpendicular to the ground and be sure to finish with the racket pointed high (toward the top of your opponent's fence). But you may also be missing because (1) you are trying too tough a shot, (2) you didn't watch the ball, (3) your wrist was flopping, (4) you didn't finish the stroke, (5) you wound up too late or (6) you tried a shot you had not yet mastered. More about the latter later. Keeping the ball in play, not trying for winners without regard to errors, is your basic ploy.

In groundstroke exchanges (when both players are in the backcourt) there are three tactical approaches. First, the crosscourt is the basic (easiest) shot on both forehand and backhand, so use the crosscourt normally unless (1) your opponent has an attacking forehand and weak backhand or (2) you have a natural chip or sidespin forehand down the line. In the exchange of crosscourts, hit the ball between 6 and 10 feet over the net to get good depth. Avoid the short crosscourts that leave your down-the-line alley open for a winner, and only try the sharp, short crosscourt when your opponent is out of position. The object of these deep crosscourt exchanges is to elicit a short ball (preferably a short, high ball) from your opponent. That gives you the opportunity to attack, but it does not give you the right to lose your head and overhit.

The proper attack, when you get a short forehand, is a deep down-the-line to your opponent's backhand. Only rarely (when you feel sure you can make an outright winner) should you try the sharp, short crosscourt since you have left your backhand court wide open. When you hit deep and down the line off a short forehand, you can come to net even if you don't volley well, since the chances are your opponent will pop up to you and all you need do is stick out your racket and tap the ball in a short crosscourt angle. Never hit this volley hard since you could miss through overanxiety or losing your head, whereas tapping the ball short crosscourt is an outright winner.

If your opponent hits a short, high ball to the left of center, run around your backhand and take it on your forehand, either hitting deep down the line or, if you can hit a reverse crosscourt, sliding one wide to his backhand. If you happen to have an excellent backhand, then hit it deep down the line (if you are sure you will make the shot) or else crosscourt. On all set-ups (high, short balls), use your favorite, most confident shot. You have worked the whole point to get a short ball, so don't blow it by trying something overly cute (a touch angle or a delicate drop shot) if the chances are you may make an error. The strategist never makes an error on a set-up.

At times, in deep crosscourt exchanges, your opponent may have you on the run and you are barely able to touch the ball. When this happens, don't go for a winner (unless your name is Rod Laver) but throw up a high ball deep to the center which will cut down the angle of your opponent's return and enable you to get back into position.

When your opponent hits you a short, low-bouncing angle shot, your return will depend on what *you* do best. If you can slide the ball deep and heavy down the line as you come to net, knowing you can make the volley and overhead, your aggressive attack will pay off. However, if your "deep and heavy slider" goes short and soft, you have made a terrible mistake in judgment. Much better to try for depth down the center than to pop up a short backhand and get passed. A short angle return by you has to be a placement since you are exposing a flank. A drop shot must also be an immediate winner or you are dead. The aggressive, confident net player will advance with underspin (on the backhand) or a chip (on the forehand), the touch player will try an overspin sharp crosscourt or a drop volley, and *you,* until you reach a higher level of the game, will simply play deep and safe. Low, short, angled balls are not yet set-ups for you.

When your opponent hits hard and deep to you, you have two choices. The easy one (you don't have to move) is the difficult one (chances of success are much smaller) since you half-volley the ball from your shoe tops. If you jump or run back two steps, the ball will rise to a better height, and you can then step forward and hit. Of course the great players often half-volley from the baseline,* but when you do so you will frequently lose control and depth, thus letting the opponent take over. By stepping back and driving, accuracy and control improve. Here is the time to decide whether you want to look

---

* Rosewall often steps back, but Ashe never does.

good missing (you will only look good to your boy- or girlfriend) or appear what I would like you to be—a heady fighter who knows his limitations.   The day will come when you will be able to take balls on the rise and half-volley them with control, but don't put this into your everyday, match-play repertoire until the stroke is mastered.

Now play a set against a good player in your area and see what you know.   He serves hard to you—possibly hard and wide.   Your *only* ploy is to get the ball over the net.   If you can get your racket on it, you can lob it back deep and to the center.   At least you are in the point and have not been damaged.   If your opponent misses his first serve and foolishly hits a short one to your forehand, your obvious ploy is to side-spin, chip or, if you know how to, topspin the ball down the line.   Top-spins are easy to hit crosscourt and more difficult (except for advanced players) to hit down the line.   The return of a short second serve to your forehand is the down the line that never misses (if you don't pos-sess one, go out and buy one, steal one or borrow one, knowing that the sidespin and chip are slightly easier to learn than the topspin).   If your opponent's serve comes to your backhand, lob it if it is trouble-some but return to his backhand if you possibly can.

On the second point, you are returning in the backhand court.   Usu-ally the serve will come to your backhand and, *unless the serve is short,* your return will be a crosscourt.   If the return is short, you can eat it up *if* you totally own a backhand down-the-line.   The shorter it is, the more time you have to pivot, step in, and hit.   Aim carefully because your opponent has just given you the big opening.   If your opponent has hit deep to your backhand, your best, safest, and easiest return is deep crosscourt to keep you in the point.   The only players who can return this serve down the line are those with solid, grooved slices—or Don Budge.   If your opponent has chosen to serve to your forehand in the backhand court, your return will be based on *what you do best.*   If you have a sidespin or chip forehand, you can hit to his backhand. Otherwise, hit deep to his forehand or, if you are the least bit uncertain, hit deep to the center to avoid an unnecessary error.

If your opponent is coming in behind serve, you have more choices, depending upon both his and your abilities.   If the serve is tough, lob—as high as you can.   If it is short, *you* are in the driver's seat so don't blow your mind.   First, hit the shot you like best.   Second, never look to see how the server is approaching net.   As a matter of fact, never look at the server *at all* (it will only take your eyes off the ball).   So your choice as to whether to go down the line or crosscourt when the server comes to net depends on what shot you hit best.

The following hint on fast serves may help your return.   Watch the toss only, looking at the area a few feet above the server's head rather than looking at his action.   You will spot the ball a split-second faster and can make your readiness move quicker.

Now it is your turn to serve.   Unless the score is 0-0 or 30-0 or 40-15, don't risk serving to your opponent's forehand if his down-the-line return could kill you.   There are very rare exceptions.   If you haven't served one ball to his forehand in over a set and you suddenly throw in a second serve wide to his forehand, you just might catch him off balance, depending upon your assessment of his mentality. For example, if you consistently return only to his backhand, he will begin to run better and better towards his backhand side. Then, in the middle of the second set, if you suddenly run him on his forehand side, he may be so backhand-oriented that he will run very poorly on the forehand for three or four times consecutively.

Your basic serve is to the backhand and it must be deep. Any short shot can put him on the offensive. Occasional variations keep him off balance, and these variations are designed to keep you from getting in trouble in case your execution is poor or he outguesses you. One variation is to serve right at him. Another is to spin one to his forehand when you are serving in the backhand court. Learn to know his return —whether he favors the crosscourt or can slide one down the line. So your basic serve is to the backhand with the two variations thrown in to catch him off-guard.

If you come in behind serve, you must know his favorite shots—short crosscourts, down the lines or lobs. Leave one side slightly open if he seldom goes for it since the reason he avoids it is he seldom makes it. If he does make it, say "Nice shot" and forget it since he probably won't chance it too often again or will err when he does. While you are developing your strategy, your opponent is also developing his, and this is the fun of competition. Be sure you know what he is capable of doing and what he cannot do. Then you know his tactics and possibly he does not know yours.

It is a good idea to acquire a knowledge of spins—your opponent's so as to be able to handle his, and some of your own so as to be able to take advantage of an opponent's weakness. A promising player I know has an excellent chip forehand down-the-line approach to his opponent's backhand, but when he finally came up against another player with a great backhand and no forehand, he was eaten alive. He could have won if he had known a topspin forehand crosscourt. He didn't. May he rest in peace.

Chapter Twenty
Checkpoints for Intermediates

The tennis boom in the United States has created millions of new players in less than five years. Roughly speaking, at least 90% of American players today are beginners, perhaps 8% are intermediates, and the very small remainder are advanced or tournament players. If you are not sure whether you have reached the intermediate level, or if you think you are beyond this stage, take this test. If your answer to the first question is "Yes," you are no longer a beginner. If your answers to most of the other questions are "Yes," you have reached the intermediate category but are not yet among the advanced.

TEST FOR INTERMEDIATES

- Can you direct the ball to the forehand or backhand side at will?
- Do you have reasonably consistent groundstrokes, but do you hit much better off one wing (probably the forehand)?
- Is your high volley better than your low volley?
- Are you better on short overheads than deep ones?
- Do spins or changes of pace bother you?
- Do you anticipate drop shots badly?
- Do you have problems hitting the half-volley?
- Are your own shots easily readable?
- Is your strategy basically limited to hitting to the opponent's backhand?
- Do you sometimes overhit set-ups?
- Do you frequently approach net on a weak shot?
- Are your passing shots inconsistent?
- In a baseline exchange do you try to hit a winner off a deep shot?
- Do you often fail to maintain depth in a baseline duel?
- Is your serve either inconsistent or not forceful enough?
- Do you "press" or jerk when you try to hit hard against a good player?

The objective of an intermediate is to become an advanced player. It doesn't happen overnight, but the process can be accelerated by practice, knowledge, and a series of goals. The knowledge and the goals are herewith given; the rest is up to you.

SPINS AND CHANGE OF PACE

A heavy topspin shot jumps forward and bounces high. Heavy underspin causes the ball to slow up and bounce low. When playing against an opponent with a big topspin forehand and a heavy underspin backhand, you must move *back* for the forehand and *up* for the backhand. By moving back, you no longer have to drive a ball that is shoulder height or above; you take the ball instead slightly above waist-level, and because you have jumped or hopped or skipped backward to get ready, you can step forward just before the hit. (Advanced players—not intermediates—often take such balls on the rise.) When you return an underspin backhand, move forward, keep the wrist stiff and bend your knees. In handling underspin the racket must be held firmly so that you move the ball rather than having the ball move your racket. An opponent will frequently come to net on a forehand sidespin down the line. This ball moves to your left and can feel "heavy" on the racket.

A right-handed slice serve moves to the receiver's right and a left-handed slice serve moves to the receiver's left. A right-handed slice serve to the forehand in the forehand court will move the receiver into the alley or beyond, whereas a left-handed slice serve to the forehand in the forehand court will move into the receiver's body. The receiver will find the closer in he stands, the less the effect of the slice: he can take the wide slice to the forehand before it has a chance to pull him really wide.

Change of pace and change of spin can "ungroove" an intermediate unless you are mentally prepared. Be ready for high loops to the baseline, backhand crosscourt slices that pull you short and wide, hard sidespin forehands down the line, drop shots, teasing lobs, sharp angles, and deep balls with no pace. Be on your toes, bouncing and ready for a drive or a loop. Watch the ball come off the opponent's racket and be ready to hop back and then step in on the big topspin, to run wide and take your wind-up as you run, to handle a hard, deep shot by blocking it, to manufacture your own pace by stepping toward the ball just before the hit, and to run up for the shot that is hit with backspin.

ANTICIPATION

An intermediate can get some weird ideas about anticipating—for example, one should watch the opponent's feet/eyes/head/hands. There are two ways to anticipate well: watch the ball come off the opponent's racket and remember where the opponent has been hitting his previous shots. Many players will hit all backhands crosscourt except on a short shot when they may go down the line. Some players will invariably hit forehand passing shots down the line and many more will forget to lob a net-rusher. Watching the ball only and never watching the opponent will enable you to start a fraction of a second early.

THE HALF-VOLLEY

The half-volley is a ball which is hit when it is only a few inches off the ground. Anyone who comes to net will have to half-volley frequently. It is not difficult when one learns the timing; it is simply a groundstroke hit with a smaller backswing and smaller follow-through. It should be hit one to two feet in front of the body. There are four rules to remember: watch the ball, don't try to hit it hard, stay down to the shot, and never hit it on the dead run.

DISGUISE

The intermediate regularly signals when he is going to drop shot or lob: he changes his wind-up and thereby gives away his strategy. The reason he changes the wind-up is because he shovels rather than drives his lob (with a little practice, he can acquire a perfectly disguised lob which will catch the net man cold). His drop shot is merely a "dump" shot that falls reasonably short but has no backspin. Several hours of practicing coming under the ball at the last minute with an open racket face and an extremely short follow-through will help you to acquire this useful change-of-pace shot. On groundstrokes the intermediate positions himself in two different ways—one for the crosscourt and one for the down the line. If you take your backswing early and *hold it,* you will "hide" your shot until the moment of impact.

STRATEGY

The intermediate has not yet experimented with sidespin, heavy topspin, backspin, and angles. He has learned to serve to the backhand and to play to the opponent's weaker side. He does not yet know how to lure a baseliner to net, how to make winners wide to the opponent's strength, or how to keep the attacker from crowding the net.

First you can learn several serves. By tossing the ball to your right, you can develop a heavy slice that will trouble most intermediates. Next you can acquire a forehand sidespin coming-in shot by letting the racket come across your body on the follow-through at slightly above waist level. If you have a topspin backhand drive, you can easily learn underspin by opening the face of your racket and following through at slightly above waist level. If you have an underspin backhand drive, you can work on developing topspin by keeping the racket face perpendicular to the ground and following through high (the racket head points to the top of the opponent's fence). By using underspins, topspins, and sidespins, the opponent can be maneuvered with deep shots to the corner, wide and sharp angles to the opponent's service line, loops, lobs, drives, drop shots, and dinks.

Some "don'ts": don't drop-shot from the baseline, don't hit short and high and straight down the middle deliberately, don't give away all your shots by failing to use disguise, don't hit to the opponent's strength unless you hit wide to his strength, don't let your opponent get grooved by hitting all shots with the same pace, don't let your opponent crowd the net by failing to lob, don't hit a putaway shot harder than necessary, don't come to net on a short ball to the opponent, and don't try shots you have not yet learned—such as lob volleys or drop volleys.

SET-UPS

A set-up is a high, short ball that can be put away for a winner. For tournament players, set-ups are high, soft serves, high volleys, short overheads and high balls that bounce near the service line. An intermediate cannot always put away what are set-ups to advanced players, but your goal should be to make near-winners or forcing shots out of "easy" balls. The worst mistake you can make is to hit the ball into the net or outside the court boundaries. Therefore precision is the key. A high, short ball is a set-up because (1) the receiver can hit down on the ball, and (2) the opponent has less time to reach the ball because the receiver is standing close in. The choices on a set-up are: a deep shot to the corner; a sharp, wide crosscourt; or a trick shot such as an extreme angle almost parallel to the net or an angled drop shot with backspin. First learn the "deep to the corner," which is the safest shot. As you get more secure in approaching this shot, add more pace so that your riposte is a putaway.

APPROACH SHOTS

When you come to net, your approach shot must be deep. If it is short and high, only a very weak or nervous opponent will fail to pass you. You can come in on sidespin (forehand), underspin (backhand) or topspin (either side), but your depth must be good. Naturally the harder you hit the approach shot or the more bite to your spin, the more difficult it will be for the opponent to pass you. However, you must hit with control: the first rule of the approach shot is that it must go in.

PASSING SHOTS

There are four passing shots—down the line, crosscourt, straight at the net man's body, and over the head. The more disguise to a passing shot, the more chance for a clean winner. Passing shots need not be hard: they can be hidden lobs or crosscourt dinks. The intermediate too often hits the passing shot with all his might, and for every winner he makes, he has racked up four or five losers. Disguise, precision, and change of rhythm/shot/direction/pace are much more successful than wild slugging.

DEEP SHOTS

The most important factor in a baseline duel is depth. The ball must clear the net by 6 to 8 feet since low skimmers fall short. If the intermediate hits short, his opponent has the edge. If the opponent hits with great depth, the intermediate often fails to be prepared and either tries a half-volley from the baseline or returns short. Play 2 to 3 feet behind the baseline against opponents who consistently hit with depth. The deeper the shot, the more topspin you should use to return the ball. Consistent depth generally elicits short balls. The worst time in a rally to try for a winner is off a deep shot; the best time is off a short one.

THE SERVE

Practice is what makes for improvement, but practicing a bad shot (one that can never be forceful) only grooves a bad habit. There is little point in practicing a serve that lacks pace. It may be caused by a bad toss, poor weight transfer, too many wiggles or frills, or failure to snap the wrist or to follow through with shoulder and arm. If the serve has no sting, discard it and start again from scratch with the help of a good pro. Once you have a good foundation, the more you practice, the better the serve will become. A consistent, forceful serve is one of the most important factors in winning tennis.

HITTING HARD

Good players get power without jerking or pressing; their power comes from transferring their weight forward just before the moment of impact. They look silky smooth and relaxed, but their shots have sting and pace. The intermediate tries for power by moving arm, shoulder, and/or wrist vigorously. The result is a jerky motion and uncontrolled power: mixed doubles partners are hit, balls wildly spray the court, and errors multiply. "Step-hit"—not "bam-bam"—brings controlled power.

Chapter Twenty-one / How Matches Are Lost

There are several hundred methods of losing a match, but the commonest cause is the failure to practice sufficiently. Constant daily practice to groove the toss on the serve, groove the strokes, groove footwork, and groove concentration are basic to winning tennis. You cannot improve your consistency, pace, control, and accuracy without working out with a racket and a ball. The lesser player gets better with practice—and the better player goes down hill without it. The more one practices, the greater is the opportunity to improve.

There are 199 other reasons for losing, the more important of which are hereby proffered. Take note of them since realization is half the battle.

LACK OF TOURNAMENT PLAY

A top player can lose in an early round if he is not match-hardened, and a player relatively new to the tournament game will be "upset" by a player who is worse than he but who has more tournament experience. Match play is as important as practice. If you haven't played a match in six months and you meet a fellow who has played four tournaments in the last four weeks, you will not be able to do justice to your game but he will to his. In 1973 John Newcombe took a few months off from the WCT Circuit to recover from an injury. He came back as fit and as strong as ever to play the eight-man WCT final, but despite numerous, regular practice sessions his game fell apart and he was nowhere close to the player he usually is.

UNFAMILIARITY WITH THE ELEMENTS

Wind, shadows, sun that shines in the server's eye or poor lights on a court lit for night play account for many "unusual" results. I once heard a rather good player sneeringly comment on the lack of natural ability of another player who went to pieces in the wind. Adjusting to the winds does not take as much "natural ability" as it does practice. Players from Chicago, Palm Springs, and San Francisco adjust "naturally" to the wind because they play in it so often. There is a twelve-storey rooftop club in New York, populated mainly by seniors, where even the worst members are good "wind" players (no pun intended) because they get so much wind experience.

The intelligent thing to do is to practice just as the gale warnings go up. You will learn to overhit against the wind and to spin the ball heavily when it is behind you. You will overhit lobs which will sail in by dint of a strong wind. You will never plant your feet because a strong gust may suddenly bring the ball right into your body. You will pretend you are serving to the opponent's baseline on one side of the court, and you will put tremendous spin on the ball to make it drop fast when you are serving on the other side. You will run five steps in when the wind is behind you and five steps back when the wind is against you. You will enjoy every minute of wind play because it is an intellectual exercise, and although you won't be at your best (no one is in the wind), your opponent may easily be at his worst.

Shadows, direct sun, and bad lights are also hazards of the game. Even if you are nearsighted and astigmatic, *you* will be the better player under these conditions than a guy with 20-20 vision if you have deliberately subjected yourself (on occasion) to such environments and if the other fellow demands perfect conditions to produce his average game. Shadows require concentration; you must follow the ball intently, more intently than ever. You will still lose it in a fast exchange, but your opponent will lose it more often.

Every player should make friends with someone who has a private court that faces in the wrong direction. Most players avoid friendly invitations from a tennis enthusiast whose court is disastrously placed with regard to the sun. You be the smart one; play there often. Pretty soon you will learn to adjust your toss on the serve to avoid the sun and to lob your opponent to death when the sun is right in his eyes. The bad lights your friend has on his court (for economy reasons?) are a godsend. You will learn to play more from the backcourt, to concentrate better and to hit a little harder because the ball is so difficult to follow.

RESTRICTION TO ONE TYPE OF SURFACE

Although more and more frequently players are learning to adjust to different surfaces, too many players will practice on one type of surface only. They groove themselves to the point where they cannot ungroove for the smallest change in court speed. The greatest achievement, and the best test of your adaptability, is switching well from one court to another—from fast cement, when there is no time for a big backswing; to slow clay, where one can watch the ball bounce, light a cigarette and then return the ball; to wet grass, where the ball bounces up from one to three inches; to medium-slow carpet, which plays like clay except for spins that pull you into the fence; to medium-fast

Laykold where it pays off to be aggressive and it also pays off to be fast as a rabbit and only retrieve; to dry, slippery, cracked clay where the technique is to wrong-foot a player by hitting where he is coming from; to bad grass, where one bounce is never the same as another and it is wise to follow to net even on your terrible, short second serve; to Plexipave, to Dynaturf, ad infinitum.

A player without great talent who learns to adjust through practice to different surfaces will be far more dangerous than the "natural" who stays on his own home courts and never learns different bounces.

INABILITY TO ADJUST TO CROWD (OR LACK THEREOF)

A good player can lose his incentive when his match is played on a back court, but a player new to the game can go to pieces when he is assigned to the stadium court. The gallery affects the player by its presence or absence. The good player must tell himself in advance: "I will probably be assigned to Court 19 for my semi-finals. This will destroy my opponent's optimistic view of his own drawing power, and as a result I will play better than ever." The "new" player who has never before competed in front of knowledgeable (or unknowledgeable) spectators must assure himself that by watching the ball only and never looking at the fans, he will be able to give 100% of his concentration to the playing of each point. He must recognize that he will be more nervous, particularly if it is his first appearance on the Wimbledon Centre Court, but if he tenses up simply because 8 or 18 or 88 people are watching, then he will understand that he needs more "public appearances." It is as difficult for the experienced player to reach his peak when no one is watching as it is for the newcomer to play his best when twenty or thirty fans are staring at every shot he hits.

FAILURE TO USE A VARIETY OF BALLS

Mr. X or Ms. Y has been playing regularly with balls that are hard as rocks. Mr. A or Ms. B buys only soft balls. Junior Player L or M gets Pop's used balls which haven't had fuzz in the last six sets. Ms. R's foursome only uses Tretorns. Player K occasionally plays with different balls—Pennsylvania, Dunlop, or whatever. He adjusts his game to new balls of every variety and, if he is smart, occasionally to used balls. He knows when the balls are beginning to float, when they come back at him with a little extra "zing," and when they seem to swell and get heavier with each rally. Player K is not the best player in the city, but he is smarter than most of his opponents.

OVERDEPENDENCE ON ONE RACKET

If you are going into tennis in a serious way, you have picked out a racket suitable to you, with the proper handle size, the right grip and the suitable weight. You should also buy an "insurance" racket which is identical in every way to the one you already own. You should use both rackets (or three, if you have three). Then, if a string pops or your racket breaks or the grip begins to unravel, you are not stranded with a totally unfamiliar bat. You must never get into the purely mental syndrome where one of your two rackets is the "lucky" one and the other (identical) racket makes you lose. If this happens to you, you have hexed yourself and you are your own worst enemy.

INABILITY TO LAST

If you have no stamina, develop some—unless you only want to play a good first set. Practice *past* the point of all possible endurance and you will be much more fit the following day. Jog, run, do push-ups, eat well, and get plenty of sleep. Stamina comes from physical fitness and from stretching yourself beyond the point of fatigue. As fit as you may be, you will never have good endurance if you only play occasionally; you will also get out of shape faster from a layoff than you will get in shape from a heavy concentrated period of practice. It takes several weeks to adjust to tennis in hot tropical weather, but you can lose everything you gained from a four-day layoff.

PRESSING TO WIN

When a player presses, he loses sight of the ball and, consequently, jerks, overhits, tries the wrong shot, forgets to move his feet, and becomes discouraged. Why did you learn all those beautiful shots if only to forget them in a match? If an opponent is making you feel "pressed" because he gets every ball back or hits so hard or lobs so well or achieves so much depth or pulls you so wide on his serve, don't forget the fundamentals and go into a tizzy. First, he may be too good for you (that is always a faint possibility). You won't beat him by losing your head; because he is better, you must stay calmer and cooler than ever. If he is hitting with greater pace, play back two to three steps farther. If he is endlessly retrieving, work only on getting the ball back deep to him until he accidentally hits a short ball; then stay calm and hit a forcing forehand deep to his backhand. If he lobs, lob back—until you get a set-up overhead. If he is running you mercilessly, work on your depth to prevent him from getting the upper hand. If he is hurting you on his serve, try to retrieve with deep, high lobs. If he attacks relentlessly, never watch him but only the ball. If he knocks off every short ball to his forehand, play his backhand. If he is still killing you, don't give up. You are up against a better player but at least you can give him a fight and force him to earn every point by his good play, not by your sloppy errors. Lunge for volleys as you have never lunged before. Be steadier than you have ever been, concentrate to the point where you see only the ball, and start faster, move more quickly and take your racket back in plenty of time. If you overhit, it means you have given up and you intend to lose by the quickest possible means.

While you are in the midst of being "killed," see if you can analyze where your opponent is winning points and where you are losing them. How many backhand returns of serve did you miss in the first set? Six? Man, you are doing something wrong. How many lobs did you try in the first four games? What, none? How many short balls did you hit, thus handing him the point on a silver trophy? How often were you passed by coming in on a ball with no pace? How many backhands down the line went wide when they would have gone in if you had tried the crosscourt? How often did he run around your second serve and catch you moving backwards? Did you miss a set-up and, if so, why? Set-ups are not to be missed. By how many feet are you clearing the net when he is in the backcourt? What can you do to make this one-sided massacre into a respectable struggle? Does your opponent have a weakness, do you have a strength and is discouragement preventing you from using your head?

INABILITY TO USE YOUR INTELLIGENCE

After you have been beaten badly, you learn what you have hitherto been incapable of doing and you must use this knowledge to acquire new skills. If you have been beaten by an attacker, work on lobs and passing shots. If the pace was too great, start developing better ripostes to hard, forcing shots. If you find you cannot last with a retriever, either learn to attack more skillfully or to retrieve yourself with more consistency.

You will only improve if you use your head, as well as your body, arms and legs. If today is windy, run out and practice in the wind, but don't leave your brains at home. Groove yourself, but in all conditions against all opponents. Don't be afraid of challenges; seek them out.

Chapter Twenty-two/The Mental Game

T he simplest ideas can help the average player raise his game to a new level.

LEARNING TO CONCENTRATE

While you are playing you remember a phone call you forgot to make at the office.   In the middle of a rally you wonder if you will have to go to Chicago next Thursday.   After you play a bad point, you think about it. You recognize the value of concentration—but you are unable to produce it.   Perhaps your mind *is* on the game but you are watching incorrectly.   You look intently at the server and you never take your eyes off him as he goes through the contortions of a service motion.   You are aware that his weight is wrong and his toss peculiar, and as a result of watching him you have failed to follow the ball.   Work out what you will do to achieve almost-total concentration.   This will test your ingenuity.   Pause now for a moment and work out your plan.

Obviously you must watch the ball from the moment the warm-up begins.   Your mind thinks "tennis ball," your eyes watch the ball come off the opponent's racket, and you automatically prepare for the return. You see the ball come over the net, you watch it bounce, and, *if you have been really seeing it,* you will be able to hit it well in front of you. You *look* at the ball as you hit it.   Your mind is attuned to the ball only, which will prevent any extraneous thought from moving in.

Don Budge once said he only saw his opponent twice—when they walked on the court together and when they shook hands at the end. When his opponent served and came to net, *Don never saw him.*   He was too busy watching the ball.   Billie Jean King will literally look at the ball for five minutes at night; she wipes everything else out of her mind and sees only the ball.   The next day she claims she can watch the ball that much better.   Now ask yourself if your tendency is to watch the opponent perform his stroke or to watch the ball only.

The harder your opponent hits, the more intensely you must concentrate—or you will lose the ball through the fact that it is coming back at you so quickly. When you serve, it is almost impossible to watch the ball's flight, but you must pick it up with your eyes as soon as it bounces on the other side. Try to follow the ball through four rallies, six rallies, ten rallies, without losing sight of it. Then see if you can do it for two games, four games, a set. Concentration is achieved only by *consciously* working on it.

BEATING THE HITTER

Another problem for many players is returning well against a power hitter. The power hitter makes placements, forces errors, rushes you so your stroke is no longer smooth or your control is gone. Decide what you can do to enable you to handle power better. Pause again and compile a list.

Reflexes must be speeded up, backswings shortened, and you must play farther back to give yourself a better chance at the return. You don't stand on or inside the baseline to return a cannonball serve; you play 3 to 5 feet back depending upon your ability. Neither do you stand in the baseline area to return bullets unless you can half-volley them from your shoetops; you play farther back than usual, although always alert to move in if the ball is short.

Even though you shorten your backswing and play farther back, you must still hit the ball in front of you. If you take it by your side or slightly behind you, you will lose all control. Do not try to return as hard as your opponent is hitting but, if you take the ball in front of you, you will be able to use his pace.

When you come to net, you will have to react much faster. If your approach shot is deep, you will be able to close in despite the pace of the return and volley the ball well in front of you. If your approach is short, you have very little chance and may find yourself eating a tennis ball. The late Rafe Osuna had extremely fast reflexes, but when Rod Laver was "on" Osuna had plenty of trouble to keep from eating tennis balls when playing net. Arthur Ashe is another player with excellent reflexes, but Laver can prevent him from volleying with his usual depth and pace because Laver's balls can be bullets.

No one plays well against the truly hard hitters—Don Budge, Lew Hoad, Rod Laver, Jimmy Connors, or Arthur Ashe. They hit winners. They pass you. Sometimes they almost knock the racket out of your hand. If you can get to the ball of a big hitter and can return it with control, then you can evolve a strategy—spins, change of pace, sky balls, or a hitting-to-the-center plan. Despite the pace of Laver, Tom Okker beat him through spins and Roger Tayor by steady center technique. Don Budge was defeated in a Pro Tour by Bobby Riggs, who lobbed him to death. Lew Hoad, one of the great hitters in the history of the game, was soft-balled by steady Tony Vincent in Monte Carlo. Lew got so disgusted when his big overheads kept floating back that he finally knocked a ball into the Mediterranean. Jimmy Connors had no answer to the short, low balls hit down the center by Arthur Ashe at the 1975 Wimbledon. Arthur in turn found his big game nullified at Forest Hills in 1975 when Eddie Dibbs ran down the almost-winners and hurled them back soft but deep.

The best way to handle power, to react faster, to get ready sooner, and to hit the ball in front of your body is to practice with the power hitters. Your wrist will get sore and you will be hit a few times, but your reflexes will get faster and faster. When your opponent hits hard to you when you are in the backcourt, cut your backswing in half and hit the ball in front of you. This will help your timing and give you power on your return.

Practicing against power doesn't make perfect, but you will improve very quickly. If there is no local pro, use a ball machine set close to you to make your reactions faster.

OVERCOMING YOUR NERVES

Every player is bothered by nerves at some time or other, but some players are a bundle of nerves every time they play. You undoubtedly have had spells of unbearable tension which have ruined you for the match. It is much easier to tell someone else what to do, so think of what advice you would give to a player who is overly tense and, consequently, plays under his capabilities. Pause while you prepare your recommendations.

All good players are nervous in a big match. As they walk on the court the heart beats faster and the knees are shaky. Nerves can be terribly frayed in a first game—or in a last game or on big points. Tournament players usually, but not always, achieve control over nervous tension shortly after play begins, but even the greatest has suffered so badly in a particular match that he was reduced to a bowl of quivering Jello.

Every non-tournament player tightens up occasionally in a "fun" match; tournament players tighten up in pressure matches, at the beginning of the season, or after a series of "bad" losses. Since tightening up is purely mental, mental schemes must be used to enable you to beat your nerves. After you have beaten your nerves in eight consecutive matches, don't be saddened if you suddenly are overwhelmed by unconquerable, destructive tension in the ninth match.

Here are a few strategies for everyone who is overly tense. The first is relaxation between points. Walk loose, breathe deeply, and let your arms, fingers, and neck relax. Do *not* start concentrating until you are about to serve or your opponent is about to serve. Relax totally until the second that the ball is to be put in play. Second, be confident. This is very easy to say but difficult when you must convince yourself and you are not quite convinced. Here each player will have a different method, but nothing helps more than six or eight great, tough practice sessions which can convince even you that you are capable of hitting certain shots very well.

Some people think of hitting freely or running hard to overcome nerves. Others go back to basics and "demonstrate" the strokes so that every point will be a perfect lesson in how to hit the ball. Some must believe that it is only exercise, that it is a privilege to be on the court, and that, even if the results are disastrous, it is a lovely day and a pleasure to be given the opportunity of running around. A few must be reconciled to defeat and work only toward "giving the other fellow a good work-out."

The best way to overcome nerves takes the most time. It involves regular practice, plenty of tournaments, and a *good reason* for confidence. Even then, one bad day can deteriorate the confidence so carefully developed.

Concentrate during points and relax between points, hit out freely and enjoy competition of any variety. Work on your game so you *can* be confident. Forget "bad losses"; everyone has them. Remember that *you are good* if you concentrate; if you let yourself down today, you won't tomorrow.

If this doesn't work, try a shot of brandy.* You will lose your tension, although you risk losing your reflexes.

FIGHTING FEAR

The players who best overcome fear are those who test themselves regularly against those they fear. The players who suffer intensely from fear are those who won't even play a practice match against a lesser player who might beat them. They avoid tournaments they are supposed to win and instead play in competitions against better players where there will be no unbearable pressures to succeed.

Mr. A is No. 5 on the tennis ladder. He likes to challenge No. 4, No. 3, No. 2, and No. 1. He intensely dislikes being challenged by someone below him. Ms. R is at the bottom of the "A" Group in her club. She is delighted to play with any "A" player—but she avoids the "B's" like the plague. Mr. L, a good local player, has stopped practicing with the good Junior players because he might lose and thereby lose face.

As soon as the fear syndrome appears, the chances of that player improving recede. Bob is the best player at the local courts. He will play anyone and everyone, including Jack, Dan, and Richard, who rank just below him. Dan and Richard only want to play Bob. They don't even want to play each other for fear of a loss. This immediately cuts them out of reaching their potential. Jack will play everybody; his potential is not limited by fear, the worst bugaboo in tennis.

The more you practice against the players whom you consider under your level, the better your chances of winning. If they beat you, you are not as good as you thought; you will have to work harder, run better, and hit the ball more cleanly to gain the domination you would like to possess. Playing someone below your level but who can beat you requires all your powers of concentration and all your competitive spirit. It's the real challenge.

* Advised for adults only.

Chapter Twenty-three
The Imaginative Player

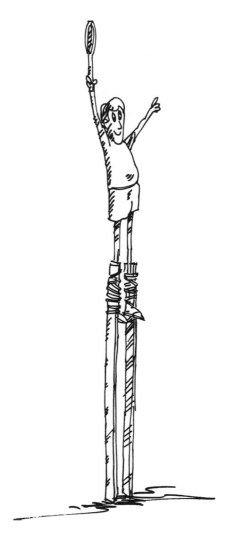

Edward and Bob are tournament players with pretty much the same tennis history. Edward has the more forcing strokes, but Bob is the better player; Edward loses to John, Steve, and Bill, while Bob beats John, Steve, and Bill. In their formative years everyone picked Edward to be the better player because his forehand was deadlier, his backhand was every bit as good, he volleyed with more sting, and his first serve was much stronger and better formed than Bob's. Bob had one thing going for him: imagination.

Edward has one style of play; Bob has a dozen. Edward plays the same on grass, cement, and clay; Bob changes his game with the surface and the opponent. Edward has a "thing" about the wind; Bob eats it up. Edward has a big, fairly consistent first serve and a good spin second serve; Bob's serve has less pace but far more variety. A good player gets grooved against Edward's big, attacking game; the same good player has a harder time getting grooved to Bob's shots since they are designed to ungroove the opponent.

Do you have one style of serve only (a "big" serve and a semipush second serve)? Do you change your game with the surface? If you are basically an attacker, do you know how to defend? If you generally retrieve, do you know how to attack when necessary?

Here's what Bob does:

He quickly finds out if the opponent can handle a wide, spin serve to the forehand in the forehand court or a serve into the body. He serves deep to the backhand as his "safety" and, although he doesn't have a really tough, flat serve, he throws in one occasionally to keep the receiver off balance. By varying his toss he gets more and different spins; he tosses to his right for a heavy spin to the forehand, in front of him for a deep, topspin serve to the backhand, and over his head for a "kick" or American twist to the backhand. He never serves doubles because his philosophy is never to "give" points. Although his second serve is not superb, it is never short. He thinks before he serves as to the amount of spin and the spot where he will place it. In the backhand court he regularly pulls his opponent wide on the backhand, then tosses in a deep one on the center service line; he has traded in power for accuracy and spin control, and his deceptively easy serve is continually disturbing the receiver's rhythm.

How many different serves do you know? Have you ever tried a heavy slice by tossing the ball far to your right? Can you play for a week without double-faulting? Do you try to place the ball every time you serve? Next time you play, think before every serve as to where you are going to place it. If you are an advanced player, see if your spins and placements can catch the receiver off guard.

Bob has no one way of receiving serve. He stands 2 feet behind the baseline, on the baseline, or 2 feet inside, depending on the surface, whether or not his opponent is attacking, the speed and/or spin of the serve, and the depth and/or accuracy of the second serve. If the court is slow, the serve is not coming in and the delivery is hard but not wide, he will stand 2 or 3 feet behind the baseline and "throw" back big serves all day long. He stands on the baseline and takes a much shorter stroke to return a fast serve when the opponent is coming in. Here his return is often a "block" (a drive with a very short backswing): it comes back fast and hard at the server, who must volley it at or behind the service line. On heavy spin serves he will try to stand *inside* the baseline to cut off the angle. On short second serves he runs around his backhand and goes for a forceful forehand to a corner. If the short second serve is accurately placed wide to his backhand, he *drives* (not slices) his backhand well in front of him, more often than not down the line deep to the forehand corner, but occasionally crosscourt so his opponent can never outguess him. He is murderous only on short serves since he is never one to let an opportunity go by. He does not "murder" deep serves; he drives them, blocks them, dinks them, chips them, and lobs them, in the process of which he discovers what his opponent likes least.

Do you alter the spot where you stand on return of serve? Is your return of serve always the same? Try driving the soft serves, blocking the hard serves, and standing several steps in for the spin serves. If you are an advanced player, experiment with chips and dinks, particularly against a net-rusher.

Bob has the basic topspin drives on forehand and backhand. Additionally, he can sidespin his forehand and slice (or underspin) his backhand. He uses the chip with moderation, mostly so he can throw in an unexpected drop shot using the same chip action. He lobs defensively (deep to the middle) when he is way out of position and he lobs offensively with excellent disguise as his "fourth" passing shot.* The sidespin forehand is not his basic weapon but a bit of change-of-pace artistry. He uses the slice backhand on many low shots, as an approach shot, and for variety in backcourt exchanges. His lobs do not have the tremendous topspin that he wishes he had, but he does hide them well

* The four passing shots are: down-the-line, crosscourt, over the head, and straight at the body.

and often catches the net man cold.   On slow clay he will hit balls that clear the net by 15 feet since this gives him excellent depth.

How many ways do you have to hit a forehand and a backhand?   Do you vary the height at which the ball clears the net?   When you get a short ball, have you ever attempted a sharp angle?   Add a little variety to the level of your skill: try "hiding" your shots, lob unexpectedly, and see if you can vary your length on low balls.   Advanced players are at a level where they can practice sidespin forehands, underspin backhands, and disguised lobs.

Bob is not as athletic as Edward and doesn't leap as well at net, but he comes to net often and always imaginatively.   He makes up for a certain lack of athletic talent by his knowledge of the court and his opponent: if the opponent scarcely ever lobs, he closes in more; if the opponent keeps trying the down-the-line, Bob "anticipates"; if the opponent can only slice his backhand, Bob keeps boring in on deep forehands down the line.   Bob doesn't hit his overhead very hard, but he compensates by deadly accuracy, which is better than speed.   As a junior he practiced hitting a dozen overheads a day for two years—and the practice paid off.

When you come to net do you know where to move?   When you hit the volley, do you know where to place it?   Do you know what shots to come in on?   A good formula for the volley is to be sure to hit with depth when you come to net, move in the direction where you have hit the ball, and volley in the opposite direction (crosscourt).

The theory behind Bob's play is the Four Tennis Commandments: Know Thyself, Know Thy Surface, Know Thy Court, and Know Thy Opponent.   By knowing himself he never tries a shot he can't make—a desperation winner off a wide shot when a lob will be the safer return. As a result he is no Rod Laver—but neither is he Joe Schlunck.   Bob knows his surface, playing steadily on clay, using his spin repertoire on Sportface, attacking on grass, wrong-footing his opponent on a slippery court, lobbing under the lights or into the sun, and playing the altitude, the wind, and even the heat for all he can.   Bob also knows his court dimensions much better than his opponent does—the necessity for depth on serve, for angles on passing shots, for serves down the center to cut down the opponent's angles, for approach shots down the line to limit the degree of the angle, for pulling the opponent wide to open up his court, for lobbing deep down the center to close up his own court, for dinks to make the net man volley up and deep drives to make the baseliner return short.   Most important, Bob knows his opponent and feeds him everything he dislikes—junk balls, bloopers, chips, a barrage of wide shots to the backhand, serves into the body, deep shots to bring him in, and lobs to chase him back.

So learn to use your imaginative powers.   You've been using your legs and arms; start using your head.

Chapter Twenty-four/Winning Matches

If you have equal or better stroke equipment than your opponent, and if you are as fast on your feet, why do you lose? Assuming that you have the same stamina and can hit every shot approximately as well but you still get beaten, your weakness is match play.

Do you lose your cool under pressure? Regaining composure is achieved by players in many different ways. Pancho Gonzalez shouts and blows off steam. Ken Rosewall hangs his head—and thinks. Margaret Court towels off deliberately on the odd games, regaining her poise and composure. Guillermo Vilas looks at Ion Tiriac for confidence, Clark Graebner used to look at his wife and Nancy Gunter at her father. Each is trying to achieve that equilibrium that will prevent him or her from pressing, blowing, or forgetting to think. Analyze and work out a winning strategy.

The ideas below may help you when you are losing a match that you should be able to win. Some are for mental stability, some to regain lost control, and some to establish a battle plan.

THE TOURNAMENT PLAYER

- Look at the ball, not your opponent. Watch the ball as it leaves your opponent's fingers on the service toss and see it come over the net. You will find that you prepare your stroke far more unhurriedly and, as a result, you will be less pressed. Watch the ball in every exchange: when your opponent comes to net, you see only the ball and you will be far cooler on passing shot or lob.

- If you find yourself nervous at a critical point, play the ball (its spins and its pace) rather than the opponent. Never let the ball play you (it means you are not getting ready soon enough) and never let your opponent play you (it means you are thinking about the opposition, which is a distraction, rather than the action of the ball).

- If you are getting wiped off the court and are not even in the match, calm down and collect your thoughts at the change-over. Take the full 60 seconds allotted on the odd games to analyze what is happening. Are you getting to the ball too late? If his backhand is coming in a ton, is there any way of breaking up his timing with chips or loopers? Are you lobbing often enough or high enough? Are all your first serves going in and are you thinking about direction and spin on each of your serves? Can you change the pace of the match by slices or sidespins or topspins? What spins or what tactics is he using? When he comes to net, are you always going for the down-the-line or always for the crosscourt? Is he mixing up his serves and can you anticipate them? If he is hitting very hard, can you shorten your backswing? Are you half-volleying too many balls, which means you are constantly trapped by deep balls? Will you have a better chance if you play back one step farther? Will a forehand sidespin return of serve offer him any problems? Are you trying drop shots when you are too far back? Have you forgotten to try drop shots when the right opportunity presents itself? Does he have you on a yo-yo and can you get off by changing your pattern of play? If your timing is bad, is it because you are not moving your feet or are taking your backswing too late or are not watching the ball or are thinking about the point you lost two games ago or because you think the crowd is against you? Are you concentrating like mad on every point? If your strokes are off, can you go back to fundamentals, eliminating all the extras, to get back your "feel"?

THE INTERMEDIATE (SLUGGER)

Although the above should be read by intermediates and beginners, the latter have problems that are very different. Mr. Intermediate loses a "friendly" match to Ms. Intermediate, and he cannot understand it because he knows he is the better player. But is he? He thinks he can hit such a hard ball that she almost never returns it. His problem: his hard balls seldom go in, and when they do they are without accurate direction.

Mr. Intermediate's problem is ball control. His motion is so swift on the stroke that he must connect at exactly the right fraction of a second or the ball will career wildly into the fence or the bottom of the net. He is concentrating so much on power that he has forgotten balance and footwork. The wrist quickly turns over in all his strokes; he does not know how to keep the wrist flat and motionless through at least 12 inches (preferably longer) of the hit. When the wrist approaches the ball in steady fashion (without turning over), the face of the racket will "stay" on the ball for a good 12 inches. Then, if Mr. "I" should mistime the ball, the wrist still has not turned and he can make a good shot.

Before Mr. "I" makes winners, he has to get the ball back regularly, with proper depth and proper direction. Why hit a ball hard when you don't know where the hell it is going?

Mr. "I's" strategy must be different from that of the tournament player. It is not recommended that he try drop shots or side spins because he still does not have ball control on basic drives. However, he, too, can learn winning tennis, and many of the shots suggested to the tournament player will be applicable to him. He, too, must watch only the ball, play the ball rather than the opponent and attempt to interpret what the opponent's ball is doing. The difference is in his riposte.

Mr. "I," like the tournament player, should try to get ready early, consider the value of the lob and, in his own way, change pace or direction *while still looking only at the ball.* Mr. "I" double-faults a lot ("Here, opponent, I want you to have this point"), throws in cannon-ball serves that almost never go in and pats or pushes in his second serve. Mr. "I" has the big return of serve—whop, boom, zoom ("Out!"). He must temper his passion of hitting winners with the thought that this causes him to lose to losers. Basically he must learn to keep the racket face on the ball for as long as possible, to acquire some steadiness and to learn direction and then sharp angle. He is a player without finesse. He loses his cool constantly; even when he has the set-up, he gives it such an enormous wallop that it could land anywhere. His thoughts should be as follows:

- Losers serve double-faults.
- Losers have cannon-ball first serves and pat-ball second serves.
- Winners will only miss two or three returns of serve a set against other intermediates.
- Winners can consistently play the opponent's backhand.
- Champions *do not* miss a set-up (they need not necessarily hit the ball 125 mph).
- Losers come to net without adequate preparation (or adequate overheads).
- Winners in the intermediate level can hit forehand crosscourts and backhand crosscourts all day long; they only try the down-the-line when the return is short or when they absolutely know the down-the-line will go in.
- Winners would rather poop the ball back, knowing it will at least go in, when they are pressed by a hard ball, than go for a big shot that has hardly any chance of going in.
- Winners play percentage tennis, making the most of their own strengths and the most of their opponent's weaknesses. If the winner has a weak backhand he plays it only as a steady shot; if the winner gets a short shot to his backhand that he can run around, he takes it on his forehand.
- Winners keep track of their own losers, not their winners. A real winner knows how many backhand returns of serve he has missed after a match. There won't be very many because, if his backhand return is failing him, he will lob or loop or even kick the ball back in.
- Winners know that even if they miss two or three volleys in a row, it is still not necessary to stay in the backcourt every point. However, after losing three games by coming in and getting passed, the winner will change his strategy.

- The winner would rather win than look good; the loser would rather hit hard than win.

THE INTERMEDIATE (POOPER)

Ms. Intermediate depends solely on steadiness and perhaps some depth to win for her.   She is at a level where she can acquire some additional skills, particularly ball control and a little more power.   While Mr. "I" is knocking balls all over the arena, Ms. "I" is pooping them in the air. This in itself is good strategy against most other intermediates.   If she can also run down balls well, she will win many matches.   But she will win many more if she can retain her steadiness while adding to her game a drop shot, a punch volley, the angle shots and a reasonably hard put-away shot on a set-up (a short, high ball).

THE BEGINNER

Winning strategy for beginners is also possible, even though you are still learning form, footwork, and balance.   You still can work on concentration and watching the ball.   You should read the above tactics for advanced and intermediate players so that you will know the direction in which you are heading.   Because you are still working on strokes, your guidelines are slightly different.   Your "strategy" takes second place to improving your form, but it is never too early to think about tactics. Your basics are:

- Watch the ball and prepare early.
- Take the proper backswing and follow-through.
- Maintain balance.
- Keep the strings of the racket on the ball as long as possible.
- Hit the ball in *front* of the body whenever possible.
- Use the crosscourt as your basic shot.   If your crosscourts are going wide, aim toward the center of the court.
- Allow a 10-foot margin in hitting the ball over the net so it will go deep (if you skim the net, the ball will go short).
- Make adjustments in timing to compensate for errors—if your forehands are going wide to *your* right (the opponent's backhand), you are hitting too late, and if your forehands are going wide to your left (the opponent's forehand), you are hitting too early.
- If the opponent hits a deep shot, step or run back at once so that you will still hit the ball at waist-level. (If you don't step back, you will have to half-volley the shot and your chances of error are extreme.)
- If your balls are sailing (hitting the fence), either your wrist has stopped at the moment of impact or you have opened the face of the racket so that it is tilted skyward.   If your balls are hitting the net, make sure you get under the ball and your follow-through ends high.

- As soon as you have acquired some ball control, hit to your opponent's weakness, which will generally be his or her backhand. Sometimes, however, it is better to play your own strength than your opponent's weakness: if you have a very good forehand crosscourt, playing this shot (even if it is to your opponent's strength) may be your best ploy.
- Winning factors are steadiness, depth and control. Steadiness means always returning the ball, depth means the area close to the baseline (2 or 3 feet) and control means the ability to put the ball deep to the backhand or to the forehand. After you have accomplished the first, work on the second and then the third.

Chapter Twenty-five
The Art of Mixed Doubles

Too many mixed doubles matches are lost because the formation is wrong, a player takes his tensions out on his partner, the value of certain points is overlooked, there is not enough poaching at net or too much from the backcourt, the importance of the lob return of serve is forgotten, not enough pressure is put on the opponents, and/or the captain of the team does not have an adequate concept of his function.

Mixed doubles becomes a lopsided game when the man is much better than his partner or the woman is much better than the man. Only occasionally are the partners well-balanced. There are cases where the man *thinks* he is the better player because he is physically stronger and can hit the ball harder, but in fact the woman has better ball control, understands the doubles game better, and is racking up more points for her team. Physical strength pays off provided the player knows what he is doing; sheer power without control is less valuable than control without power.

This chapter is designed for those playing lopsided mixed. If the members of the team are evenly balanced, then mixed is played like any other doubles (see *Doubles Strategy*).

DON'T BE A BULLY

If one or both women in the mixed game is a beginner or an intermediate, points can be won without hitting her in the eye or making her cower when the opponent has a set-up. The mark of a great player is not his ability to knock the opponent unconscious. If he tries it just once, he will learn all about the game called ''Retaliation'': when he is at net, he will become the target on every high volley set-up and overhead.

When the mixed doubles teams are extremely uneven—e.g., if the women are much better than the men—there are two ways of playing the game. If it is not a tournament match, the weaker players are "fed" balls. The woman serves at three-quarter pace to the man's forehand and hits medium-paced shots to give him a rhythm. When he is at net, she hits short lobs or gives him a chance to knock off a volley. This is "social tennis," designed to give players with limited experience a great deal of pleasure. It is seen in Pro-Am tournaments, where an Ashe or a Smith serves at three-quarter speed and where a Laver or a Newcombe never hauls off on a drive-volley in case a "celebrity" runs in the wrong direction. When the mixed doubles is a tournament match, the competitive player wants to win, and he will serve hard, hit hard and poach, although he will always avoid hitting the intermediate player with a ball on the fly (volleying or smashing directly at a relative novice). Anything goes in a tournament (big serves, drop shots, crazy spins, hard drives from the baseline) as long as the ball doesn't come close to hitting someone who is defenseless.

In all the years that I have played and watched social and tournament tennis, I have seen a lot of intermediate and advanced male players drill a lesser female opponent, but I have never seen an intermediate or advanced female player ever deliberately drill a lesser male opponent. Social conditioning goes a long way.

MIXED DOUBLES FORMATION

The folklore of tennis has changed frequently in the 100-year history of the game. Few teaching pros now advocate the closed stance, teach only the backhand slice, or forbid their pupils from gripping the racket with two hands. However, one old adage with no rationale to defend it still remains: the stronger player should play the backhand court. The male player in mixed doubles automatically demands the backhand court because he is stronger. If you ask him why, he will say the critical points are played in the backhand court, he can take balls down the middle of the court with his forehand, and he can poach better with his forehand volley. But what if he is a left-hander or his partner cannot hit a backhand reverse crosscourt from the forehand court or his backhand volley is his strength?

There is no logic to the old saying that the critical points are played in the backhand court. There are actually more points played in the forehand court. If the man is playing the forehand court and the opponents are serving at 15-40, he has a chance to win the game on that point. With the man returning in the forehand court, his team has a better opportunity to take the lead: if he wins the first point, it is 0-15; if he also wins the third point, it is 0-40 or 15-30.

If Rosie Casals always plays the backhand court in doubles with Billie Jean King, and if Ilie Nastase always plays the forehand court in doubles with Jimmy Connors, then why should Rosie and Ilie reverse their usual roles when they play mixed together? The answer is they shouldn't— and they don't. They won Wimbledon in 1972 with Ilie in the forehand and Rosie in the backhand.

The proper way to determine who plays which court is to analyze the weaknesses and strengths of the team. If the woman has a natural forehand crosscourt and lobs well off the backhand, there is a good argument for her to play the forehand court; if she can also hit her backhand return of serve from the forehand court so that it goes reverse crosscourt (to the server's forehand alley), she should definitely play the deuce (or forehand) court. However, if her strength is her backhand crosscourt, and if she has an excellent forehand which she can hit as a reverse crosscourt from the backhand court (her return will go to the server's backhand), she should play the ad (or backhand) court. If her backhand is her weakness, but she can lob off it, and if she can run around a lot of backhands in the backhand court, taking them instead on her forehand, it is logical for her to play the ad court. It puts the pressure on the server to serve wide to her backhand, and if the score is 30-40 and the opponent's first serve is a fault, the woman receiver in the backhand court can stand wide in her alley, literally "asking" the server for a forehand or putting pressure on the server to aim for the very small spot where she is forced to return with a backhand.

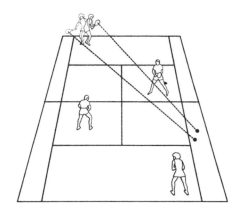

Woman can hit reverse backhand crosscourt or sharp forehand crosscourt. She should play forehand or deuce court.

The better player in mixed doubles is the captain, and he or she will determine in which court the partner will play. If the better player is the man, he will ask his partner what side she usually plays—or, if he has played mixed with her before, he will know how she hits reverse backhand crosscourts from the forehand side and reverse forehand crosscourts from the backhand side. Her backhand lob may be far more effective in the forehand court and her backhand crosscourt may be very consistent, low and wide. His decision will be based on the percent of good service returns she will make: if almost all of her returns from the backhand court will be cut off by the poacher, he will play her in the deuce court; if her crosscourt returns in the backhand court are reasonably consistent, he will play her in the ad court.

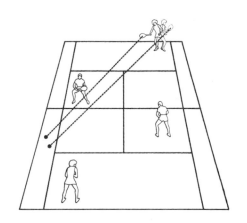

Woman can hit reverse forehand crosscourt and sharp backhand crosscourt. She should play backhand or ad court.

WHO SERVES FIRST?

The better player always serves first. If the opponents are foolish enough to have the man serve first when the woman is stronger, they have given away not one but two games: the weak player drops serve for 0-1, then the strong player on the opposite side serves first and holds for 2-0.

When a new set starts, the stronger player should again serve first; if he or she doesn't, the team is "giving" a two-game edge to the opponents. When a new set starts, each team can also change their formation—for example, if the woman was receiving in the backhand court, she can now receive in the forehand court. If any mistake was made in the first set formation, it can be reversed in the second set.

If the man is the better player but decides to be a gentleman and ask his partner if she would like to serve first, he is a loser; if she accepts his offer, they deserve each other.

If the woman plays better than the man, she serves first. Under no circumstances should she act "feminine" by offering him the balls; she must insist on serving first if she wants to win.   If the man has hurt feelings because he isn't "first," he should avoid playing with women who are better than he.

HELPING ONE'S PARTNER

The captain, by his remarks, the expression on his face, and his enthusiasm or lack thereof, can make or break his partner.   If he talks after every point, she will lose concentration.   If he analyzes what she did wrong after every shot she misses, she will be confused and depressed. If he sighs or looks glum when she fluffs a sitter, he might just as well have yelled at her.   If his partner is not playing well or is not a good player, a series of helpful criticisms will not make her into a champion.

When the woman is better but the man insists on being captain, the team will get nowhere.   The lesser player should never be the team strategist.   The weak man is fighting the Battle of the Sexes and he would rather dominate his partner than defeat the opponents.

Getting the most out of one's partner is an art that consists of 1 cup of encouragement, 1½ pounds of compliments, 1 tablespoon of tactics— and a generous dash of cheerfulness.   Mix them all together and you get a happy partner.

The phraseology of helpful remarks, as well as the tone in which they are issued, are the keys to whether the partner can accept them and follow their advice.   You can't make a beginner play net well if he or she is afraid of getting hit, or return crosscourt if he or she has no ball control, or run for a drop shot if he or she has not yet developed anticipation.   Be happy when your partner gets the ball over the net.   Pour on thick compliments mixed with sugar-coated suggestions: "That's excellent playing—you're doing well enough so you could try a high lob now"; or "Well done—you're running so nicely that you could get even more short balls by starting earlier"; or "If you stand four feet behind the baseline, I bet you return the next serve"; or "Good try on the volley—pretend they're going to hit every ball to you at net, and you'll have an even better chance of making a winner."

This may sound saccharine to you, but it won't to your partner.   If Rod Laver made these remarks to you, you would glow with pleasure and play like a dream.   It's a bit more encouraging than "No, No, No! I told you to stand closer in!" or "Can't you even lob?" or "You're dead on your feet.   Get your tail moving or we'll lose this match."

Some captains like to think of themselves as gruff football coaches, yelling at the team to spur them on to victory, or as Davis Cup captains, pouring on a constant stream of unsolicited technical advice. The shouts work in reverse on the tennis court, and the skillful comments are usually wrong.   The less said, and the more pleasantly it is phrased, the better the chances for winning.

If the woman on the team is stronger, the man should refrain from any remarks other than "Nice shot," "Great playing," or a very occasional "I'm sorry" when he misses for the umpteenth time.   His ploy is silence and concentration.

SERVE AND RETURN OF SERVE

The two most important shots for all levels of players are the serve and the return of serve. An error on either causes the immediate loss of a point. The rules on serve are:

- Never serve a double-fault to the weaker opponent. It can mean the service break.
- Get your first serve in. Fine doubles players get the first serve in 80% of the time. The stronger player in mixed doubles should get his first serve in at least 70% of the time, and the weaker player should try for 50% or better.
- Serve to the opponent's weakness, which is usually the backhand. Mix up your serves (wide to the forehand or straight at the body) if you have a good serve.
- Anticipate the return of your serve. The wide forehand may always elicit a wide, sharply angled forehand crosscourt. The serve to the opponent's backhand may always float up or he may sometimes lob over your partner's head.
- When you are trailing in score, your first serve must always go in. You can't afford to give the opponent an easy second serve at 0-30 or at 15-30 or 30-40. This is particularly true when serving to the stronger opponent. If your first serve doesn't go in, you are forced to try a tough second serve when down 0-30, 15-30, or 30-40. If the opponent has a big shot and he is smart, he will invite you to serve to his big shot by leaving it wide open, thereby leaving you very little room to serve to his weaker side. An example: in the forehand court, when you are down 0-30 or 15-40, and after your first serve has been a fault, the opponent with the strong forehand plays close to the center service line. You have no "room" to serve to his or her backhand; if you serve to the forehand, it must be a wide one to "hurt" the opponent—and so you are pressured into going for too good a serve.

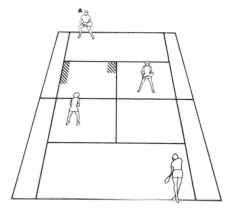

The receiver (A) with a good forehand leaves his forehand side open at 0-30 or 15-40, thereby inviting the server to hit the second serve into the narrow area of his protected backhand. The shaded areas in the service court are the only possible choices. To prevent being put in this pressure spot, get your first serve in.

The return of serve offers many selections, several of which are excellent as regular returns or as variations to keep the opponents off balance and guessing. The alternatives are: a hard, low crosscourt; a sharply angled, dipping crosscourt hit to pull the opponent wide and/or to force him to bend low for his first volley; a lob over the net man's head; a hard, low shot down the net man's alley. The worst returns are, in order, a netted,* out, or wide return; a medium-high ball to the net man; a soft, high, floating crosscourt which either the net man or the incoming server can pick off; a short lob to the net man; or a soft floater in the alley of the net man.

Too many doubles players try only the hard, low crosscourt. This return results in too high a percentage of errors and it also allows the server and net man to groove their tactics. The incoming server can

---

* It is better to have the ball go over the net, even if it is a putaway, than to have it not go over at all: the weak player on the other side may be sleeping or overanxious, thus granting you a reprieve.

usually guess where the return is coming and the net man can poach freely if the shot is not hit sharply. Therefore, it is good to vary the one shot with occasional lobs over the net man's head, a hard one down his alley (particularly if he is poaching a lot), or a dipping crosscourt to the incoming server's feet.

The weaker member of the team has a more difficult time with the return of serve, either because the serve is coming in too fast or too wide to handle well or the net man is poaching on most of the returns. The net man fakes a poach to lure the weaker one to hit down his alley, but he is waiting for the shot. The safest return is therefore a very high lob over the net man's head. It forces at least one of the opponents to go back toward the baseline. This gives the strong partner a chance to poach off the next return. Obviously the weaker player will sometimes lob too short, giving the opponents a putaway, but more often the ball is put in play and this opens up the court for the partner.

THE LOB

The lob is one of the most important factors in mixed doubles, even at the highest level. A team that never lobs is allowing the opponents to close in at the net; a team that lobs with disguise keeps the opponents farther from the net and therefore more susceptible to a low, dipping shot; a team that uses a lot of high, defensive lobs is succeeding in keeping the ball in play and driving at least one opponent to the baseline.

The weaker woman in mixed doubles will often use the lob defensively against a heavy hitter or an astute poacher because she cannot match power with power. Her lobs must be high and deep so the net man can't pick them off. The stronger partner will use the offensive lob (a disguised topspin shot that moves toward the fence) to wrong-foot the opponents, but he will also use the high defensive lob when he is well out of position. Regretfully, when the weaker player is the man, he feels lobbing is a sign of weakness, an admission of failure, a loss of masculinity.

For the purpose of this discussion, I will assume the woman is the weaker player. Psychologically, she has usually been indoctrinated into the role of being weaker and so she can adapt to the weaker member's strategy. When the man is the weaker player, he struggles against the concept of his role unless the stronger partner is also a man. This ruins the match, irritates the partner, and prevents the team from doing as well as it should. I don't know how good women players can put up with such men; many of them won't.

In doubles, most lobs should go down the line because most lobs are returns of serve. The times to lob crosscourt are when the woman is at net and the man is in the backcourt (lob over the woman, even when she is crosscourt from you) or when both players are at net (lob over the woman, even though this means you must lob crosscourt). If the woman is at net and the man in the backcourt and you choose to lob down the line to the man, he can come in on the run and volley the ball away. The rules on lobbing are:

- On return of serve, lob down the line.

- If both opponents are at net, lob over the woman.
- If the male opponent is crosscourt at net from you and the female opponent is on the baseline, lob down the line to the woman.
- If the female opponent is crosscourt at net from you and the male opponent is on the baseline, lob crosscourt over the woman's head.
- Whenever you are way out of position, the high, defensive lob gives you a chance to get back into the point.
- When an opponent hits an overhead and you run it down, try a high, defensive lob. Even in top doubles you will see one team lob three or four (or even more) times in a row during the same point. As long as the lob is very high and reasonably deep, the point is not automatically over. The opponent's overhead has a tendency to get more tentative rather than stronger, particularly if you manage to get back three or more consecutive overheads.
- The weaker woman can never lob too much, especially if her lobs are high and deep and if she lobs a lot to the other woman.

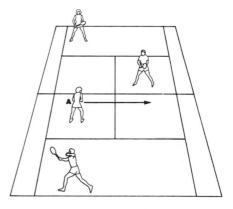

The woman at net (A) has been lobbed over. Her partner has run back to get the ball. She should have run to her right; instead she has put her team in the "I" formation.

A short overhead is a putaway. Good women players can knock them off for winners and should always handle their own. A weak woman player should take her own short overheads whenever her partner is too far away to run in and take the ball himself. The weak woman has no alternative if her partner is out of position. If she cannot hit every short overhead away and end the point immediately, she should let her partner take them whenever he is reasonably close to the ball. The only exception is when the game is "social doubles"; the woman should then take her own overheads because she needs all the practice she can get.

Often the woman at net is lobbed and she can either barely get it (meaning she can't do much with it even when she hits it) or she knows she won't be able to touch it at all. If her partner is in the backcourt, she runs to the other side of the net and her partner crosses over to take the ball. If both are at net, she *must* try for the lob unless her partner yells "Mine." As soon as she hears him call, she runs to the other side of the net—or, if she thinks her partner is going to lob, she runs crosscourt to the baseline. The worst offense of a mixed doubles player is to fail to cross over to the other side when the lob goes over the head. The team is left in the "I" formation, with half the court open.

If the woman is frequently lobbed at net, she moves back two or three steps from her regular position. If the woman is never lobbed, she closes in at net the moment the receiver hits the ball.

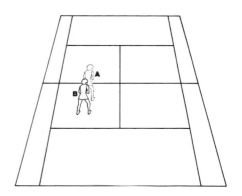

Position A is where the woman stands if she is never lobbed. If the opponents lob frequently, she moves back to Position B.

The man cannot come in behind his serve if his partner is being lobbed over regularly. But there is a trick he can use to shake up the lobber. The server and his partner deliberately take a stance that is almost the "I" formation. She stands close to the center service line at net and the server stands close to it on the baseline. As soon as the receiver lobs, the net woman on the opposing side runs to the other part of the court while her partner, the server, comes in on the lob and takes it as a volley. It is a perfect pressure tactic against a woman receiver who only lobs well and who cannot hit very aggressively crosscourt or down the line.

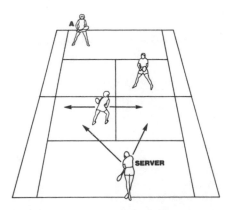

*Alternative 1 against a lob return of serve—
Player A only hits lob return of serve. The
server (the stronger player) therefore stands just
to the right of the center service line while
his partner (the weaker player) stands to the left
of the center service line at net. If Player
A lobs down-the-line, the net woman runs
to her right, leaving the server to cover the lob;
if Player A lobs crosscourt, the net woman
runs to her left and the server covers the lob
on the right side. The advantage to this
ploy is that the server can come in, taking
the lob on the volley. The server's partner
(the woman at net) must bend her knees and
get way down when her partner serves since
she is directly in line with his target.*

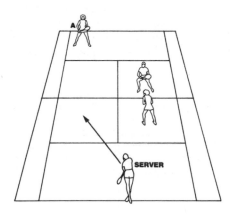

*Alternative 2 against a lob return of serve—
The receiver, Player A, regularly lobs down-
the-line. The server and his partner therefore
use the Australian formation: the net woman
stands in the right court instead of the left,
and the server comes in down the left line
to cut off the lob. When A changes her tactics
and starts to lob crosscourt, this alternative is
no longer effective.*

There is an alternative, more popular method of handling a down-the-line lobber—the Australian Formation. The server and his partner both start out on the right side of the court. The partner remains on the right unless the receiver lobs over her head. The receiver is now forced to lob crosscourt when she is grooved to lobbing down the line. Pressure is put on her to do something different—and to do it well. If she still tries to lob down the line, the server comes in and volleys the ball away.

The curious thing about this analysis is that, first, a weak woman in a mixed doubles match doesn't even have a clue that her best shot is the lob. You seldom see a weak woman player who lobs regularly. However, two of the best doubles teams in tennis history were lobbers—the Kinsey brothers in U.S. national competition (they won the U.S. title in 1924 over Aussies Pat O'Hara Wood and Gerald Patterson) and Italian stars Sylvana Lazzarino and Lea Pericoli (they beat all but the very best women's teams with high defensive lobs). On those rare but very special occasions when one does see a relatively weak woman lob, the opposing team has no reply. They simply let her lob the woman to death while the man is nailed to the backcourt. To every parry there is a riposte, and the answer is in a change of formation.

Whenever the man (assuming he is the stronger player) hits the overhead, it must be in the direction of the opposing woman—unless the other half of the court is open. If the man does not have a consistent, reliable overhead, his team is going to lose or his tongue will be hanging out before the first set is over. A good woman lobber is therefore worth her weight in gold (or oil).

Breaking up the woman's lobber requires: (1) a good overhead on the part of the opposing male and (2) frequent changes of formation to force the lobber to outguess the riposte.

THE MIDDLE SHOT

The stronger player takes most of the center shots. If the man is the better player, he is not supposed to play "hog" just because the ball is down the center; if his partner is playing the ad court and she can handle a short forehand well, there is no reason for him to yell "Mine!" and take it on his backhand. However, if it is a high, poopy, motherly shot down the center and he has the big forehand putaway, he has a right to end the point since there is a chance his partner might blow it. The cocky male who yells "Mine" when he really doesn't know if he will end the point is simply yelling to bolster his ego. It ruins the team's formation. Similarly, the woman player with a reasonably secure forehand should not insist on hitting all her set-ups if she cannot put the ball away and if her partner can. (The definition of a set-up is: a ball that can and should be put away by the opponent, thus ending the point.) If the man cannot regularly put the shot away, he should let the woman hit the ball when it is on her side of the court so that his team is not out of position.

Many intermediate women are not sure of their volley. They are delighted not only when the man takes the center ball but even when he moves into their court area to jump on the volley. If a woman is insecure in her volleying, she wants to guard as little territory as possible and leave the lion's share of the net to her partner.

The woman who volleys well wants to handle her own shots. If she volleys better than the man, she should take some of his shots. If the woman and the man are equally good at net, the one who volleys the last ball should take the next shot down the middle. This is a doubles rule which players automatically follow, except when a team is unevenly balanced; then the stronger or more agile player takes the middle shot.

POACHING

A poach is a movement out of one's territory at net into the partner's area. There is no such thing as "poaching" when both members of the team are at net; it occurs when one is at net (the potential poacher) and the other at the baseline. The opponent hits in the direction of the baseliner, but the opposing net man surprises him by crossing over and volleying the ball.

A successful poach is an immediate winner; an unsuccessful poach is a disaster. A proper poach is not just a usual point winner; it also puts the pressure on the opponents to outwit the poacher or to hit the ball so sharply that the poacher will either miss or not reach the ball. The opponents try tactical ploys such as lobs over the potential poacher's head, shots down his alley, heavy balls aimed directly at him or wide spins far away from him. Meanwhile, the poacher fakes and double-fakes, feinting to his right while intending to move back to his left. His movements, real and feinted, distract and confuse the opponent, making him change his mind at the last minute or teasing him into watching the poacher out of the corner of his eye.

If the poacher can't volley, he inspires no fear. Ergo, only a good, agile volleyer can poach; a nonvolleyer is seldom successful. The intermediate player should poach only a few times a set, when the high, soft return is anticipated and the volleyer is sure he or she can knock it off. Weak players who are timid at net should almost never poach. Women who see the ball well, and who are as good or better than their partners, should poach when they see the putaway. Not only are they making more points than they are losing, but they are pressuring the opponents to go for better shots.

The strong man player sometimes overestimates his poaching ability and goes for too many shots in his partner's territory. Since the weaker player in mixed doubles is supposed to win somewhere between 10 and 40% of her points, her stronger partner has to bear the burden of winning 60 to 90%. Therefore he should make 75% of his poaches. The stronger player usually thinks he need only make half his shots. If he only makes half and his partner only makes 10%, they will lose handily.

PRESSURE PLAYS

Some unusual formations can be played to upset the rhythm of the opponents. Normally, two medium players can defeat a strong man and a weak woman; the better balanced team will hit every ball to the lesser opponent. But the lone strongman can intimidate and unnerve the other team by forcing them to hit for a smaller target. He does this by heavy poaching and by protecting his partner's weakness. An example:

Partners A (woman) and B (man) have more or less the same ability. Ms. C is quite weak but she has a strong partner in Mr. D. Ms. C has a terrible backhand and a fair forehand, so her partner (Mr. D) asks her to play the forehand court.

When Ms. C serves to Ms. A in the forehand court, Mr. D asks her to stand almost in her alley; he will try to cut off everything at net. As Mr. D poaches, Ms. A tries to hit wider and sharper crosscourts. The pressure is so great that Ms. A forgets to lob over Mr. D's head!

When Ms. C serves to Mr. B in the backhand court, she again stands in the alley while Mr. D covers most of the net. But Mr. B is hitting his backhand crosscourt so sharply that Ms. C is losing her points. So Mr. D changes his formation. He has Ms. C serve right by the center service line and then cover the forehand court. Mr. D, who is very quick, stands at net almost by the center service line so that he can cover the backhand crosscourts and just about every shot except a clean backhand down the line in the alley area. Mr. B feels the pressure and tries too close a backhand down the line; it goes wide.

After losing the first set, Ms. A and Mr. B settle down. Ms. A begins to lob over Mr. D's head with excellent success. Mr. B's down-the-line backhand goes into the alley beyond Mr. D's reach, and Ms. C can't quite handle them. Mr. D discards this tactic and tries something new.

Mr. D realizes that Ms. A is not very fast. When Ms. A serves in the backhand court to Mr. D (A does not come to net behind serve), Mr. D varies his return—a wide backhand crosscourt that pulls Ms. A wide and deep in her alley or a sharp drop shot. When Ms. A anticipates the wide crosscourt, D feeds her a drop shot which she doesn't reach. A and B have a quick conference and decide to imitate D's tactics:

Ms. A stands by the center service line when serving in the backhand court to Mr. D. After Ms. A serves, she runs to cover the forehand court. Her forehand is her better shot and she runs better for a forehand drop shot. Meanwhile, Mr. B stands on the center service line at net, ready to cover any backhand crosscourt drop shot. Mr. D can no longer use his crosscourt backhand drop shot successfully (Mr. B is on top of it). Mr. D therefore goes down the line to Ms. A's sharp forehand. Ms. A likes this much better since she can hit forehand crosscourts to Ms. C.

Ms. A and Mr. B win the second set because they respected Mr. D's tactics, learned from them, and then adopted them. If they had not kept their heads and changed their formation, they would have come apart.

Mr. D is a clever player because he tries to keep the opponents off

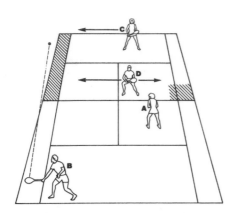

Player D is a very good volleyer and can cover all but the wide shots. Player B is unable to hit a backhand crosscourt into the narrow (shaded) areas that D cannot cover. Player B therefore tries to hit his backhand down-the-line in C's alley so that D cannot poach on it. B feels the pressure to make too good a shot and his ball goes wide.

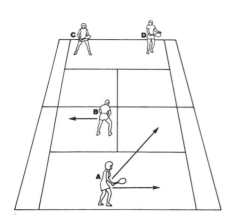

A and B have wised up. Now when A serves to D, she runs to her right for a deep forehand or crosscourt to her right for a drop shot. B covers the net on the backhand side, thereby preventing D from drop shotting crosscourt with his backhand. D now has to hit down-the-line to A's better side (her forehand).

balance, to play to weaknesses, and to make them hit to the smallest target. Mr. D is an excellent mixed player because he knows what his partner can and cannot do. Ms. C is only a fair volleyer on the forehand side and a terrible volleyer on the backhand (she uses a forehand grip, turning her elbow up to the sky). Mr. D does not ask Ms. C to play net or to stay in the backcourt; she can do either, depending on her confidence. Mr. D suggests only that Ms. C cover a small area of the net if she chooses to play there; he will cover the rest. Ms. C knows that Mr. D will cover lobs over her head, so she is not afraid to play close in—unless the balls are coming too hard at her. Because of Mr. D's attitude, Ms. C is more relaxed and less apologetic about her relative lack of skill. In the last tournament she played with Mr. X, he growled at her and Ms. C could hardly hit a ball.

SUMMARY

Mixed doubles is a team sport. The partners must work well together, with the captain (the stronger player) determining the strategy by making the ball go to his opponents' weaknesses and his partner's strength. He knows the high percentage shots he must make to compensate for losers from his partner. He never serves a double-fault to the weaker player, he takes extra care to get his first serve in when he is behind in his own service game, he runs around the opponent's second serve on big points, he roves the net to unsettle the other team, using fakes and feints and double-feints, he encourages his partner to lob over and over, he is not too proud to lob himself when he is out of position, he mixes up his serves and his returns of serve so the opponents can never get set, he takes the set-ups whenever he can and he never growls when his partner misses.

The weaker player relies heavily on the lob. She is not yet a good tactician, but when a lob goes over her head, she runs as fast as she can to the other side. She covers only a limited area at net and expects every ball to come directly at her (this keeps her ready for the volley). She covers her own lobs when she knows her partner cannot get to the ball. She poaches only when she is reasonably sure she can knock the volley away. She tries to get her first serve in and to anticipate where the return will go. She follows the tactical plans of her partner—the Australian Formation. By the time the match is over, she knows she has learned a lot about the mixed doubles game. As her skills improve, her game will improve even more.

Chapter Twenty-six / Doubles Strategy

T he top-flight singles player is not necessarily a great doubles player: the strategy is different, less court has to be covered, and good teamwork is essential. Bob Hewitt and Frew McMillan have won most of the major doubles titles in the world (French, Italian, Wimbledon, and World Championship Tennis) but neither has ever been ranked in the World's First Ten in singles. Betty Stove has to her credit the Wimbledon, French, and U.S. Doubles Championships but has never been a finalist in the singles. Elizabeth Ryan did not win the Wimbledon singles, but she took the Wimbledon doubles twelve times and the mixed seven times. Owen Davidson and Judy Dalton have between them won nineteen doubles and/or mixed titles in the Australian, French, Wimbledon, and U.S. Championships, but neither has ever taken a major singles championship.

Strategy for the doubles player varies according to his or her achievements in the game. At the very top level the important factors are quick reflexes, a great volley, overhead, and lob, the ability to get one's first serve in 80—90% of the time, a low, dipping return of serve, and the knowledge of where to be at the proper time. At a much lower level the requirements are less rigid: the lob becomes more important, drop volleys are never tried, and there are no cat-and-mouse tactics. Choose your tactics based on your own skills—don't start poaching before you have learned a putaway volley, for example.

BEGINNERS AND LOW INTERMEDIATES

- Pick up the balls quickly when the point is over and walk or trot rapidly back to your position. If you dawdle, you are wasting three other people's time and they won't play with you again. In the summer, dawdlers force partner and opponents to stand in the hot sun while, with snail-like precision, they pick up a third ball or meander with irritatingly sluggish movements back into the arena. In the winter these tortoises waste a good 15 minutes of valuable and expensive indoor court time. Almost all good players walk quickly after the point (eager ones run); almost all poor players plod. Please jog.

- If your partner is better than you, insist that he serve first. If your partner politely replies, "Oh, go ahead, you serve first," stick by your guns: the better player *always serves first in each set.*

- Don't serve double-faults. If you get your serve in, no matter how easily it sets up for the opponent, there is at least a chance the opponent may overhit. If you serve double-faults, there is no chance. Good doubles players will sometimes go an entire season without serving a double-fault; great doubles players almost always get their first serve in.

- Don't try to hit winners off returns of serve; you will make too many errors. Aim your service returns crosscourt. If the net man cuts off too many, lob high over the net man's head. The lob is the most important shot in beginner and intermediate doubles. The player who is too proud to lob because he would rather hit power shots that sail out will have a difficult time finding partners.

- Guard your alley. When you are standing at net, you are there for more than decorative purposes. Pretend, when your partner is serving and you are at net, that all returns will come directly to you or in your alley. It is the one area of the court that your partner cannot cover. If you do get passed down your alley, don't get despondent. It happens to the best of players. Your second thoughts should be whether the opponent mis-hit the shot and how you can anticipate the ball if he tries it again.

- If one of the opponents lobs over your head when you are at net and your partner is in the back court, run as fast as you can to the other side (if you have been standing near the left alley at net, run to the right alley at net). Conversely, if your partner is lobbed over and you are in the back court, run as fast as you can to retrieve the shot and hope that your partner crosses over quickly. From this position (running across the court to cover a lob over your partner's head), the best reply is a deep, high lob.

- If your partner is at net and one of the opponents has hit a deep ball which puts you in trouble, and if you decide the best return is a lob, then lob but at the same time yell "Back!" to your partner. If you don't yell and if you happen to lob short, your partner may wind up eating a tennis ball. There is no way for your partner to know what you are doing unless you tell him. If he is warned, he has time to get back and possibly retrieve the overhead. If you are at net and your partner lobs and you hear him shout "Back!" back up as fast as you can.

- If you are about to hit a ball and your partner calls "Out!" don't hit the ball. If his judgment is good, the ball will sail out. Do the same for your partner when you think he is going to hit an "out" ball. Occasionally you or your partner will misjudge and call "Out" only to find the ball has landed in. Intermediates play far too many "out" balls and so it is worthwhile protecting your partner and having him protect you with an "Out" call. In the beginning you both will be abashed when a ball lands in, but you will get better with practice.

- Never hit a high or a medium-high soft ball to the net man. If he is any good at all, he will put it away. You will accidentally hit many high balls from time to time, and if it is an accident there is nothing you can do but forget it. Your partner will also commit such errors. This is never done intentionally so don't berate him or comment on his mistake.

- On the beginning and intermediate level of doubles, the match is won by the team that makes the fewest errors, not by the team that makes the best shots. Therefore steadiness (getting the ball back) and the ability to retrieve (moving as soon as you see the ball leave the opponent's racket) are primary. As you achieve steadiness, you will get better control of direction of your shot. When you can get back most shots and keep them away from the net man, you will have jumped to the high intermediate or even the advanced level.

- Never poach (cross over into your partner's area to cut off a high ball) until you have achieved an adequate volley. If you miss 40–50% of your volleys and you step over the center line to cut off a ball, the chances are you will make an error or you will not put the ball away, thus leaving the whole area of your court open. A poach must always end the point; if you can't put the ball away, you are stranded in an untenable position on your partner's side of the court.

- You should not follow your serve to net when you are in the beginning or low intermediate level. You will make too many errors. The only time you should be at net is when your partner is serving or when your opponent hits a short ball, thus forcing you in. Practice your volley as often as you can and be alert whenever you are in the net area. Once you can put away your volleys or hit them with precision—that is, depth—you are ready to try the serve-and-volley tactics.

HIGH INTERMEDIATE AND ADVANCED DOUBLES

- The shots that are most important at this level of the game are the volley, the half-volley, the overhead, and the topspin lob. Don't expect to achieve them quickly (some fine doubles players have never been able to hit topspin lobs, but at least they acquire a disguised lob). Half-volleys (shots hit close to the ground just after the ball has bounced) are learned perforce by serving and coming to net: there is no backswing, a short follow-through, and the head must be kept down (if you look up, you might as well play blindfolded).

- When you come in behind serve, don't try to volley on the dead run or you won't be able to move sideways to cut off an angle return. Serve, run in, stop, volley, then move in two steps further.

- Whenever you cannot decide where to volley, hit the ball deep down the center. It is the safest shot in the game.
- When you are coming to net behind serve, spin the serve to give yourself time to get into position at net. If you serve a cannonball, you won't get three steps in before you have to hit the return.
- Never let a volley drop. When you see a high ball, move into it; don't wait for it to come to you.
- Get your first serve in at least 75% of the time. (Try for 90%.)
- It is not as important in doubles as in singles to serve only to the backhand in the forehand court. Sometimes you can "read" all your opponent's forehand returns. If you know they are all going hard to your forehand volley, you have an edge. However, if your opponent dips his forehand returns and makes you stretch or volley from your shoe tops, you will want to direct most of your serves to his easier-to-read backhand.
- Don't let your opponent get grooved to your serve. Change the angle, the pace, and the spin so he cannot get planted. Don't forget the jamming serve (right at the body).
- Keep your returns of serve low and dipping to force the server to volley up.
- When the server's partner is poaching and you cannot angle wide enough with safety, lob over the poacher's head or (occasionally) hit one directly down his alley.
- If the server is volleying up because of your low return, try coming in behind your service return.
- Play your opponent's weaknesses. One of them may have a weaker overhead, a fragile forehand, a tendency to serve short on second serve, an inability to maneuver quickly, a pattern play on the backhand, or a difficulty handling low underspins. If you spot a weakness, discuss it with your partner and pound it.
- If one opponent is returning serve so well that you are missing your volleys or setting them up for the net man, don't be ashamed to stay back and come in on the first short return.
- If your opponents lob you high to the backhand, be sure to hit with enough depth to protect yourself. Most backhand overheads are hit too short.
- If you or your partner hits a good offensive lob, both of you should come to net behind it. If you are at net and your partner hits a great offensive lob, be ready to poach on what will probably be a high return.
- When the opponents are regularly hitting down the center, let the player who has hit the last shot take the ball. He will be on the move and is usually in the best position, whether you are both at net or both on the baseline.
- To avoid any conflict when both you and your partner go for the same ball, one of you should be the captain (the player who calls "yours" or "mine").
- Although drop shots are seldom used in good doubles, drop volleys are often outright winners when at least one opponent is in the back court.

- A talented player should never neglect working on his lob-volley. It is a dangerous loser if it is not played perfectly—but it's a morale-breaking winner if it catches the opponent off balance.
- Use the "fake" (pretending to poach but not doing so) to tempt the opponent to hit down your alley. If you are very quick, you can "double-fake" (pretend to poach, then go back, then leap for the poach). Fakes and double-fakes keep the opponents off balance; they start to watch your movements instead of the ball.
- Poach on every high ball. It puts the pressure on the opponents to keep the ball low and wide, and this should cause them to make more errors.
- If you have been trapped on four or five winner lobs over your head, play two steps farther back, but be ready to move forward for any short or high return.
- Practice the "cat-and-mouse" game of sharp, low angles when the ball travels almost parallel to the net. When you are at net and you have to return a ball that is below net level, this is one of the most effective returns provided your shot bounces low (below net level) and has angle. If the ball clears the net by a foot or more, the opponent will jump on it and volley it away.
- Change a losing game. Don't go down to defeat with dignity but switch your ploys. Try the Australian or tandem formation: when you serve to the forehand court, your partner stands at net in your forehand court and you, in turn, cover the backhand side. This forces the opponent to go down the line instead of crosscourt, thus changing his groove. Other ploys: deep lobs; soft, dipping shots instead of hard boomers; chips, chops, and underspins instead of topspins; wide, sharp angle serves; more poaching or less poaching; and probing constantly for the weakness.
- If one partner has a bad patch, the other partner should encourage (not criticize) him. If you know your partner, you can do what will help him best. If he is injured, take all the set-ups and do most of the running. If he is nervous, try to get him to relax. If he is returning serve poorly or lobbing badly, stand back. If you are the one who is having the "off day," tell your partner to stand back when you return and have him take the majority of the center shots. If your partner doesn't glare at you, yell, or overinstruct, it is very possible you can get back in the groove before it is too late.
- Move with the ball. If you hit a sharp crosscourt angle, your partner should immediately cover his alley and you should move to the center, leaving your own alley unguarded. If your partner hits the sharp crosscourt angle, you then cover your alley and your partner covers the center. If you hit a down-the-line shot, you must cover your alley and your partner moves over to cover the center. This always applies when you are both at net. If your partner is at net and you are in the back court, he must cover his alley when either his shot or your shot goes into the alley he is facing; if you hit your shot down the line, your partner (at net) has to move toward center, although not as much as if you were both at net. If you are both on the baseline and one of you has hit a ball to the opposing alley,

there is no need to follow this "cover that alley and the center, leaving the other alley open" formation.   The theory of moving with the ball applies almost totally to the net man or net men, not to the two baseliners.

Chapter Twenty-seven
The Champion's Strategy Notebook

When a new pupil asks me for a lesson on strategy, my usual answer is, "Before you learn tactics, you need ball control." You cannot execute any skillful ploys until you have the ability to hit hard, deep, short, and high at will.   If you have all the shots, including drop shot and drop volley, it's so much the better.   Bobby Riggs did and was one of the complete players of the game.   So were Chuck McKinley and Manuel Santana.   So are Ken Rosewall and Ilie Nastase today, although Nastase does not always use his repertoire wisely.

By having ball control, the player can exploit a weakness.   If the opponent does not play net, you can bring him in with low angles, then lob or hit a passing shot.   Knowing all the shots enables you to force the opponent to play a game he is not used to.

SERVING AND RETURNING SERVE ON KEY POINTS

I find out as much as possible about my opponent's game before I go on the court, but I am always learning during the match.   For example, I know ahead of time he has a good serve, but in the course of play I'll find out where he serves on key points.   In my case he would probably go to my backhand, which is my weakness.   But there's more to it than that.   He knows on a key point that he has to get his first serve in. Since he is limited to the area of the service box, I will try to run around my backhand to put the pressure on the server: he now has to go very wide to my backhand while still getting the first serve in.   That's pressure.   If his first serve is a fault, I will run around my backhand, slice short, and come in.   This means two of us at net, and he has to hit a low volley past me.   While waiting to receive serve, I would position myself so that my forehand side was wide open, luring him to go wide to my forehand (just what I want) or forcing him to serve with no room to my backhand.   I do not try it until he is serving at 30-40, so he has not seen me do it before.

John Newcombe is the master of putting the pressure on the server at key points.   He leaves his forehand wide open and threatens to run around any serve to his backhand. I watched him use this tactic against Roy Emerson at Wimbledon when the match went to 11-9 in the fifth, and where a pressure ploy made the difference in getting the service break.

The server uses a different tactic on a key point. I would avoid serving to the forehand at 30-all or 15-40 because, at my height, I could not get a wide enough angle. You have to have a winning serve if you go for the forehand side in the forehand court. The opponent can hit his forehand from this position either down-the-line or crosscourt, and it is much harder to read than his backhand. On key points I would move the ball around: I often served straight at the body to jam the opponent's follow-through, or on the 40-30 point I would go to the forehand a lot. By serving to the opponent's forehand in the *left court,* I could anticipate the down-the-line to my strong forehand volley. This was making the opponent play to my strength, which is as important as going to the opponent's weakness.

One of the most dangerous opponents, from my point of view, was Frank Sedgman. He would come in on return of serve and cut off my volley. The difficult opponents are those who hit bullet returns or who cut off the server's volley. Tony Roche did not worry me because he never used either tactic. Tony would not take advantage of the natural edge of being left-handed. I never saw him run around his backhand in the ad court at 30-40, second serve; he never put the pressure on the server on key points. He won too many matches in long five-setters because he couldn't break serve enough. Even a Laver or a Connors, with all their strength and power, must run around second serve for change of pace.

Threatening the volleyer by coming in yourself is a pressure move that should be used cautiously. The play is no good if you hit a low, short one and the server stays back. It's too late for you to go back: you have made the move and are committed to go all the way in. Therefore it is advisable to come in only on the opponent's second serve, and it should be a relatively weak second serve. Rosewall, Sedgman, Gonzalez, Olmedo, and I would come in with a backhand slice that made the server volley up. That's the tactic on key points that makes the server worry.

Developing a good serve, even if one is a small player, is vital to prevent the opponent from taking away the offensive. Harold Solomon's big weakness is his bad serve. Because he is small he hasn't got the natural power of a tall man hitting down. This means he must generate power by more body motion—a forward and backward rock, followed by a body thrust at the ball. A Tony Trabert or a Dick Savitt does not need body motion, but a Solomon or a Segura does. I rock and thrust —and I would like to see Harold do the same.

SERVING IN SINGLES

The players today, particularly on the fast surfaces, come in behind every serve. Jimmy Connors does not. If a player with a big serve does not come in, how can the opponent hurt him? The server can instead come in on a good approach shot off return of serve.

When a champion develops a pattern of play, it is a handicap because it grooves the opponent. I like the element of surprise. When the server can come in on serve or off the opponent's return of serve, he has two options. His game has more variety and the opponent cannot get grooved. It takes good nerves to serve, stay back, and come in off the next return, but it is effective: the receiver hits a short return of serve because he is expecting the server to come in, only to discover the server is coming in off the short return of serve. If the receiver returns deep because he thinks the server is staying back, and if instead the latter comes in, the server has an easy volley.

The placement of the serve depends on the ability of the player to whip a really wide one to the forehand in the forehand court. Only a few players—Arthur Ashe and John Newcombe today and Ulf Schmidt a decade ago—are good enough to try it. Because I am small, some players will try to angle me with a wide serve to my forehand. I can guess they will try it at 30-0 when they have nothing to lose, but at 30-all they will go for the safer serve to my backhand. The big guys try the wide-to-the-forehand serve against Connors and myself, but the effectiveness is gone if we have anticipated their strategy.

One almost never serves to the forehand in the forehand court except at 30-0 or 40-15 because the forehand return is so hard to read. By serving to the backhand in the deuce court, one can anticipate that the return will go *to the center*. Almost no one can hit the reverse backhand crosscourt consistently in singles. To put it differently, playing to the right side of the court with the left side of the body is unnatural.

In the backhand court, one can and should serve to the forehand. The receiver cannot hit a reverse forehand crosscourt consistently, particularly off return of first serve, and so you can anticipate a down-the-line or a down-the-middle return. I have always served to Rosewall's forehand in the backhand court and the return is often to my forehand volley. I can then get him out of position immediately with a crosscourt volley. Then why do so many players serve to the backhand in the backhand court? Either because they are stupid or they do not have a forehand volley.

THE SINGLES RETURN OF SERVE

Pancho Gonzalez will often return serve short intentionally, but at the same time he moves up to rush the volleyer. Gonzalez will give Stan Smith the "nothing" return—a soft, low, dipping ball. John Newcombe will use the same tactic against Smith, particularly when Newk is returning serve off the backhand, but he does not come in to cut off the volley. Instead, Newk "reads" the volley and passes Smith with a lob.

If I had been Smith's Davis Cup coach when he played Newk, I would have offered him a counterattack to Newk's "nothing" return. This would be to hit the big serve, follow in but stop at the service line, or let the ball bounce and come in on the next shot, or stop, fake, and come in. Instead Smith came in all the way and volleyed weakly because Newk's return was so low. Rosewall also likes to play Smith with low, short returns—but Muscles either moves in or threatens to move in.

On a key point, the low, short return is a great play. Laver uses it well and deliberately off his backhand slice, and the opponent is then a sucker for a lob. Laver uses this return against Newcombe just as Newcombe uses it against Smith. Gonzalez is the master of this shot, probably because he could never hit as hard as the other players. It takes an elastic, flexible player to hit the low dipper. Don Budge and Dick Savitt could never do it, but they hit so hard it did not matter. Most big players, Gonzalez being the lone exception, will go for speed because they are not limber enough for touch. But Gonzalez, as big as he is, is so flexible that he can get into position at the last minute and he can improvise at the last second. A player such as Erik Van Dillen has no flexibility. In a Pro-Celebrity match, where hitting bullets at the Celebrity is like knocking off pigeons with a machinegun, Van Dillen will try to dink (to avoid fatalities) and is unable to keep the ball in court.

There is usually a riposte to any strategy. When I served to Gonzalez and he hit his short, low slice and came in, I would let the ball bounce so I could have more alternatives. Then I could hit deep or lob or drop shot, depending on his position.

The short, low return of serve, often called a dink, is very tough for many volleyers. They handle speed better. That's why Laver has two returns—a boomer and a dink. Women players don't use the short, low return often enough. If I were on the Virginia Slims Circuit, I would use it a lot against six-footer Karen Krantzcke. It's an excellent play against a tall player because it sets up the next shot. Amazingly, most players will dink in doubles and never try it in singles, because in doubles the player is forced to hit short and low. Julie Heldman hits a lot of dinks to the feet, but she does not come in. She would be a lot tougher if she did; here, however, it is a question of confidence in the volley. The late Rafael Osuna of Mexico was always threatening to move in and cut off shots, but he had a special gift because he was so fast. He and Connors, as you will see later, could cut off approach shots because of anticipation and speed of foot.

Vijay Amritraj has the flexibility to hit dinks, but he never opts to do so. He is all power and hits all his shots straight. He never lobs off the backhand. When he played Rosewall at Forest Hills, he either made great shots or bad ones. His backhand is superb, but it is readable. It is easy to volley Amritraj's shots because the opponent knows Vijay will hit hard. The opponent can also crowd the net because Vijay won't lob or dink.

READING THE OPPONENT

There are many ways to read what the opponent will do. If, as in the case of Vijay, he never lobs or dinks, you can read "power return."

You "read" where the opponent will serve on a key point because you remember what he has done on previous key points.

Beginners and intermediates at first are unable to read drop shots, chops, and slices because the game is new and they have had no experience against a variety of strokes. Advanced players can read any shot that is not disguised. Tournament players go a step further: they read by watching the motion of the stroke. The player is supposed to watch the ball at all times; but, as he advances to a higher level, he acquires some peripheral vision so that he can see the ball and still recognize what the opponent is doing. It is not easy because one still must concentrate on seeing the ball.

To learn to read a player, watch the arm and shoulder motion, the footwork, position, and stance. If the opponent is hitting away from his body, the shot is aimed down-the-line; if he is hitting around his body, it's going crosscourt; if it's in between, it's going down the middle. When a player is completely extended and going to be late, he must either go down-the-line or lob. You get your clues by where the ball is, whether the opponent is late or off balance, and how far he is reaching for the ball. If you hit a ball low and away from your opponent and you sense he is slow in moving to the ball, you can predict lateness and the consequent down-the-line or lob.

The advanced player automatically reacts to the open racket face of the opponent (underspin), the flat face (a flat ball) and to the sharp pull-up on the follow-through (topspin). The easiest shot to read is the chop, but unfortunately the only great players to use it are Jack Dreyfus, Joe Cullman, and the late Bill Tilden. The advanced player can also learn to read the dropped racket head on the forehand: it cannot be topspin and the ball must go high.* He reads a heavy slice on serve when the ball is tossed far to the right, an American twist when the toss is over the head, and very little slice or a flat ball when the toss is well in front.

The hardest shot to read is a disguised drop shot. Instead you sense it from the position of the opponent on the court, the frequency with which he uses the shot, and the score. At 40-0, when the opponent has lots of time and is in midcourt, he may drive long or he may go for the drop shot. Determining the odds on whether or not your opponent will drop-shot is a matter of your knowledge of his patterns.

The better you know your opponent, the more you can read him. He may have a particular area from which he likes to hit a favorite shot. Arthur Ashe, on backhand return of serve in the backhand court, goes crosscourt. He only goes down-the-line if he has to. His favorite shot is the hard backhand return of serve crosscourt because he has so much room. Billie Jean King hits her forehand approach shot down-the-line with sidespin. (Incidentally, this may be the best shot in the game.) After I hit a forehand crosscourt I usually moved up. Rosewall will hit his backhand anywhere, and it's very difficult to read. The easy shots

* There are exceptions. Harold Solomon, Bjorn Borg, and Bill Tilden could drop the racket head and still topspin.

to read are serves that always go to the backhand at 30-all (the server never goes straight for the body) or the forehand down-the-line approach shot that never varies.

When you drive a good crosscourt with angle and the opponent is running full speed, he will be slightly late and out of court so he will go down-the-line. Only a Nastase, Gonzalez, Okker, or Laver can go crosscourt when running at full speed because the crosscourt requires the arm to come around the body. The reason most passing shots are down-the-line is because the player has no time to turn. The pattern of the opponent is down-the-line when he is forced wide from both wings because he does not have enough time to hit the crosscourt.

A player learns to read an opponent through experience. When Tony Trabert and Ken Rosewall were meeting on the Pro Tour, Trabert would hit a backhand high and down-the-line to Rosewall's forehand. Rosewall finally got smart, started reading Tony, and came in to cut off the shot with a forehand volley. Those who have played Arthur Ashe know he serves to the right a lot on the right side. Brian Gottfried comes in from three-quarter-length (between the service line and the baseline) with a slice, but no one reads him enough. I know he is coming in. He takes a gamble by hitting the ball on the rise but no one cuts him off. I would move in to threaten to cut off the shot. It is hard for Gottfried to come in with a really firm shot, but he does it amazingly well and puts the pressure on his opponent.

The hardest player for one to read is Rosewall. He can slice short or deep, hit angles, drop-shot, and lob. The easy players to read are those who lob a lot or not at all, who have a pattern play, and whose game lacks variety.

COMING TO NET

Most players come in either on serve or when the opponent has hit short to them. There are other times to come in—e.g., off return of second serve—as pointed out earlier. I come in when I have hit a short, low ball for three reasons. If I do not come in, my opponent will; even if he is already at net, by coming in I put the pressure on him; and I was always able to do it better than anyone else. Jimmy Connors has just started to use this ploy. When Stockton (or Gottfried) comes in, Connors hits a low, short one and comes in, too. Obviously to be effective the ball must be kept low, and many players can keep it low on the backhand slice. Generally I would get the volleyer to go down-the-line because I kept the ball so low. One does not have to be in the top echelon of tournament competition to try this ploy.

The deep approach shot, when the opponent is on the baseline, is much more commonly used. The ball must be firmly hit, and it should bounce low. It can be hit with slice, topspin, flat, or sidespin. I avoid topspin because the ball bounces up and the opponent can lob you. It is better to force the opponent to return a ball that is bouncing just above his shoe tops—then he has to hit up. That is why I like slice, sidespin, or a flat ball. There need not be any backswing on the deep approach shot, because the momentum of the run is all you need. If the ball is high, then you can stop and hit with a big swing. You can even topspin or fake the opponent with a drop shot because you have time. However, topspin in that area of the court is usually not as good. When you are hitting a low ball on the run well in front of you, it is difficult to hit a heavy topspin shot. Depth is vital: the opponent has too easy a shot if your ball lands between the service line and well inside the baseline.

There are other times to come to net. If I lob a high shot, I come in. If my opponent hits an overhead from behind the baseline, I press him by coming in. If my opponent hits a shoulder-high shot from behind the baseline, I come in because his shot will be short or high. If he passes me, that is his great shot. Very few players can muscle the ball into a great shot, the exceptions being Hoad, Budge, Kovacs, and Savitt, among others.

If I throw a low, short shot to the net man's feet, I know he will play short—so I come in. If he then drop-volleys, I am on top of it. If he half-volleys, it will be short because the ball is so low. I would take my chances against anyone half-volleying a low ball, except for Whitney Reed. He preferred the half-volley to the volley and he had perfect control. (Reed's control was the best in the world, although Gonzalez was not far behind.)

The minute I sense the opponent is off balance, I move in to close the court and put on the pressure. Fred Perry, the British three-time Wimbledon Champion, was superb at this maneuver. If his opponent was rushed and late, Perry would be at net in no time flat. The ball would be moving and the opponent would be moving—and Perry would be moving, too.

If I drop-shot I come in. There is no reason to stand back and admire the shot; I come in and put the pressure on.

EVERYDAY TOURNAMENT STRATEGY

The short, low, angle shots are effective against the net man, and they are also an excellent means of bringing a reluctant opponent to net. If the opponent happens to be a great groundstroker, why let him play his own game? By forcing him to net you cut down his rallying ability. Connors does it to Solomon. I used to use it against big players who were not quick enough. I could not match length with them, and if I let them force me from the baseline I was dead. Bitsy Grant, one of the famous clay court players in American tennis history, used the low, short angle against Frankie Parker. Bitsy could hit the low angle off either wing. Riggs was also masterful at this shot. The big players never use it because they have so much power they do not need it.

If I hit high and deep to my opponent and he returned high and deep to me, I would be in like a flash to cut off the shot on the fly. This is the tactic to use against a Solomon or Dibbs: if they insist on hitting high and deep from the baseline, come in and cut off the ball. That forces them to play lower to you.

In cutting off the ball, the volley must be deep. If it isn't, you're dead. Even if your name is Arthur Ashe and you volley short, Harold Solomon will murder you with a passing shot and Rod Laver will annihilate you with a lob or a passing shot. When Jimmy Connors was to play Ken Rosewall in the 1974 U.S. Open final, I told him he had to volley so firm and so deep that Rosewall would have no time to pass him. The greatest passing shot artist of the decade was crushed by deep, firm volleys.

No one can hit deep volleys on every point, and so eventually, when two players are evenly matched on a particular day, it comes down to five factors: knowing the percentage game; understanding the value of surprise; having steel nerves; being aware of the key points; and having a balance in reserve. On any particular day, sixty or eighty players (perhaps even 100) are capable of beating any one of the top five in the world. Once a player has a win over one of the Big Five, his chances of jumping twenty or forty or even eighty notches go way up.

The percentage game has been discussed in detail—when to serve to the forehand, when to come to net, when not to drop-shot or drop-volley, when to run around second serve, etc. Now we come to the value of surprise.

If you can read a player, there are no surprises. The opponent who can vary his spins, depth, angle, and pace and has no given groove is full of surprises. I have mentioned the volleyer who does not always come in on serve so he can crush the receiver's short return of serve, the volleyer who comes in when his opponent is already at net, the server who jams the receiver, the quick-footed man who comes in on the opponent's down-the-line approach shot, and a number of other maneuvers. There are more:

If the opponent is a topspin genius, he'll beat you every time if you topspin back; slice low. If the opponent slices, return with topspin. The point in tennis, after a certain level, is not just worrying about getting the ball in play or overhitting; it's to prevent the opponent from having full control of his strokes. This means you need three paces (medium, slow, and fast) and the ability to slice and topspin on the backhand, to hit with topspin or sidespin on the forehand, and to hit flat when necessary on either side. You must lob well—and know when to lob. If you are behind the baseline, running laterally, at 30-40, it's the obvious time to lob. Lesley Hunt, for all her other abilities, tries to pass with a big shot at this stage and makes one in twenty. The percentage is not there; it is the difference between winning and losing. It's the choice between the spectacular and the defensive: which is the most appropriate at this juncture?

Nerves are obviously a factor in a player's confidence and relaxation, his ability to rise to a major challenge without crumbling, his capacity to make arm, wrist, legs, body, and mind function quickly and without flaw when the pressure is on. It takes growing up to get to the stage where nerves and pressure make you play your best, but the player who is out of competition for too long forgets the ploys and reactions that must be instinctive. Too much competition satiates, too little competition deprives. Players get "up" too soon or "down" too quickly, sometimes from too much or too little play, sometimes because the competition is too strong or too weak. It's different for each individual, since too much pressure or not enough, too much competition or too little, works differently for each personality involved. It is the real challenge of the game, and you have to meet it if you want to stay on any competitive level. If you can stand your losses and accept them without excuses (everyone is beaten badly by lesser ranked players on occasions), you probably have the resolution to continue. The more important the contest (the finals of Forest Hills or Wimbledon), the greater the pressure. You can take it if you make the only pressures on yourself, but if others are pressing you too, you may start playing "not to lose" rather than "to win."

Nerves show when a great player fails to put away a relatively easy overhead, when he loses serve on a double-fault, when an easy coming-in shot falls short, when a drop shot is executed from the baseline on a key point, or when the player overhits or underhits, gets too loose at a critical point, and fails to play to the score. Sometimes emotion takes over. There is a bad call and the player goes to pieces. He screams or he keeps it inside—but the effects are equally disastrous (except that in the former case he/she gets bad press notices). One famous player served thirteen consecutive double-faults in a Davis Cup match; another froze on every low volley; a third never hit a forehand in during the final set of the match; a fourth led 6-0, 5-0, match point in Madison Square Garden, only to lost the next thirteen games. It has happened at some stage to everyone—to Rod Laver, Billie Jean King, Margaret Court, and Bobby Riggs. Do not let it destroy you when it happens to you.

The key points are easy to learn. There are two sets of crucial points: one gives you the edge and the other allows you to close out the game, the set, and/or the match. In the first case, the big point is the first one, and the next biggest point is the second one. If you have 30-0 and you do not play stupidly, you will hold serve. If you have 0-30, your chances are excellent for breaking serve. The second group of key points comes when you are about to hold serve, break serve or lose serve. A score of 40-30 on your serve at 4-all or 4-5 is vital to winning or losing the match; another key point is at 30-40, your favor, when each has been holding serve. In the course of a match, some key points will arise, perhaps at 3-2 in the second set, and every top player watching will know it is a turning point because of the way the match has been going. Here is an example:

Billie Jean King is playing Julie Heldman in the semi-finals of Forest Hills. Heldman beat her the previous year in the same tournament. Heldman has the first set and leads 3-2, 40-0 in the second; she loses that point and the game. Billie Jean is back in the match and has a huge edge, both because of her reputation and because she broke serve when her opponent led 40-0 on serve.

Other players have had chances to close out a match, but when they let one chance slip, the opponent suddenly sprang back and took over. Some more examples: Phil Dent has Jimmy Connors 30-0 on serve at Wimbledon. The score is 9-8 in the fifth for Phil. He loses that point and the match.   If he had won it, Jimmy would have been eliminated early and would not have been No. 1 in the world that year.

Stan Smith is playing Ken Rosewall in the semifinals of Wimbledon. Stan has two sets to none and match point in the tiebreaker of the third. He loses that point.   Rosewall takes that set and the next two sets.

Manuel Orantes wins the Spanish and Italian championships, then gets to the semifinals of the French.   He is beaten by a relative unknown, Patrick Proisy.   Lew Hoad watches the match and makes an astute observation: "It will take Orantes one to two years to recover from this match."   It took two years for the Spaniard to climb back up the ladder.

Guillermo Vilas has Orantes 5-0 in the fourth and is leading by two sets to one in the 1975 U.S. Open.   Half the spectators leave because it is well past the dinner hour and the match is apparently over. Orantes makes one of the most amazing comebacks, flashing off a couple of winners, taking seven straight games for the set and then winning the fifth.

Lesley Hunt meets Chris Evert in the first round of Wimbledon.   The score is 8-all in the final set when the match is called because of darkness.   Everyone, including Chris and Lesley, knows that Chris will take the next two games when the match is resumed the following day.   And it so befell.

Lesley could have won the match if it had not been called.   She was charged with adrenalin and confidence or what sports reporters commonly call "momentum."   A player gets to a certain peak in a match, then loses one crucial point—and the pattern of the game shifts.   Player X has 6-0, 3-0 against Player Y.   Then Player X slips momentarily or gets a bad call or worries over a weak shot, and Player Y catches fire. A player who misses an easy shot at 30-0 has no problem; it can be disastrous to miss at 30-40.

The great competitive player has the ability to block out a bad shot or a bad call.   Fortunately I was gifted that way.   I gave 100% whenever I played and I was ruthless on the court.   When I was beaten, I could not sleep for two days, particularly when the match was close.   I lost to Rosewall in the 1962 Wembley in five sets, and I could not sleep afterward.   Another match that lives in my memory forever is Santa Barbara when I lost to Jack Kramer after leading 5-0.

A top player always has a letdown after taking a major international title.   It takes three or four days to come down from the clouds.   The winner at Forest Hills invariably loses the next week.   Those losses count only on the record, not in the mind of the champion.

The last factor in the making of a champion is the reserve he keeps to pull him through a marathon.   For this he needs fitness and the ability to pace himself.   If he is getting tired and the opponent has 40-0 on serve, he lets the game go.   He never lets a game go when he is serving. He knows if he wins his serve 100% of the time, he's in good shape. Newcombe and Kramer, probably more than any other players, won 6-4 sets (one service break only).   Kramer seldom dropped serve, and when he lost two service games in a set it was startling.

In pacing oneself, the object is to try to be ahead, not to try to catch up. Therefore there are two goals. First, get the first two points of the opponent's serve to get the all-important break. Second, try to serve first in the fifth and final set, particularly if you are small or your serve is weaker. The bigger player generally hits harder and the smaller one runs more, and it begins to show in the last stages. During the quarterfinals of Wimbledon, Newcombe and Emerson had a five-set match. Emerson served last and lost 11-9 in the fifth. The smaller player was forced to keep up rather than allowed to surge ahead. It's tough on Rosewall when he serves last—and I do not like it a bit if I play Gonzalez and he serves first.

In the latter stages of the match, when fatigue sets in, judge your chances according to the shot and the score. At 30-0, if my opponent has an easy putaway, I do not kill myself. I will drive, leap and scramble at 30-40, his serve, or 30-40, my serve, because the point means a crucial game and undoubtedly the match. Reserves are seldom endless, so guard them well and use them at the vital points, which is the reason you have stored them.

Chapter Twenty-eight / Counterpoint Ploys

Tennis is a game of confidence. It's easy to win when you are playing well and hard to win when you are playing badly. That's axiomatic. However, a player who is having a bad day can still win if he can change his style of play (if, for example, he has two styles, not just one), if he understands his opponent's game (what the opponent will probably do in a given situation), and if he uses the point system well (the knowledge of how to play the 30-40 and 40-30 points properly).

Jimmy Connors is a perfect example of a champion who plays to the point system, combines great groundstrokes with an excellent net game (two styles of play), and understands the potential, the weakness, and the percentage shots of each opponent. In England a year ago, Connors was having a rough match against Harold Solomon. Harold, who makes his living with his passing shots, had match point against Connors. Jimmy was not attacking successfully and knew he could not win by blanketing the net, so he fell back on his groundstrokes when his net attack became uncertain. Connors does not have excessive topspin on his forehand and therefore he gets much better *depth* than such heavy topspin players as Bjorn Borg, Chuck McKinley or Solomon. When Jimmy plays from the baseline, he has plenty of room for his shots against another baseliner; by hitting a deep forcing shot on one side, he opens up the other side. Even if Jimmy could not be at his aggressive best, he could depend on his groundstrokes to create openings. Because he had something to fall back on, he was able to pull out a match that was practically lost against a solid baseliner like Solomon.

Knowing the important points, having both ground game and net attack and understanding one's opponent is the biggest edge in tennis— big enough sometimes to enable a player to beat an opponent who is at his best. In the finals of the 1974 South African Championships between Arthur Ashe and Jimmy Connors, Ashe was hitting the ball solidly and was probably at the top of his game. The knowledge of what Ashe would do in a given situation, plus Connors's incredible speed in counterattacking, was the factor that gave Jimmy the edge over his opponent. He anticipated a number of Ashe's down-the-line shots, but instead of running them down on the baseline Connors tore in diagonally to cut off the shot with a volley. You have to know your opponent (for example, if you give him a sharp, low crosscourt, he tends to go down-the-line) and be fast as a bullet (come in on the diagonal to cut off the down-the-line), but it is part of Connors's repertoire. In other words, Connors set up a pattern play in which he could read Ashe's response.

Connors is an admirable champion because he has determination, he tries for every shot, and his nerves are under control. The only strokes he lacks are drop volleys and drop shots, and, although these are not absolutely vital, they would add to his game when he plays a top baseliner such as Solomon.

Small players like Connors do not have to serve and come to the net every time. Those who do get killed—they get passed on the second shot. But small players continue to come in on serve against Ashe and Smith, whereas if they stayed back, neither Ashe nor Smith would come in on the opponent's second serve. There are few players courageous enough to come in on the second serves of Rosewall, Connors, Solomon, or Evert (all small players); Ashe and Smith could not do so successfully because they are not flexible enough. Play the game according to whom you play: don't come in on second serve against a big fellow who will only hit the ball back that much harder. Stay back and rally, waiting to hit aggressive approach shots before coming in. The only time a player can take chances is when he is leading 40-0 or 30-0.

It is always astonishing that players fail to use their talents to the fullest. Why do so many players insist on coming in behind second serve against the game's hardest hitters? When I played Barry MacKay or Dick Savitt, I stayed back when I served, waiting for the first opportunity I had to come in. MacKay would try to come in against a groundstroker on his second serve and lost many a match as a result. Mike Franks and Tom Edlefsen were fine players, but they would serve and come in even though they were not that quick. The opponent would make them volley up and then either lob or pass them on the next shot. Jack Kramer set a pattern for all young players to follow, whether or not they could do it. If Kramer served and came in to net, they, too, would do the same.

Players should realize their potential and understand their limitations. When a 30-year-old serves, comes in, then doesn't make a winning first volley, he wonders what has happened. He refuses to realize that he is slow, not flexible from the waist up and that this makes him volley weakly. He would be much better off if he stayed back until he got the opening (a short shot), then hit it hard and deep to prepare for the relatively easy volley.

So many players come to net behind serve and then wonder why they lose. Tory Fretz, as an example, would be a far better player if she did not come to net behind every serve. She does not make the first volley tough enough and she does not have the necessary agility. The time for her to serve and come in is at 30-0 or 40-0. If she stayed back she would get better results. If she throws in a big first serve, she can expect a rather short return and can then make an excellent approach shot.

Rosie Casals hits too hard for her weight and size and would be more successful if she scrambled rather than tried to play so aggressively. Casals's idea is to overpower the opponent, but she is too small to do so. Despite the fact that she has the biggest serve in the game for her size and that she is one of the quickest and has the most agility and talent, she tries to make winners off returns of serve and so makes too many errors.

Very few players understand point values. As an example, Julie Heldman might have beaten Billie Jean King in the semifinals of the 1974 Forest Hills if she had used a better choice of shots. At 15-30 she tried a drop shot from behind the baseline. That shot can only be tried at 30-0 when the risk factor is not so great. It should never be done at 15-30 or 30-40 unless the drop shot is executed at or inside the service line.

Nervousness can be the worst problem for a player. The champion gets nervous, but there are no hesitations and the strokes are not tentative. He does not worry about what his opponent is going to do. If he did, he wouldn't win; he would just play a close match. I make up my mind that if my opponent aces me that's my bad luck. I am not as concerned about what he is going to do to me as about how I will impose my game on him. I don't start worrying that if I hit to his right, he'll hit to my left. If I hit the ball hard and low, what is he going to do to hurt me? Worrying about what the other player is going to do breaks down one's own game. This does not mean that one does not analyze the opponent. One must discover how he plays, which are his best strokes, how fast he runs, and how he plays the important points. Perhaps I know he lobs better or passes better than I, but I think positively and know I am quicker than he.

Improvisation is a great factor in the winning game. It is an almost intuitive sense of what to do, and some players have it while others don't. The intuitive player is caught in No Man's Land—the area between the service and the baseline—and he half-volleys for a winner. When he is forced in a corner, he has the flair for something spectacular. A winning half-volley from near the baseline will demoralize an opponent in a big match. Perhaps Evonne Goolagong has the ability to improvise more than any other player, although Rod Laver and Ilie Nastase are also tremendously imaginative.

Goolagong is one of the great players in the game today, but she has not yet developed the ability to counterpunch against a clever ploy of the opponent. In the 1974 Forest Hills final, Goolagong was in a position to beat Billie Jean King. She ran up the big leads but couldn't close out the match, primarily because her second serve was faulty.

Billie Jean was coming to net on Evonne's weak second serve, and the latter then tried low, dipping shots to Billie Jean's feet which the old champion handled very competently. Evonne had three choices as a countermeasure. First, she could concentrate on not missing first serves since her second serve was ineffective. Second, she could have lobbed much more despite the fact that King has a deadly overhead. It would have prevented Billie Jean from closing in, and the next low, dipping shot would have been that much more effective. Third, she should have come in herself to cut off Billie Jean's approach shot with her own volley. King is not as quick as Goolagong, and that's what Evonne should have gambled on. Billie Jean volleys better and has a better serve and overhead, but, most of all, Billie Jean plays the points better.

Today's younger players range in age from seventeen to twenty-two; they have brought a new standard to the game. Connors, Borg, Vilas, Ramirez, and Solomon are making it tough for Pasarell, Riessen, Smith, Richey, and other twenty-eight-to-thirty-year-olds. The latter cannot cope with the new standard. Players such as Connors and Borg will get better, whereas Smith, Pasarell, Riessen, and Graebner have reached a plateau and there is no way for them to improve. *They cannot scramble and they lack agility.* The proof of this thesis is demonstrated in the play of Ken Rosewall who, at thirty-nine, still plays well, albeit not as impeccably as he did when he was younger. But Rosewall has both ball control and the ability to scramble. The players of the future will combine ball control with a big serve and great groundstrokes with great volleys. They will have far fewer flaws in their armor than today's champions.

I have usually included Arthur Ashe in my list of older players who cannot cope with the flexibility of the young giants. But in 1975 he proved me wrong. He showed imagination, flair, an improved forehand volley, a better analytic mind, and a lot of guts.

Jimmy Connors is one of the young stars who is demonstrating the future of the game: the new champions will be able to play from the baseline or at net. In the past the top players had only one style—groundstrokes or volley. Connors has shown that the champion can play both ways at the same time. His opponent never knows what he is going to do, whether he will stay back or come to net. These groundstrokers are able to handle the biggest serves in the game, as Rosewall has proved so convincingly in his matches against big-serving John Newcombe. Newcombe has the cannonball, but it is not enough to annihilate a Rosewall. The groundstroker can beat the big server if the latter is not that quick.

If Chris Evert could volley, no one would beat her for the next five years, even though her serve is not that strong. I am always surprised at the way her opponents play her. There are two tactics that should be effective against her. First, one should play her short and low, making her move up to the service line and reach for the ball. Second, the opponent should force her on return of serve by coming in on her serve at full speed, taking the ball on the rise. A woman with a good forehand should run around Chris' second serve and attack. This should be done only when the first serve is a fault and at 0-30, 15-30 or 30-40, which are the pressure points. It is at this time that the player knows how important service is and so he or she has a tendency to tighten up. Jimmy Connors knows that when the score gets to 4-all, 15-30, his opponent will almost inevitably miss his first serve (he is overanxious to hit it well since the point is crucial). Jimmy is therefore mentally geared to run around second serve and attack. Connors knows that he must have these scores—the pressure points—with him when he uses this tactic.

When a player is losing, it is not the time to take chances. If he does take chances, he will lose faster. Instead, he should understand the most effective shots. Connors knows that when he is playing behind the baseline he must go for the crosscourt rather than the down the line. He can make the crosscourt deep or short and still keep it effective. If he hits the down the line short, he is dead. When a crosscourt is hit to Connors, he does not run along the baseline toward his alley but instead runs on the hypotenuse of the triangle (on a diagonal) to cut off the angle. If Connors hits a low, angled crosscourt to the opponent's backhand, he knows the opponent will hit down the line and so he comes to net on the diagonal and cuts off the shot with a crosscourt volley. When Connors hits down the line from the baseline, he goes for depth. The idea of the game is to have the opponent behind the baseline, in the alleys or very close to net, making him reach for the ball.

Most players do not understand the most effective return of serve. Should one hit it down the middle, crosscourt, or down the line? The answer is down the middle, but the ball must be low and short if the server is coming to net. If the server stays back, the shot must be hit deep. Players must develop a pattern. When a player returns serve, he should understand that the server is limited to a relatively small box. Furthermore, the thinking player remembers what the server does: perhaps last time at 30-all the server went for the backhand. The receiver can take a position to make the opponent serve where he wants him to. He simply leaves his forehand open or his backhand open. John Newcombe is a master of forcing the server to do what John wants. At 30-40 Newcombe stands in his *backhand alley* to receive serve, forcing the server to hit to his forehand. At 30-40 the server gets nervous because the point is so critical and there is so little room to swing in the big serve. Of all the players in the game today, Newcombe has the most imagination. He uses this strength of putting the pressure on the server, but he does not do it at 40-0; he waits until he has the opponent 30-40.

Tony Roche could have been the best player in the game if he had played these 30-40 points like John Newcombe did. A left-hander such as Roche with an excellent topspin forehand should have run around second serve every time on this critical point, but he never did. He simply played it safe and chipped his backhand. The question is whether this was the safe play.

Player A can win more points than Player B and still lost the match. Player A takes four games at love, earning 16 points. Player B wins six games at deuce, which gives him a total of 24 points and gives Player A

12 points. So Player A got 28 points, Player B got 24—and Player B won. The key points are 30-15 and *every point thereafter* and the most important games are 4-3 and *every game thereafter*. I used to aim to win the first two points to get that big 30-0 lead. If I had 30-0, or if I had 0-30 on my opponent's serve, I had a 70% chance of winning the game. So one strives to get the first two points to get that big advantage.

The most telling example of bad judgment from an excellent player and a great tactician was shown by Bobby Riggs in his famous match against Billie Jean King. He was serving to King at set point for her. The first serve was a fault, and then he went for a serve to her forehand at 30-40. It was a possibility on first serve—but never on second serve with set point down. Because King played so well and proved to be the better tactician against a male famous for his cool nerve and tactical sense, Riggs will never be as great a competitor again. Poor judgment in a major pressure match leaves permanent scars.

Chapter Twenty-nine
Great Matches of Strategy: Connors vs. Laver, Newcombe, Ashe, and Orantes

Major matches are won by a combination of three factors. One needs the technical skills to guide and control the ball, the tactics to probe the opponent's weaknesses, and the nerves to hit the the strokes and carry out the plan when the pressure is on. I have taken four matches that were important in the tennis career of Jimmy Connors, two of which he won and two he lost. The first two were the biggest money matches in tennis history, played specifically for a television audience on a medium-speed carpet indoors, and by winning them both Connors earned himself a small fortune. The other two were final-round matches in the major championships of the world—Wimbledon and Forest Hills—and in both cases Connors was defending the title he had won the previous year. He was beaten in an unexpected upset on the fast grass of Wimbledon by Arthur Ashe, and he lost on the slow clay of Forest Hills to Spain's Manuel Orantes, who had never before won a Big Four title.

JIMMY CONNORS *d* ROD LAVER
6-4, 6-2, 3-6, 7-5/LAS VEGAS, 1975

Rod Laver and Jimmy Connors had not met in tournament competition until their head-to-head match was staged by Caesar's Palace in Las Vegas and televised by CBS. The winner was to receive $150,000. Laver had twice won the Grand Slam but was slightly over the hill. Connors had probably not yet reached his peak but was the current No. 1 in the world.

I was sitting on the court as Connors's coach in this match. Jimmy's ploy was to rush Laver by hard, firm returns of serve and deep, hard volleys. Laver's weakness was his excessive topspin which often made the ball bounce short and always made it bounce high. Jimmy hit the ball on the way up or at the top, never giving Rod time for the next shot.

Laver has always been one of the hardest hitters in the game. When he turned pro, he discovered his second serve was being torn apart by Hoad and Rosewall, and rather quickly he developed better length. His pro years saw one other big change in his game: he learned the value of dink returns and topspin lobs, and so touch shots were added to his power. He now had several options when the opponent attacked, whereas before he could only rely on bullets.

Connors seemed to have no weaknesses and many strengths. He does not have the touch shots, but his anticipation is excellent, he plays percentage tennis, he can serve and come in or serve and stay back, he will attack at the slightest opening, and he will never stay in the backcourt when he has his opponent on the run. He (along with Newcombe) has the most aggressive first volley in the game, and he also has the best return of service in tennis today. Add to that his speed of foot and his iron nerves, and he had to be the favorite in this match.

Connors played so well in the first two sets that it looked to be a straight set victory. As the third set began, Jimmy stopped coming in on every forcing shot, and he played as though Laver were already demoralized. But Laver is mentally tough; he never gave a gesture of dissatisfaction in the first two sets, and this helped him to play inspired tennis in the third and fourth. Rod broke Jimmy at 3-2 in the third, getting a particularly vital point on a slice ball that Jimmy could not get under. Rod began to serve so well that Connors never even got to break point thereafter.

Laver was the better player as the fourth set began. He broke Connors for 2-1 and was unlucky not to hold serve for 3-1: at 30-15 he just missed on a backhand volley. Games went with serve until 4-all. Jimmy was serving first, and this really put the pressure on Rod, who was down two sets to one and serving last. If Laver had been serving at 4-all, psychologically he would have been in a better position; even if he lost the game, he would have a chance to break back. Connors held for 5-4, and now it was Laver's turn. He was down five match points in this game and twice saved the point with a service ace. Rod smelled success and he served and played like a champion to pull even. There was one point where Jimmy threw up a lob, Rod failed to return it, and Jimmy thought the match was his. The lob was out.

One might have expected a letdown from Connors as he served at 5-all. He had lost five match points, and the crowd was cheering loudly for Laver because of his remarkable comeback. But gutsy Jimmy played fantastically to hold for 6-5. As he changed sides I made three suggestions. First, he should return serve more to the center because at this stage Laver could not afford to take the chance of making a great volley. Because of the tightness of the situation, Laver could not risk deep, decisive volleys. Second, if Laver stayed back, Jimmy was to come in and force Rod to pass him. Third, although Jimmy had mainly been going down-the-line on his passing shots, I suggested he go crosscourt. That is exactly what happened: at 0-30 Connors returned serve down the center, Laver volleyed and Jimmy then hit the passing shot crosscourt. (Connors got a little lucky because the ball hit the tape.) At 0-40, Rod served and stayed back; Jimmy came in. Rod lost his serve at love, and Jimmy pocketed $150,000.

JIMMY CONNORS *d* JOHN NEWCOMBE
6-3, 4-6, 6-2, 6-4/LAS VEGAS, 1975

Connors and Newcombe had played each other three times, once in a WTT one-set match in Houston, once at Forest Hills, and once in the Australian Open final just four months before.

Newk had won all three times. The Forest Hills encounter had been a good lesson: Newcombe had constantly forced on his forehand, and Jimmy had tried to go for too many winners on return of serve. Still, it had been a close quarterfinal, with Newk winning 6-4, 7-6, 7-6 and going on later to take the title. In 1974 Connors took every major event in which he played except Australia, where he lost to John. While Newcombe was beaten by Rosewall at both Wimbledon and Forest Hills, Connors had annihilated Rosewall in both those finals.

Again the match was held at Caesar's Palace in Las Vegas—and again CBS televised it live to a huge audience, although not one that compared to the King—Riggs encounter.

I sat on the court as Jimmy's coach for this match, too. We both had guessed what Newcombe's plan would be. John would try to vary his serve, mixing up wide ones with serves directly to the body; on key points he would try to press Jimmy by running around his backhand on second serve; in the ad court he would frequently serve down the line; he would dink backhand returns of serve to Jimmy's feet if Jimmy came in; his second serve would be as deep and almost as forcing as his first; he would come to net at every opportunity; and he would probably play well under pressure even though he had had very little competitive play in the last four months.

As it turned out, Newcombe's serve let him down and he was a little slower than usual. Jimmy, on the other hand, showed nerves of steel. They were playing for $250,000 (the largest purse ever for a tennis match), but also prestige and pride were resting on the outcome. The more that is riding on a match, the better Connors usually plays.

Jimmy won the first point by serving so wide to Newcombe's fore-hand that it put him in the alley. It is tough for a lefty to serve wide in the forehand court without getting into trouble, and it was a hell of a way to open the match. Connors deliberately did not follow his serve to net so that Newcombe would not have a target. Connors's pattern on serve was to be "no pattern." Sometimes he would come in on serve, and sometimes he would come in off Newcombe's return of serve. Therefore, if Newk dinked the return, Connors could come in on the second shot. By staying back at times, he kept Newk from getting grooved.

John's first serve was off due to the pressure of knowing his second serve would be attacked. He served a lot of double-faults because he tried to make his second serve too good. The Connors and Rosewall returns of serve are so deadly that the opponent often "overserves." Jimmy not only had a superb return of serve day, but he served the best of his career. He kept moving the ball: there was always the danger, if Connors kept serving to Newcombe's backhand, that John would get grooved and start to anticipate it, especially at 30-all.

In the course of the match Jimmy lost his serve only once, and that was when Newcombe hit a fantastic backhand crosscourt return of serve angle shot at 30-40. Jimmy had served the ball right into him, and John either got lucky or made the best calculated shot of the match. At no other time was Jimmy ever in trouble serving. Meantime, John was in trouble over and over on his own serve; he found himself at 30-all too many times. His big serve had deserted him and so, as it turned out, Jimmy served more aces than John. When Connors was ahead, particularly in the fourth set, he would serve wide to John's forehand—but he did not follow this serve in so that he cut down Newk's chances of hitting a winner by having Jimmy as a target. I was surprised that a lefty could serve so well wide to the forehand.

Repeatedly Connors played to John's weakness—the backhand. He came in down the line to Newk's backhand and John could not return down the line. This is the one poor shot in Newcombe's repertoire, since he can only dink to the feet or hit crosscourt.

Throughout the match Jimmy anticipated beautifully, particularly on return of serve, and was unbelievably quick with his hands. He not only hit out freely from both sides but he was also consistent. Newcombe, on the other hand, could not confuse Connors with a variety of serves since Jimmy was "guessing" him.

Analyzing these two head-to-head matches is an interesting exercise. It enables one to compare patterns (or nonpatterns) of play and the way one champion eventually was able to dominate or outsmart another. Big money and prestige were on the line, and the pressures were enormous. The mark of the truly great champion is to win when the pressures of winning (and losing) are greatest. Stroke or tactical weaknesses are exploited in such encounters. Connors took the loot and the glory, but Laver's play was so superb in the last half of his match against Jimmy that one can only regret he is past his prime.

ARTHUR ASHE *d* JIMMY CONNORS
6-1, 6-1, 5-7, 6-4/WIMBLEDON FINAL, 1975

Connors, as defending champion, was highly favored over Ashe, whom he had beaten in all three of their previous meetings. Ashe had struggled in the semifinals to beat Tony Roche 5-7, 6-4, 7-5, 8-9, 6-4, whereas Connors had overwhelmed hard-hitting Roscoe Tanner 6-4, 6-1, 6-4. Tanner had beaten Connors just a few weeks before, and with Jimmy reversing the results so easily it seemed he was playing at the top of his game.

I wasn't in England, so I saw the match on television. The most noticeable factors were Connors's poor return of serve and Ashe's intelligent tactics, coolness, and unshakable forehand volley.

Ashe talked to Tanner after the latter's match against Jimmy, and Tanner warned him against playing the Connors game of big serves, hard, aggressive ground shots to the corners, and booming, deep volleys. The harder Tanner had hit, the better Connors had returned the ball. Ashe therefore decided on a totally different strategy: serves at three-quarter pace, forehand chips, low balls down the center, and plenty of lobs. This wasn't the typical Ashe game, but Arthur felt it was better to give up the "big serve" in order to get more first serves in. He also planned to keep the ball low and short to Jimmy, since Connors is much more aggressive on balls that bounce waist-high or above.

Ashe has an excellent wide-to-the-forehand serve in the forehand court (in this case, it was wide to lefty Connors's two-handed backhand). Since Connors knew that Ashe could pull him wide in the forehand court, he should have stood in farther to cut off the angles. But Connors chose to copy his good friend Ilie Nastase, who stands 2 feet behind the baseline to return serve because he topspins every return. The dangerous factor in this tactic is that it allows the server more time to come in and the server can also drop-volley. Nastase gets away with standing way back because of his agility and flexibility. Connors is not that flexible on return of serve.

Ashe had a new plan, but Connors had only the old plan which was to use Arthur's pace to hit aggressive returns. By the third game of the first set, Ashe was succeeding with his chips, lobs, and low, short balls to the forehand. With the score 1-1 and 40-15 for Connors on his own serve, he netted, hit out, and then overhit on a smash to lose the game. He only won one of the next eleven games to be down 6-1, 6-1.

The low short ball to the center is good against any player but particularly good against two-handers. This is Chris Evert's weakness, too, since she is forced to come in—and her coming-in shot is not that good when the ball is under net level. Connors handles high balls and wide balls extremely well because he is a counterhitter. The weakness in his game was revealed by Ashe, and Connors had no riposte since he cannot drop-shot fluently and he cannot hit with enough topspin to clear the net and return deep and hard.

The surprising part of Ashe's game was his consistent, strong forehand volley. This has always been his weakness, but it has been played so often that perhaps it may turn out to be his strength. He got down to the ball beautifully and the volley action was shorter and more precise.

I have watched Jimmy play many matches, and this was the worst I have ever seen him return serve. When one stroke is off, the rest of the game usually begins to suffer; in this case it was Connors's first serve; it simply wasn't going in often enough. The deliberate way in which Ashe had changed his style of play could account in large part for the break-up in Connors's game. What Connors expected as an Ashe weakness turned out to be a strength: Ashe didn't miss a forehand volley until the fourth set!

Jimmy was in the match only in short spurts. He was down 2-3 in the third, having lost his serve, but pulled himself together to break back when Ashe missed an overhead. At 5-all in the third Connors was twice down break point, and momentarily it looked like the old, confident Jimmy when he took that game, then returned serve beautifully to take the set. He led 3-0 in the fourth but won only one of the next seven games. Ashe chipped, lobbed, dinked, and volleyed, letting Connors make the errors.

The television cameras showed Arthur on the changeovers sitting in a chair with his eyes closed as though he were meditating. His body was relaxed as he regularly found and kept his composure. He never varied his plan, and small lapses in the third set and early part of the fourth were immediately forgotten. Arthur Ashe seemed a man of iron. He is a great human being and a gentleman, and in this crucial final his strokes, his tactics, his composure, and his nerves overcame the many failures in previous years. He won the biggest title of his career by using every facet of the game.

MANUEL ORANTES *d* JIMMY CONNORS
6-4, 6-3, 6-3/FOREST HILLS FINAL, 1975

This time the surface was slow clay (Har-Tru) and Connors's opponent was Manuel Orantes, who had never won a big title other than the Italian championships in 1972. The Spaniard is an excellent clay court player with an effortless game. Manuel can lob, drop-shot, hit approach shots, or rally from the back court. If his opponent comes to net, he has enough topspin to hit good passing shots but he doesn't overroll, and so in rallies his forehand goes deep. His backhand slice is both accurate and effective on clay because with the same motion he can drop-shot.

The night before the final, Orantes was involved in what seemed to be a hopeless match against Guillermo Vilas. Vilas was leading by two sets to one and 5-0 in the fourth. That was at 9:00 P.M. An hour and a half later Orantes had won the match 4-6, 1-6, 6-2, 7-5, 6-4. In the other half Connors had been a bit lucky against Bjorn Borg. If the latter had won the fourth set, the outcome might have been different.

Orantes played a brilliant final, soft-balling Connors, hitting disguised passing shots with extreme precision, and even coming in himself to make winning volleys. Connors might have taken him too lightly because of the long five-setter Manuel had the previous evening and because Manuel had never before reached the finals of Forest Hills.

I had suggested to Jimmy that he play Orantes's forehand, which he did in the early part of the first set. Jimmy's good friend Ilie Nastase had told him to play Orantes' backhand, but Jimmy didn't concentrate on either side exclusively, except for those few games in the middle of the first set.

All of Manuel's errors were bunched in the first two games of the first set. This might have been from stiffness and fatigue from the previous evening's semifinal, but thereafter he established an unshakable rhythm.

Only in Davis Cup and in head-to-head television encounters are coaches allowed on the court to help their players. Coaching is forbidden in tournaments, and that's one rule I'd like to see abolished. If coaching were permitted in the finals of the French, Wimbledon, and Forest Hills championships, the tennis could be that much better. It certainly has been beneficial to Davis Cup play. If I could have talked to Connors on the odd games in his match against Orantes, I would have told him to come to net more to cut off the soft balls and to break up Orantes's rhythm. He could have come in more often on serve—and particularly on return of serve, since Orantes's returns were soft and Jimmy should have volleyed them. One can also drop-volley a soft ball for surprise.

While Borg's high-bouncing forehands and backhands set up for Connors (he could hit down on the ball), Orantes's balls were sliced low off the backhand and he forced Jimmy to dig up on his approach shots. Manuel probed Jimmy's biggest weakness, which is not getting under the ball enough. When Jimmy got a short, low ball and tried to attack off it, he netted or hit long. Even when he made his approach shot, it lacked the sting that he always has on a faster court or against a harder ball, and Orantes passed him frequently.

The underspin backhand of Orantes was impeccable, but his forehand was also superbly consistent. The only time it wavered was when Orantes was leading 4-2 in the first set and Connors pounded his opponent's forehand in long exchanges to level at 4-all. Thereafter Orantes played superb clay court tennis, maneuvering Jimmy with soft balls, lobs, drop shots, and beautiful passing shots. He broke Jimmy at 15 to win the first set 6-4; he then knew his opponent could not hurt him if he continued his steady, accurate, soft ball tactics.

Connors had two other chances to forge ahead. He broke Orantes's serve in the fifth game of the second set after Manuel was leading 40-0. Again Jimmy vainly tried to attack, but he couldn't generate the pace he wanted or achieve the required depth without falling into innumerable errors. Jimmy's last chance was in the third set when he was down 0-2, then won three games in a row and had break point for the next one. But the attacker was stymied because his opponent would feed him only low balls or drop shots or spinning lobs. Orantes was in a groove that kept Connors from getting a groove, and Jimmy could find no countermeasures.

Orantes had never played a better match. He analyzed his opponent to perfection. Most players would agree that the scores would be reversed on a fast court, but Orantes proved himself a supreme clay court artist with the strokes, the tactics, the composure, and the nerves to win a major title over another great champion.

Chapter Thirty
A Tennis Glossary Or.
How to Talk a Championship Game

Ad (Advantage).   *See Scoring System.*

Ad in.   Game point for the server.   (See *Scoring System.*)

Ad out.   Game point for the receiver.

Ace.   An unreachable serve (the receiver is not able to touch the ball). An ace refers only to a serve; any other unreachable shot, viz., groundstroke, volley or overhead, is called a placement.

Aetna World Cup.   An annual match between male professionals representing the U. S. and Australia.   It is played in Hartford, Conn., during a specified week in the winter, and the contestants are among the top players in their respective countries.   The Aetna World Cup is a special event promoted by WCT (World Championship Tennis).

Age division.   Junior and Senior events are restricted to players under or over a certain age.   In the Junior division, there are tournaments for players 10-and-under, 12-and-under, 14-and-under, 16-and-under and 18-and-under.   In the Senior division, events are for players 30 and over, 35 and over, 40, 45, 50, 55, 60, 65, 70 and 75.   There are National Championships in most of these categories.

Alley.   An area of the court parallel to the sidelines that is used in doubles only.   A player who hits the ball in the alley in singles loses the point; an alley ball is "good" in doubles.   See *Court Diagram.*

Amateur.   A player who does not accept prize money.   The major spectator tournaments throughout the world are professional events, and almost every player who competes in them is a pro, the lone exceptions being a scattering of Juniors, some intercollegiate players who are on college scholarships and players from the Soviet Union.

Amateur events.   Events restricted to amateurs.   There are very few left, the majority being Junior tournaments (*See Age division*) and college events. The U. S. National Amateur entries consist totally of Juniors or college players.

American twist. A serve that is hit with the face of the racket crossing from left to right. When the ball bounces, it moves to the receiver's left (into his body on the forehand, away from his body on the backhand), assuming both server and receiver are right-handers.

Approach shot. A shot behind which the player advances to net. It is not meant to end the point but to put the player in a good position to make the next shot a winning volley and his opponent in a bad position to hit a passing shot.

ATP. The Association of Tennis Professionals, an all-male group that includes almost all the best current pros in the game. The executive director was originally Jack Kramer (it is now Bob Briner) and the legal counsel is Donald Dell. The ATP does not recognize the authority of individual nations over its members which is a source of conflict among the ATP, ILTF and various national tennis associations. ATP members pay annual dues of $400. The only top player to date who has not joined the organization is Jimmy Connors.

Australian grip. A grip popularized by the Australians during the last 15 years. There is a slight, almost imperceptible change between forehand and backhand grips, but the grip is very close to an Eastern backhand. The Australian forehand stroke style resembles the Eastern forehand style—the same kind of wind-up and follow-through but with a less firm wrist. The advantage of the Australian style is that one doesn't have to change grips.

Backboard. A high board, often placed on the side or the back fence of a court, which is used by players for practicing strokes. A good backboard is usually 12 feet in height and 15 or 20 feet wide.

Backhand. A ball hit on the left side of the body by a right-handed player, or on the right side of the body by a left-handed player.

Backswing. The arc or swing the racket makes preparatory to its forward swing to meet the ball. The backswing is typically bigger on slow courts or against soft shots and it is typically smaller on fast courts or against hard shots when there is less time to prepare.

Bad bounce. A ball that bounces crazily because of a defect in the surface of the court, not because of the spin of the ball. There are frequent bad bounces on grass (especially wet grass), on rough clay, on tapes that serve for lines or on cracked courts.

Bad call. A ball that is called out when it was actually good.

Ball boy. A boy who picks up balls quickly when the point is over, thus saving wear and tear on the contestants.

Ball machine. An electric machine that throws a series of balls over the net automatically. Some ball machines can be adjusted to throw a variety of balls—high ones, hard ones or medium-paced shots, alternating from left court to right court.

"Big." A term used by some players to indicate the ball was over the baseline. Not in common usage.

Big game. See *Serve-and-Volley Game.*

Block. A short stroke with almost no backswing and very little follow-through that is often used against hard serves. Block volleys have almost no backswing and a follow-through of less than a foot. They are used against hard shots to the body of the volleyer.

Bonne Bell Cup. An annual contest between female players representing the U. S. and Australia with prize money awarded to the players. There are six singles and three doubles matches, with the top two American singles players each meeting the top two Australian players. The site alternates annually between Australia and the U. S.

Cannonball. A bullet-like serve. The cannonball only refers to hard serves, not to hard overheads, groundstrokes or volleys.

Carry. A ball that is caught on the racket, held and then thrown back, very much like a jai alai shot. The player who carries the ball loses the point. It is often hard to judge a carry, and if there is no umpire, the player who does so is supposed to call it on himself. Often an opponent or an umpire will ask the player: "Was that a carry?", a legitimate inquiry. Good players almost always know when they have carried a ball by the sound (there is no clear "hit" tone).

Cement. A term commonly used by Californians to refer to Portland cement concrete, a common California surface. Cement courts are hard on the feet and hard on the balls, but the bounce is predictable and no daily maintenance is required. Most cement courts are fast, but a retriever or steady player can still do well on them.

Center marks. A short line, usually two inches in the center of each baseline (see *Court Diagram*). The server must remain on the right side of the center mark when serving into the forehand court, and on the left side of the center mark when serving into the backhand court. If he steps on the line, the serve is a fault.

Center service line. The line on each side of the court that goes from the middle of the net to the service line, thus separating the forehand court from the backhand court (see *Court Diagram*).

Change of pace artist. A player who mixes up his shots. He hits some balls hard, some high and deep, some sharp angles, some drop shots and he also varies his spins. In other words, the pace is never the same.

Changing sides. Changing sides on the odd game, viz., *when the total number of games played* in a set add up to 1, 3, 5, 7, 9, etc. In tournament play, the time limit allowed for changing sides is 60 seconds.

Challenge Round. An archaic term describing the old-style Davis Cup finals (see *Davis Cup*).

Chewed up. A term that refers to balls whose fuzz has worn off after considerable play (or after a short amount of play on a rough surface). Balls get chewed up quickest on asphalt and California cement.

Chip shot. A groundstroke hit with a volley-like action. It is usually used either as a return of serve or as an approach shot (see *Approach shot*). A chip shot has underspin, which makes it a good approach shot, and it is an abbreviated stroke, which makes it useful against a big serve.

Choke. A freezing up of the normal stroke due to nerves. The free backswing may become stiff, the follow-through stilted, the feet planted, the ball taken late, the legs rigid, and the timing impossible.

Chop. This was a popular shot in the 1920s and 1930s. It is rarely seen today except among the old-time players. It resembles a chip but it is a much longer stroke, with a full backswing and follow-through. The old-style player used it instead of a forehand drive. It is an underspin shot and therefore lacks the power of a drive.

Circuit. A series of consecutive tournaments with most of the same players signing up for the entire series, although this is not a prerequisite of all circuits.

Clay. A generic term for courts composed of clay, dirt, composition, crushed shell, cow dung (throughout India), etc. These courts are composed of finely ground materials that are compacted together by being tamped down firmly. They get dusty in the wind (the top surface blows off), hard as rocks during a dry spell, soft as mush after heavy rains and full of bad bounces after the court has been played on for a few hours. Clay courts are slow (one can chase down balls that would be placements on faster surfaces), they require constant maintenance to keep them playable, lines must be painted or tacked on, they are relatively cheap to install, and they are soft on the feet. They are the favorite surface of many players and are disliked enormously by players who learned to play on a faster surface. There are far more clay courts in the world than courts of any other type.

Close call. A euphemism for a bad call. Those who call the ball close are, euphemistically, cheats.

Closed stance. Stepping sideways just before or after the hit so that the weight moves sideways rather than forward. Three decades ago many pros taught a closed (sideways) step: the left foot stepped toward the right alley on the forehand, the right foot stepped toward the left alley on the backhand. This prevented the body weight from moving into the ball and therefore power came primarily from arm or wrist rather than from weight transfer. No one teaches this approach any more. Players will sometimes be forced into hitting a ball with a closed stance as when they are run wide and end up with the body moving sideways.

Closed tournaments. Events restricted to a certain category of players. For example, some pro tournaments exclude amateurs and amateur events exclude pros. There are quite a few regional events which restrict the entries to players (amateurs or pros) coming from that region.

Continental grip. A grip popularized in Europe many decades ago. It resembles an Eastern backhand, but the one grip is used for both forehand and backhand. The Continental is similar to the Australian grip although the style is different: the Continental forehand has a lot of wrist movement and the racket head points upward (the wrist is cocked). This gives disguise, touch, and wrist power.

Contract pro. An archaic term for a pro who signed a contract to a professional promoter to play only for him. Today pros sign up only for circuits (a specific number of weeks) or commit themselves to specific tournaments. One of the last of the contract pros is Cliff Richey, who signed with WCT. Several years ago WCT signed a pact with the ILTF not to sign up any more players to contracts.

Court diagram. See illustration.

Crosscourt. A ball that is hit from one side of the court to the diagonally opposite side—in the case of two right-handers, a forehand crosscourt would go to the opponent's forehand and a backhand crosscourt to the opponent's backhand.

Cut. A term used only by those who don't know tennis terminology—e.g., "He gave the ball a terrific cut."

Davis Cup. A men's international competition played between nations. It is an elimination event, with the countries split into zones—two zones in Europe, one in America and one in Asia. The zone winners play semifinals, with the winners meeting in the final. Each match (or tie, as it is often called) consists of four singles and one doubles; two players are selected for the singles and they each play two matches. There is no prize money although some countries pay their players and give them bonuses if they win. Amateurs and pros are eligible to play but contract pros are barred. The Davis Cup used to be a purely amateur event until most of the world's best players turned pro. Until 1973 the winner of the previous year automatically got into the finals without playing a match, then played the winner of all the other nations in what was called a Challenge Round.

Deep. Description of a ball that lands in the area near the baseline.

Defensive shot. A ball hit without power, often a high, soft shot, to enable the player to get back into position.

Deuce. *See Scoring System.*

Deuce set. A set that goes past 5-all, viz., 7-5. Before the tiebreaker was introduced, there were many long deuce sets since a player was required to win a set by at least a margin of two games.

Dewar Cup. A five-week indoor circuit in England for men and women players during the fall.

Court diagram:

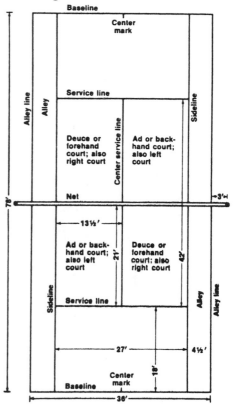

Dink. A soft, dipping shot that clears the net by a small margin and bounces low (under net level); also any soft shot. Retrievers are sometimes called "dinkers."

Double fault. Failure of both first and second serve to go into the proper court, resulting in loss of the point.

Doubles. A game played with two players on each side. After the serve is put into play, a ball hit in the alley is "good." The players alternate in serving games and alternate in receiving. If A and B are playing C and D, A serves a game, C serves a game, B serves the next game and D the fourth game. In A's service game, he serves the first point to C in the forehand court, the second point to D in the backhand court, the third point to C in the forehand court, etc., until the game is won. If C chooses to play the forehand court, he must do so in every game until the set is over.

Down-the-line. Hitting the ball in a line parallel to the sidelines. If two right-handers are playing, a player hitting his forehand down-the-line would be hitting to his opponent's backhand; a player hitting his backhand down-the-line would be hitting to his opponent's forehand.

Draw sheet. A sheet that shows how players will meet in a tournament. In an elimination event with 32 players, the draw sheet will show 16 matches in the first column (the first round), eight matches in the second column (the second round), four matches in the third column (the quarterfinals), two matches in the fourth column (the semifinals), and one match in the fifth column (the final).

Drive. A forehand or backhand groundstroke featuring a full backswing and follow-through.

Drop shot. A ball hit off a groundstroke with enough underspin to make it drop to the ground just after it clears the net and to have very little or no forward motion after the bounce. Sometimes so much backspin is put on the ball that after it bounces, it will go *back* over the net.

Drop volley. A shot similar to a drop shot except that it is hit off a volley.

Dump. Deliberate throwing of a match.

Dump shot. A ball hit very gently from a position close to the net so that it barely goes over the net. A dump shot differs from a drop shot in that there is no underspin or backspin.

Eastern backhand. The "V" between thumb and forefinger is either on top of the rocket handle or slightly to the left.

Eastern forehand. The "V" between thumb and forefinger is a quarter turn to the right from the Eastern backhand.

The Eighteens. The age division for players eighteen and under.

The Elbow. A synonym for the choke. A player who has "the elbow" is a victim of nerves.

Fast surface. A court that allows hard-hit balls to travel very fast after bouncing. Fast surfaces are wood, grass, cement and some carpets.

Fault. The failure of a serve to go into the proper service box. There is no penalty on the first fault and the server is given a second chance. See *Double fault*.

Federation Cup. An international female competition between nations which is played in a designated city during a one-week period. It is an elimination tournament, with each match consisting of two singles and a doubles. This is the female version of the Davis Cup, although the latter is played over a one-year period in many different countries.

Fence ball. A wild ball that will hit the fence before it bounces.

Fifteen. The first point of a game (see *Scoring System*).

Finals. The last match of a tournament (see *Draw sheet*).

"First one in." A remark frequently made by a player in a nontournament match to indicate that, on the first point of the first serve, there cannot be a double fault: the player can keep on serving until the ball finally goes into the proper court. This is only done on the first point of the first service game for each player; it is not permitted in tournament play.

Follow-through. The finish of a stroke after the racket has hit the ball.

Foot-fault. A fault on serve caused by one foot touching the line or stepping inside the court or going over the center mark before the ball is hit. Jumping in the air is not a foot-fault, even if both feet are well in the court, provided neither foot makes contact with the ground before the ball is hit.

Forehand. A ball hit on the right side of the body by a right-hander or on the left side of the body by a left-hander.

Foreign seed. A term seldom used today since tournaments no longer separate foreign and domestic seeds because the game has become so international. Twenty years ago, and for many years before that, tournaments such as the U.S. Championships would have only a few foreign entries. These players would be separated from each other and from the top domestic players by placing them in different quarters of the draw. See *Seed*.

Forest Hills. A section in the borough of Queens (part of New York City) in Long Island, New York, where the U.S. Open is annually played. Not to be confused with Forest Lawn, a cemetery in Los Angeles.

Forty. The third point of the game. See *Scoring System*.

Fourteens. A designation for players fourteen years old or younger. See *Age division*.

Fuzz. The nap on a ball.

Game. A segment of a set, which in turn is a segment of a match. See *Scoring System*.

Game point. A position in which a player needs only one point to win the game (he is either at "40" or at "Ad"). See *Scoring System*.

Good call. A ball that is called good by a player although it *seems* as though the opponent hit it out.

Grand Slam. The winning of the four major titles of the world in one year. These titles are the Australian, the French, Wimbledon and the U.S. Championships. Only four players in history have won the Grand Slam—Don Budge, Rod Laver (twice), Maureen Connolly, and Margaret Court.

Grass. A court composed of grass. There are grass courts in Australia, England, the United States (mostly in the East), New Zealand, and India but hardly anywhere else.

Grip. The position of the hand in relation to the racket. The four grips are known as the Eastern, the Continental, the Australian, and the Western.

Groundstroke. A ball hit after it has bounced. Groundstrokes can be either forehands or backhands.

Gut. Strings of the racket that are made from the intestines of animals.

Hacker. A player of nondescript tennis ability.

Half-volley. A ball hit just after the bounce, when it is as low as 6 inches off the ground. It is actually not a volley but a groundstroke.

Handicap tournament. A competition in which players are given points or games or must win extra points or games to even the differences between the weaker and the better players. As an example, a poor player might start every game at "30" or even "40," while a top player might have a handicap of "minus 40" (he would have to win three points just to get to "love").

Hard courts. Surfaces that are hard and cohesive such as cement, asphalt or any of the acrylics that are painted over asphalt—Laykold, Dynaturf, Plexipave, etc. Hard courts require no maintenance. In Europe the term *hard court* refers to a clay court.

Heavy-duty balls. Balls that have a thicker nap and last longer than regular balls. They are frequently used on very fast courts since the heavy-duty balls are more sluggish and slightly slow down the play.

High-altitude balls. Special balls made for high-altitude play (regular balls float too much in rarefied air).

High ball.   A ball that bounces to shoulder-height or higher.

Hitting down on the ball.   Following through with a downward motion, which can be done effectively on a high, short ball.

ILTF.   The International Lawn Tennis Federation, the world governing body of the amateur tennis world and, in part, of the professional world, although their degree of authority has been disputed by the Association of Tennis Professionals and World Team Tennis.

Independent pro.   A playing pro not under contract to a promoter or to WTT or WCT.

Invitation tournament.   A competition open only to players invited to participate.   The object is to insure the event a high standard of play, and so hackers seldom are invited.

Junior.   A player eighteen or under (see *Age division*).

Junior Vet.   A player thirty-five or older (see *Age division*).

Junk-ball artist.   A player who uses a variety of spins.

Let.   A call to replay the point.   When the ball hits the net on serve but lands in the correct court, a let is called and the first or second serve, whichever it may be, is replayed.   A let is also called because of an interruption of play, such as a ball rolling into the court from another court.

Linesman.   An official in a match who calls "out balls" on a particular line.   A linesman can call the baseline, the sideline or the service line. In an important match, there are usually linesmen sitting on every line.

Loaded draw.   A draw in which many of the good players wind up in the same quarter.   This can happen in a 64 draw when only eight players are seeded: since the next eight players are drawn out of a hat, they might be bunched together in one quarter (see *Seed*).

Lob.   A ball that is intended to go over the net man's head by a safe margin or any very high ball that would go over an imaginary net man's head.

Lob-volley.   A lob hit by a volleying net man over the opposite net man's head.

Long.   A term that indicates a ball that landed beyond the baseline.

Loose.   A description of a player who looks as though he has no nerves and whose body seems totally relaxed.

Love.   Zero points (see *Scoring System*).

Low ball.   A ball whose bounce is not as high as the net.

Marathon set.   A term seldom used since the introduction of the tiebreaker.   When tiebreakers are not used, as in the Davis Cup, a set can go on to 16-14 or even 20-18 if the players are relatively even.

Match. A contest between two players (a singles match) or four players (a doubles match). Matches are either the best of three sets or, in some major tournaments, the best of five sets. Women are never required to play more than three sets, although there have been two exceptions: the Billie Jean King—Bobby Riggs match was the best of five sets and the final of the International Mixed Doubles at Dallas is the best of five sets.

Match point. That time in the match when a player is one point away from winning.

Mini Circuit. A series of tournaments for women players who are just under the top echelon.

Mixed doubles. Man—woman against man—woman.

The Nationals. The National Championships of a country. The U.S. Open is considered the Nationals in this country, but there are also a number of other National Championships—the National Clay Courts, the National Hard Courts, the National Indoors, the National Intercollegiates, the National Interscholastics, the National Juniors, the National Junior Hard Courts, the National Junior Clay Courts, etc. There are national titles in every division from the age of twelve to the age of seventy-five. Some age groups have four different national titles on four different surfaces.

Net. The barrier that separates the opponents. It is 3 feet high at the center and 3 feet 6 inches high at the net posts.

Net umpire. An official who sits with his hand on the net and advises when a serve ticks the net. His other functions are to call "carry" and "not up" and to keep a running duplicate score card.

New balls. Freshly opened balls. In most tournaments, new balls are used for each match and new balls are usually given if the match goes to three sets. In the biggest tournaments, new balls are given after every nine or eleven games.

No-Ad. A system of scoring invented by James Van Alen in which points are counted as "1, 2, 3, game" rather than "15, 30, 40, game." In the regular system, a player has to win a game by two points; under No-Ad, the first player to get 4 points wins the game. Therefore at 3-3, both players are at game point.

No Man's Land. The area of the court between the service line and three or four feet inside the baseline. It is called No Man's Land because it is a difficult area to handle deep, hard balls or shots into the ankles.

Not up. The call after a ball has bounced twice. Sometimes a player hits the ball just as it is about to bounce twice (or just after it has) and then the call is difficult to make.

Nylon. Strings made of nylon used in racket instead of gut. Nylon is cheaper, lasts longer, and the strings will not snap in wet weather.

However, the string job tends to loosen up with time. Most tournament players use gut but some will have an extra racket strung with nylon. Most beginners use nylon since they are not at the stage where they can feel the difference.

On the line. The call that means the ball was good. A ball is still in play as long as it touches any part of the line.

On the rise. Taking the ball as it is coming off the ground when it has not yet reached its full height.

Open stance. Feet facing the net as the ball is hit. The open stance is used by a number of top players on forehands: the feet face the net but the shoulders pivot. This style is seldom taught to beginners or intermediates. See *Closed stance* and *Sideways stance*.

Open tennis. Unheard of before 1968, accepted today. It means pros and amateurs are allowed to compete in the same tournaments. See *Closed tournaments*. Before 1968, professionals were barred from playing any of the USLTA or ILTF events.

Overhand. No such word in the tennis player's vocabulary.

Overhead. A ball hit when it is over the area of the head with a swing similar to the serve. It is also known as a smash when it is hit hard.

Overspin. See *Topspin*.

Passing shot. A ball that passes the net man. The three passing shots are the crosscourt, the down-the-line and the lob.

Percentage tennis. Playing the shots or using the strategy that gives you the best chance to win—e.g., hitting deep down-the-line on a forehand approach shot against a right-hander. The term was introduced by Jack Kramer in the mid-1940s.

Permanent fixture. The net posts, the lights on the court, the chairs around the court, the linesmen, etc. A point is never replayed if the ball hits a permanent fixture; the player who hit it loses the point.

Pick-up shot. A return off a ball that bounds near the ankles. As long as it is not a carry or a double-bounce, it is a good shot.

Placement. An untouchable winner off a groundstroke, volley or overhead but not off a serve (see *Ace*).

Playing to the score. A term used in percentage tennis. An example: at 30-40 the server tries to get the first ball in instead of going for an ace.

Power. The speed of the ball.

Pressure. Attacking or simulating an attack to force the opponent to make an excellent shot. If the attack is not forceful, no pressure is put on the opponent.

Pro. A player who competes for money prizes in tennis or accepts money for teaching.

Pro set.   The first player to get eight games wins the set and the match. This scoring was introduced by Jack Kramer when he was a promoter of pro matches.   Pro sets are now used when a tournament is behind schedule or when an event is played off in one day or sometimes for third-place playoffs.

Pro Tour.   A circuit or series of exhibitions or tournaments involving any number of professional players.   In the 1920s and 1930s, pro tours consisted of two to four top players competing in exhibitions throughout the countries.   Today the two most famous pro tours, WCT and Virginia Slims, stage a series of tournaments involving most of the leading players.

Psyched up.   Keyed to peak form for a particular match or tournament.

Quarters.   The quarterfinals of a tournament.   See *Draw sheet.*

Racket face.   The strings of the racket.

Racket head.   The racket face and the wood or metal surrounding it.

Racket press.   A wooden or metal clamp that fits over the racket head to prevent it from warping.   Presses were used frequently in the old days before rackets were made of laminated wood.   Now they are used mainly in hot, damp climates (they are not necessary in air conditioned areas).

Rally.   An exchange of balls over the net.   Some beginners mistakenly say "volley" instead of "rally"—as in "Let's volley some."   See *Volley.*

Ranking.   A rating of players at the end of the season or year to indicate who had the best records.

Ready Position.   The correct stance of a player when he is waiting for the ball.

Receiver.   The player who is returning serve.

Referee.   The person in charge of the entire tournament, not to be confused with the umpire who is in charge of a particular match.

Rest period.   The 10-minute intermission between the second and third sets in a best-of-three-set match or between the third and fourth sets in a best-of-five-set match.   Rest periods were optional in almost all tournaments until 1973: if one player requested the rest, it was granted.   Today many tournaments have discarded the rest period because the tiebreaker prevents marathon matches.

Retriever.   A player who relies on running down a great many balls to win matches.

Return of serve.   The return of a service by the receiver.

Reverse crosscourt.   A ball hit on a diagonal from the left side of the body to the right court or from the right side of the body to the left court, assuming the player is right-handed. Example: a player in the forehand court hits a backhand to the opponent's forehand court.

Reverse twist. A serve in which the racket face comes over the ball in a right-to-left motion. It was popular in the old days and is used on rare occasions by good players to confuse someone who doesn't understand spin.

Riordan Circuit. A series of winter prize money tournaments organized by Bill Riordan for male independent pros. The circuit is played at the same time as WCT. One of the regulars on the Riordan Circuit is Jimmy Connors who has refused to sign with WCT. The Riordan Circuit has a few top stars and some promising young players but not as many of the top ranking players as WCT.

"Rough or smooth." An antiquated call when spinning for serve. Rackets used to have color trim for decorative purposes at the top and bottom of the racket head. "Rough" meant the reverse side of the trim and "smooth" the top side. Now players spin for serve by calling the manufacturer's label, viz., M or W on a Wilson racket.

Round of 16. The second round in a draw of 32 or the third round in a draw of 64 (see *Draw*).

Round Robin. A nonelimination tournament in which each player plays every other player. The winner is the one who has taken the greatest number of games.

Sanction fee. A payment to an association for the privilege of holding a tournament or an exhibition.

Satellite Circuit. The male version of the Mini Circuit. It provides a series of tournaments for men pros who are just below the level of WCT and the Riordan Circuit.

Scoring System. A tennis match is composed of points, games, and sets. Points are scored as "love" (no points), 15 (the first point), 30 (second point), 40 (third point), and "game" (the last point). The server's score is always given first: if the server has won two points, the score is "30-love"; if the server has won three points and the receiver one point, the score is "40-15"; if the server has won no points and the receiver one point, the score is "love-15." A player has to win a game by a margin of at least two points. Therefore when each player has won three points, the score is not called "40-40" but "deuce" to indicate that one of the players must now win by two points. The player who wins the next point has "advantage" (or "ad"). If it is the server who wins that point, the score is "ad in"; if the receiver wins the point, the score is "ad out." If the player who has the "ad" wins the next point, he has the game; if he loses the next point, the score goes back to "deuce." A game can have many deuces if neither player can win two points in a row from deuce.

Player A serves the first game, Player B the second game; Player A the third game, Player B the fourth game, etc., in regular rotation. A player serves the first point from behind the baseline and from a position to the right of the center mark to the opponent's forehand court (see *Court diagram*), the second point from behind the baseline and from a position to the left of the center mark to the opponent's backhand court, etc., until the game is over. The players change sides on odd games (see *Changing sides*).

The first player to win six games takes the set, provided he has won the set by at least two games. Players can win sets by scores of 6-love, 6-1, 6-2, 6-3 or 6-4 but not by 6-5. In the past, sets could go on forever if neither player could get a two-game edge. Today, in most tournaments, a tiebreaker is played when games reach 6-all to determine the set winner (see *Tiebreaker*).

Most matches are the best of three sets: the first player to win two sets takes the match. Some major men's tournaments are "best of five sets": the first player to win three sets takes the match.

Second serve. A "second chance" for the server if he does not get his first serve in.

Seed. Placement of a leading player in a tournament draw. The best player in the tournament (the No. 1 seed) is placed in one half of the draw and the second best (the No. 2 seed) in the other half. If the tournament has 16 players, four can be seeded (the four best) and they will be placed in different quarters of the draw. A tournament with 32 players can have up to eight seeds and an event with 64 players can have 16 seeds. Seeding was adopted to prevent the two best players from meeting in the first round and from having all the good players bunched into one half of the draw. The seeding changes with each tournament: Joe Schlunck may be the No. 1 seed in the Podunk City tournament but he would never be seeded No. 1 at the U.S. Open. Seedings should not be confused with rankings.

Semis. The semi-finals of a tournament. See *Draw sheet*.

Senior. A man player forty-five or over or a woman player forty or over. See *Age division*.

Serve. The stroke that starts the point. Customarily it is hit by tossing the ball in the air and hitting it with arm and racket extended high above the head. The rules do not prevent a player from serving the ball at waist level (see *Underhand serve*) but the serve must be hit from a tossed ball, viz., one cannot bounce the ball and then hit it. If the serve does not go in the correct service box or if the player's foot touches the line or the court, the serve is a fault. The server gets a "second chance" with a second serve. If this is also a fault, he loses the point.

Serve-and-volley game. A style of play in which the server follows his delivery to net. Players with big serves and/or big net games usually follow this pattern of play, which is sometimes called the Big Game. Most of the leading men players of today and many of the leading women players follow their serves to net, the exception being on very slow surfaces. Thirty years ago there were few net rushers; twenty years ago there were many more; today there are far more serve-and-volleyers than baseliners among the men pros.

Service break.   Winning the opponent's serve; losing your own serve.

Service court.   The box in which the serve must land (see *Court diagram*).

Service line.   The line bounding one side of the service court that runs parallel to the baseline.

Set.   A division of a match composed of at least six games.   See *Scoring system*.

Set point.   A stage of the match when one of the players need win only one more point to take the set.

Set-up.   A short, high ball that is always a winner for a champion and almost always a winner for a good player.

Seven and Nine.   A notation that indicates when new balls will be given out in a big match.   In this particular case, new balls are given as the match starts and the players use them for the warm-up and for the first seven games.   Thereafter new balls are given every nine games. If the ball change is made on "nine and eleven," the players use the new balls for the first nine games, then get new balls every eleven games.

Seven-six.   A set score that indicates a player won in a tiebreaker after the game score reached 6-all.   See *Tiebreaker*.

Sideline.   The long lines on either side of a court that are the boundaries in singles (see *Court diagram*).

Sidespin.   Spin that is put on a ball by letting the racket face come across the ball as well as forward (from right to left when hitting a forehand).   Sidespin is used most frequently on forehand approach shots down-the-line.

Sideways stance.   A stance half way between the Closed and the Open stances.   The side of the player is totally toward the net on the backhand and partially toward the net on the forehand.

Singles.   A game of tennis played between two opponents.

Singles sticks.   The sticks that are put up in both alleys to raise the net to a height of 3 feet 6 inches (at the center of the net, the height is always 3 feet) when singles matches are played.   Although many clubs, parks and private courts do not have singles sticks up at all times, they are always placed in the proper position for tournament matches.

Sitter.   See *Set-up*.

Sixteens.   (1) The second round in a draw of 32; or (2) an age division for players sixteen and under.

Slice.   (1) Underspin on a groundstroke; or (2) spin on a serve created by the racket face coming forward and across the right side of the ball.

Smash.   See *Overhead*.

Social doubles. A nontournament doubles match that is supposedly played for fun and exercise.

Spin. A rotation of the ball, either sideways, forward, or backward, created by brushing the racket face in a particular way across the ball. See *Underspin, Sidespin* and *Topspin*.

Spin for serve. Spinning a racket with the other player "calling" the way it will land—"M" or "W" with a Wilson racket, for instance. If the player guesses right, he can choose to serve first or to receive first or he can pick the side he wants to start on or he can decide to make his opponent choose first. Most players do not realize they have a multiple choice. If the player elects to serve first, his opponent can choose the side he wants to start on; if the player elects to start on the sunny side, his opponent can then choose whether he wants to serve or receive; if the player elects to make his opponent take the decision, the opponent must then choose to serve, receive or take a particular side of the court.

Steady. An adjective used to describe a player who seldom misses a ball. Lesser players often use the term derogatorily about an opponent who beats them.

Stiff. Descriptive of a player whose arms or legs are not flexible. It is never used to describe a straight back.

Sting. The pace of a ball when it feels hard on the racket.

String job. The act of stringing a racket or the tension of the strings after they are in the racket. Tension varies, with most good players preferring tightly strung rackets (tensions of 55 to 60 pounds). A racket with tension of 40 pounds is loosely strung; if the tension is 65 pounds or more, it is often called "board tight."

Stroke volley. A volley hit with a groundstroke action—a full backswing and follow-through, for instance.

Sudden Death. The ninth point in a nine-point tiebreaker (or the thirteenth point in a 13-point tiebreaker), which always means set-point for both players. It can also mean match-point for one or both players, depending upon the number of sets, if any, each player has won.

"Take two". A call from the receiver to the server when there has been an interruption in play. The receiver sometimes makes this call when he has knocked back the first serve but called it a fault or when he is not sure if the serve was good or out. In tournament play, there are no calls of "take two" unless an outside ball has rolled into the court or a stranger suddenly walks through the court or a bird sits on the net or a similar incident occurs that temporarily halts play.

Tanking. The act of throwing a match. See *Dump*.

Tarpaulin. A temporary covering for a court (usually a grass court) to protect it from the rain. Usually it leaks or water seeps under the sides. It is used to assure the spectators that one day the match will resume.

Tennis bum.   A once-popular term to describe successful amateurs in the days when players were given large sums of "expense money" under the table.

Tennis elbow.   A painful ailment in the area of the elbow, the treatment of which is rest or exercise, heat or cold, cortisone or an operation, depending upon your doctor.

Tension.   The tightness of a string job in the racket.

Third place play-off.   A match between the two losing semi-finalists in a tournament.

Thirty.   The second point in a game.   *See Scoring System.*

Tie.   A Davis Cup match.

Tiebreaker.   A 9-point, 12-point, or 13-point game usually played when games reach 6-all to determine the winner of the set.   Wimbledon uses the tiebreaker at 8-all but does not allow tiebreakers in the last set.

Topspin.   A type of spin created by having the racket face come up and over the ball while the racket is moving in a forward direction.   The easiest way to impart topspin to the ball is to start with the racket head pointing slightly down or perpendicular to the ground and under the level of the ball and to finish with the racket head much higher than ball level and well in front of the body.   Heavy topspin is created by pulling up sharply after the hit.   Normal topspin enables the player to control the ball well.   It causes the ball to bounce forward faster and higher than a flat ball.

Toss.   The lifting of the ball into the air with the fingers of the left hand when serving with the right hand.

Touch.   The ability to do special things with the ball—drop shots, lob volleys, dinks, or sharp angles.

Touching the net.   An error if the point is not yet over, causing automatic loss of the point.

Tramlines.   The alley (British terminology).

Twelves.   The age division for players twelve and under.   See *Age division.*

"Two and two".   A popular abbreviation for "6-2, 6-2."   "Four and three" means "6-4, 6-3."

Two-handed grip.   The holding of the racket during the hit with two hands.   This style of play, particularly on the backhand, has grown very popular.   The 1974 Wimbledon Champions, Jimmy Connors and Chris Evert, have two-handed backhands.

Umpire.   The man or woman who calls the score in a match.   He or she often calls the lines as well when there are no linesmen.   The umpire makes decisions on the rules of the game but is not permitted to overrule a linesman's call except in World Team Tennis.

Additionally, a player may appeal the umpire's ruling to the referee.

The umpire may, with reason, grant a "let," reprimand, or default a player, call a line when a linesman is "not sighted" (did not see the ball) and—always—make all interpretations of the rules.

Undercut. See *Underspin*.

Underhand serve. A legitimate serve hit at waist-level rather than over the head. When it is used as a "trick serve," it usually has a great deal of spin and can be a point winner.

Underspin. Spin created by having the racket face come under the ball as the racket is moving forward. It is used most frequently on backhands, particularly on backhand approach shots and on low, short balls under net level. Underspin slows down the ball (it makes the ball spin backwards), but it is an effective shot on grass because it causes the ball to bounce low. It is avoided on passing shots because it makes the ball rise before the bounce, thus making it easier for the net man to volley.

USTA. The United States Tennis Association, the ruling body of American amateur tennis and the promoter of the U.S. Open. Whether the USTA controls men's professional tennis is a subject of dispute between the ATP and the USTA. Until 1975, the name of the organization was "United States Lawn Tennis Association."

VASSS. The Van Alen Simplified Scoring System. James Van Alen introduced the original 9-point tiebreaker, Sudden Death, No-Ad and VASSS. The latter is a method of scoring games by 21 points or 31 points (a "game" in VASSS is a set).

Virginia Slims. A women's professional circuit begun in September, 1970. The current Virginia Slims Circuit consists of ten tournaments played in the winter and spring, with prize money of $75,000 per tournament. All the world's leading women players participate in some or all of the events. It is now run by the USTA in conjunction with the WTA, but from 1970 to 1973 it was run privately and against the wishes of the USTA.

Volley. A ball hit in the air before it has bounced, usually from a position close to the net. Not to be confused with a rally.

Warm-up. A period of rallying before the match begins. In tournament play, there is often a time limit on the warm-up.

WCT. World Championship Tennis, a professional circuit organized in 1968 and run by Lamar Hunt, Al Hill, Jr., and Mike Davies. WCT signs up players for its circuits, which are played in the winter and spring months. Until 1976, WCT staged three tours at the same time, with thirty-two men in each of the Red, Green, and Blue groups. In 1976 there were two tours running at the same time, with sixteen players in each group. Prize money for each tournament is $60,000. There is a WC of T Final ($100,000) for the top eight singles players and a WC of T Doubles Final ($100,000) for the top eight teams.

Western grip. The "V" between thumb and forefinger is almost under the racket handle. The Western forehand was popular in the 1920s and 1930s on California asphalt because it is so effective on high balls. Its popularity declined because it was difficult to use against low balls (although Bjorn Borg and Harold Solomon have made it respectable again). The Western backhand is hit with the same face of the racket as the Western forehand, which means the elbow turns upward awkwardly. This shot has not been taught by self-respecting teaching pros for the last four decades.

Wightman Cup. A women's annual competition between Great Britain and the United States, with the site alternating between the two countries. A match consists of five singles and two doubles, but there are only three singles players on each team (Nos. 1 and 2 each play both the opposing Nos. 1 and 2).

Wimbledon. The "Lawn Tennis Championships" played on the grass courts of Wimbledon, England, the last week of June and the first week of July. It is still considered by many to be the most prestigious title in the world although it does not offer the largest prize money. The tickets are sold out months in advance.

Wood shot. A shot that is hit (accidentally) with the frame of the racket, even if the racket is made of metal.

WTA. Women's Tennis Association. Most of the women pros of the world are members. The Association was organized by Billie Jean King in 1973 and she became its first president. The current executive director is Jerry Diamond. There has not yet been any conflict of authority between the WTA and the USTA, and the USTA assumes it does have final control over all American women pros.

WTT. World Team Tennis, organized by Dennis Murphy, Jordan Kaiser, Fred Barman and Larry King. In the first season (spring-summer of 1974), WTT sold franchises at $50,000 each to promoters in 16 cities and organized a player draft and a series of matches between the 16 teams. The ATP, the USTA, and the ILTF disapproved of World Team Tennis, but over thirty ATP members signed up. In 1975 the number of WTT teams diminished to ten. While many spectators liked the WTT format, others did not. Team owners lost approximately $300,000 each in the first season.